# Eight Immortal Flavors

# Eight Immortal Flavors

### by Johnny Kan
with Charles L. Leong

---

Including new recipes kitchen-tested by Master Chef
Sun Pui Wong, Executive Chef, Kan's Restaurant

---

A California Living Book

Revised Edition
Copyright © 1980
California Living Books
The San Francisco Examiner Division of the Hearst Corporation, Suite 223, The
Hearst Building, Third and Market Streets, San Francisco, California 94103

Design/Production by David Charlsen

Printed in the United States of America.

Library of Congress Catalog Card Number 79-53192
ISBN 0-89395-060-2 (Paper)
ISBN 0-89395-032-7 (Cloth)

# Foreword

I count myself fortunate in having had the privilege of knowing Chinese cuisine from my earliest childhood. The city of Portland, Oregon, where I grew up, had a Chinese colony of some size, and several of the Chinese families were good friends of ours. Not only did I enjoy delectable meals in their homes, but also we had a Chinese cook who constantly delighted me with delicate Chinese specialties.

The Kan family were especially close friends and neighbors, and I often played with the Kan children and their cousin Johnny Kan, who came to visit from San Francisco's Chinatown. This was the late Johnny Kan of the famous Kan's restaurant on Grant Avenue in San Francisco. Whenever I reach the City of the Golden Gate, I go immediately to Kan's to feast on fine Chinese food.

I have traveled much since those days and eaten food in many parts of the world. More and more I've grown to appreciate the subtle elegance of Chinese cuisine. It is truly, as most food experts agree, the equal of the French cuisine. Indeed, the classic cooking of China antedates the French and it has been perfected through many centuries. The delicacy of Chinese cooking preserves the firm texture and full flavor of meat and fish and the crisp, fresh quality of vegetables. The subtle flavorings are used to enhance the food, never to overpower it.

I have long believed that Americans should use more Chinese recipes and cooking methods in their kitchens, and it was with great delight that I heard Johnny Kan was working with Charles Leong, an historian of Chinese life in America, and with the artist, Jake Lee, to produce a Chinese cookbook. I knew it would be outstanding. It is.

Johnny Kan always had a fine taste for good food. His mother was an excellent cook and an ingenious one. No matter where the family lived, even in such a remote Mother Lode town as Grass Valley, California, she could create delectable Chinese dishes with the ingredients and utensils at hand. I remember the first dinner I had at Kan's Restaurant when Johnny brought me a dish made with steamed clams and eggs — a magnificent Chinese specialty which his mother had embellished. Johnny Kan inherited his mother's artistic ability with food, and from his youth he had been associated with it. In the 1930s he was connected with — of all things — a Chinese soda fountain, where he devised "Chinese" ice creams based on such flavorings as lychee, ginger and Oriental preserves. He owned and operated several restaurants, and I consider Kan's the outstanding Chinese restaurant today.

Charles Leong, John's old friend and collaborator, is a writer who has contributed to and researched for *Reader's Digest, Sunset Magazine, Ford Times* and many other publications. An authority on Chinese life in America, he now is an editor of the *Young China Daily,* a San Francisco Chinatown newspaper founded by Dr. Sun Yat Sen, father of the Chinese republic. He is a gourmet and an excellent amateur cook. Some forty years ago, when Charles was editing the *Chinese Press,* a Chinese-English language newspaper, John Kan prepared a series of articles for the paper entitled "The Romance of Chinese Food." Thus began the germ of an idea. Both John and Charles traveled extensively in the Far East to enlarge their knowledge of Oriental food.

Jake Lee, the artist who so effectively punctuates the food that Johnny and Charles discuss, is also an old friend and food lover. He is a well-known West Coast illustrator and a noted water colorist.

This book with the charming title, "Eight Immortal Flavors," represents the collaborative efforts of these three brilliant artists. They worked together on a subject that is close to their hearts.

"Eight Immortal Flavors" covers a vast range of Chinese cookery. Here are the "Greats" of classical cuisine; these will delight the purists. But here too are many simple dishes that can be prepared with the ordinary skillet and everyday ingredients. You need not rush out to the nearest Chinese market to buy special utensils or exotic foods. Of course, if you are an experienced cook, and a true lover of Chinese cuisine — as I am — you will wish to graduate to the elaborate specialties. It will be most rewarding.

And finally, if you wish some pleasant hours of leisurely reading, browse through "Eight Immortal Flavors." It is well stocked with background material and unusual historical information. It will rank with many of the important books on European and international cookery.

JAMES A. BEARD

# Contents

# Preface

It is less than twenty-six years ago that the first Chinese cookbook written in English was published in the United States. Since then many more have been written and published. Why, then, have we written yet another book on Chinese cooking?

Today's changing conditions of modern-day living and attitudes on food have challenged us to write for you what we hope will be the most definitive guide to date on Cantonese cookery.

The American family menu, furthermore, reflects this jet-age world which is bringing international cuisine into closer focus. World War II exposed hundreds of thousands of armed forces members to global gastronomy. Though Chinese restaurants have been a part of the American scene for many, many years, family consumption of Chinese foods was barely noticeable until less than twenty years ago. Presently an average of 35 million dollars a year is spent in America's supermarkets for frozen and canned American-packed Oriental products. And surveys indicate even a greater potential.

In spite of this growing interest in Chinese food, it is surprising that a comparatively small number of Americans actually know what real Chinese cuisine is. Much less do they know the proper way to cook it.

An example of this was an advertisement, placed in many nationally circulated magazines by the manufacturers of a well-known condiment sauce, which featured a recipe called "American Chop Suey." The ingredients included macaroni and butter! In the first place, Chop Suey is no more authentic in Chinese cuisine than Irish stew. Some people may think it is. But to concoct a "recipe" with macaroni and butter, mixed with bean sprouts, is even more surprising. All we can say is that *Chop Suey* deserves this added insult.

So let's say that another good reason for writing this book is to play the part of gourmet-wise Sir Galahads, defending the authenticity of true Southern Chinese cooking and spreading the gospel of its virtues. We began our joint mission twenty years ago with a serial column we wrote called "The Romance of Chinese Food" for a newspaper read avidly by Chinese-Americans all over the country. At the time we hoped that, someday, all those facts about Cantonese cooking might be preserved between book covers.

Now with our dreams come true, we can continue our missionary zeal with this consistent message: "Tell the truth about Chinese food." Chinese cooking, with a recorded history of 47 centuries, is one of the world's oldest and is the essence of the highest art of cuisine. To misrepresent it constitutes an unforgivable sin. The fact that this book is the *very first* written within the heart of San Francisco's Chinatown — the recognized mecca for the best Cantonese food in the world, outside of Hong Kong — authenticates further the recipes selected from an unfathomable range of the best in Chinese food offerings.

With all these important factors in mind, we, the co-authors — both descendants of Cantonese parents — have written this book while bearing in mind the possible culinary quandary of an American-born Chinese housewife who has forgotten how to cook the dishes her mother once prepared for the family. Thousands of Chinese live in small towns all over the country where Chinese vegetables and certain other ingredients are not easily obtainable. Yet their parents ingeniously managed to cook in Chinese style by substituting and adapting American food materials, all of which resulted in wonderfully palatable dishes.

They transformed domestic vegetables, such as cauliflower, spinach, Kentucky Wonder string beans, tomatoes and even potatoes into tasty dishes of another world simply by combining them with meats, fish and poultry, a touch of a rare Chinese spice, sapidities, or with just plain soy sauce. Through the Chinese technique of undercooking American vegetables by quick toss cooking, the results were great indeed. So even in San Francisco, where vegetables grown from native Chinese seeds were abundant, American vegetables took their rightful place as part of the Chinese household menu!

As with a sumptuous Chinese banquet, the writing of this book required the participation of many persons — which added to the enjoyment of writing it and, at times, caused dismay to these same persons, because of the checking and re-checking necessary for absolute authenticity and technical perfection. Our special thanks are due to James A. Beard, the international food expert and consultant, gourmet and writer of books and articles on food, who not only encouraged us to write this book but who also graciously wrote the Foreword; to Ming Jang, Executive Chef of Kan's restaurant, for many of his precious secrets; to Master Chefs Yin Choy Chin and Fred Leong for their valuable technical assistance; to Francis Lai, the Chinese gourmet who helped with the sequences in the Chinese Tidbits chapter; to Kenneth Joe for the fine calligraphy; to Danny Kaye for his enthusiasm and encouragement; to C. Y. Lee for his story of the Kitchen God; to Mrs. Marguerite Fenner, chief home economist of the Pacific Gas and Electric Company for her invaluable suggestions and for the use of the PG&E's testing kitchen facilities; and to our other epicurean friends who gave us the constructive criticism which only sincere friends ever dare to give.

*San Francisco*
*October, 1963*

# EIGHT IMMORTAL FLAVORS

---

Caught in the reflection of lanterns in early night, the yellow roofs of the Imperial City gleamed like gold. Sandalwood permeated the air. Princes and princesses all wore the costumes of royalty distinguished by waveline patterns of blue. Eunuchs and serving girls moved quietly everywhere.

Thus an Emperor of ancient China, resplendent with all the pomp and pageantry of his proud imperial court, languidly sampled minute portions of the vast array of gastronomical delights of the empire, offered by a retinue of servants in a continuous parade. First, a famous, delectable, cured ham of the faraway western provinces; then selected golden cartilages from shark's fins. Deer tendons followed, and the paws of a bear. Freshest silvery fish and shellfish still swimming until just a moment before cooking time, made their appearance, preceding the rarest exotic herbs and plants for the forest and fields. The choicest of all domestic fowl and meats were his.

Dependent on the whim of His Highness, or the importance of the occasion, the chefs of the imperial household were prepared to concoct a dazzling panorama of superb dishes, perhaps one hundred fantastically elaborate creations or even as many as two hundred of the finest examples dramatically prepared in every conceivable cooking method known to man.

The soft sound of lutes muted the clatter of dishes while the Emperor dined.

Within a trumpet's echo of the Imperial City, somewhere in a nearby village, a peasant and his family ate with native gusto a simple but tasty meal of noodles and greens cooked with a pinch of salt and oil.

Emperor and peasant both were enjoying authentic examples of Chinese cooking, the oldest cuisine in the world. Both were savoring some of the basic *Eight Immortal Flavors* of Chinese foods.

The fine art of Chinese cookery had its beginning in the ancient China of five thousand years ago. Like the great musical compositions of the old masters, ancient Chinese recipes are in their own way a harmonious blend of ingredients. When executed by a dedicated chef, versed in the proper technique, the resulting dish can be like a symphony directed by an inspired conductor. It is a cuisine which has been developed through thousands of years and one which now is being "discovered" daily by people all over the world.

## *What is Chinese Food?*

It has been said that the history of a people is reflected by what and how they eat. China, with a civilization and culture which invented printing, gunpowder and the compass and which enjoyed exquisite jade and silks when the masses of the Western world were still living under primitive conditions, naturally was a nation where the culinary arts would be developed to the highest degree of perfection. The satisfaction of the most fastidious, sophisticated tastes is one of the demands of an ancient and refined civilization. The vast geographical spread of China, with its diverse climates, types of agriculture and variety of animals, produces edibles which make for easier payment of the demand.

Soil and synthesis — and as often as not just the hard fact of survival — all are factors in the Chinese discovering the edible qualities of such exotics as gingko nuts, lotus roots, bamboo shoots, and birds' nests.

Chinese food *is* distinctly different. It is comparable to the finest food of any country in the world. Carl Crow, the American author of *Four Hundred Million Chinese* and other books has said: "So far as I am personally concerned, there is no meal I enjoy better than a good Chinese dinner. I would not anticipate an unhappy future if I knew that I would have nothing but Chinese food to eat all the rest of my life. . . ."

What are the qualities of Chinese cooking which have earned such praise from a non-Chinese? By itself, in its elemental stage, beef is just beef and a tomato is just a tomato. What is it that makes a blend of these two ingredients become Chinese in character, and therefore, a new gastronomical adventure? The housewife is increasingly interested in the methods and ingredients used in Chinese cookery: how vegetables retain flavor, crispness and natural color by not being overcooked; how the pungent sweet-and-sour sauces and the mouth-watering black beans sauces are blended; how to prepare chicken in twenty different styles; how to cook meats and seafood Chinese style in ten different methods.

We can give you the key to Chinese cooking in words. But you must be willing to experiment and practice the fundamentals in order to become an accomplished Chinese cook. Also, you must be philosophical. For Chinese food is more than just nourishment for the body. Chinese food is poetry of the kitchen pots, too. What but an old, sophisticated civilization would name a chicken filet and ham dish *Yin Yang Gai* — a dish symbolizing marital bliss? Chinese cuisine abounds with scores of dishes blending backgrounds with legends.

In our chapters on Chinese Utensils and Techniques, and Native Condiments and Sauces, we will explain and expand in some detail on the various factors which make Chinese food what it is.

## *Octaval Taste*

Perhaps it is more than coincidental that the Chinese sense of harmonized food tastes is based on *eight* fundamental flavors. Chinese descriptive prose seems to have an affinity for this particular numerical turn of phrase — in legend, in literature, in living.

Legend proclaims that objects which possess the power of charm are called the Eight Treasures. The Buddhist faith also possesses eight emblems. Literature abounds with such references as the Eight Immortal Poets of the Chinese Golden Age of writing. Ancient China is dotted with place names bearing such titles as the one found right in the vicinity of Peking — "The Hill of the Eight Sanctuaries."

At banquets today one is seated at round tables accommodating ten persons. But during the imperial regime of Old China, a formal dinner was always set on traditional square tables which seated eight guests and which were euphemistically known as "Eight Immortals' Tables."

This numerary background, including the traditional ritualistic setting for dining, coincided so perfectly with the elements of Chinese cooking that we quickly determined what the title of this book should be.

## Eight Immortal Flavors

Two centuries ago, the great poet and scholar Yuan Mei wrote: "There *is* a difference between dining and eating. Dining is an art. When you eat to get the most out of your meal, to please the palate, as well as to satiate the appetite, that — my friend — is dining."

How to achieve this goal? Do as the Chinese do. Regard the preparation of food as a fascinating art. Explore the Eight Immortal Flavors.

Now then, what *are* the Eight Flavors which can inspire you, too, toward being a philosopher of the kitchen pots? Memorize and recite with verve and rhythm — sing-song like — thus, in a swing of two words in each cadence: *Hom – Tom, Teem – Seen, Foo – Lot, Heong – Gum*. Translated into English, they are, in their classical order of reference:

*HOM* — Salty. Since the Chinese taste range is so wide, there are many degrees of saltiness. The range includes all of the textural and taste sensation differences among steamed salt fish, rock salt chicken, and salted preserved eggs.

*TOM* — Bland. A flavor? To the Chinese, yes. For example, there is the satisfying blandness of cooked rice grains. White bread, for example, has a barely perceptible flavor of "baking," while it is also bland. And it is all the more so when contrasted with a spicy flavored meat in a sandwich. The Chinese impression of bland is "not salty," for whatever the dish may be.

*TEEM* — Sweet. As with salty, there are degrees of sweetness. Also, the term *teem* or sweet really does not mean necessarily a syrupy sweetness. A Chinese will delight over the flavor of a lotus root and cuttlefish soup, for instance, and exclaim "Ah, what a delectable sweetness to this masterpiece!" He means that the dish has an indefinable natural sweet quality. The lotus root soup does not have a thick sugary sweetness at all. It is, in fact, a reddish clear broth, an essence of purity with a seafood undertone, not "sweet" in the usual Western sense at all.

*SEEN* — Sour. One of the flavors which is more characteristically Chinese, in the sense that we have more dishes blended in this category than in American cooking. You may be familiar with the various "sweet and sour" combinations such as pineapple pork, rice vinegared pigs' trotters, pressed almond duck, and whole rock cod. Other dishes of this nature include pickled mustard greens and kidneys, toss-cooked. A favorite home dish is pickled bamboo shoot membranes steamed with sliced beef.

*FOO* — Bitter. Not half as bad as the categorical description sounds, in Chinese food the flavor is *not* medicinally bitter. This taste belongs exclusively in the Chinese cuisine. Bitter Melon (*Foo Gwa*) is named literally for its flavor. It has a slightly bitter taste, but, also a cool, quinine-like touch. Certain cooking herbs have a bitter undertone too. Very mature mustard greens used for soup have this characteristic. Bitter melon combinations have an unusually exhilarating quality once you become educated to the taste.

*LOT* — Hot. This refers to "hot" as in mustard, or chili peppers. While the Chinese do not have anything like a Texas-type *chili con carne,* we do have such dishes as curried duck and chicken. We have pungent ginger root for garnishing. Another hot item is an appetizing home dish concocted with chopped preserved cabbage, diced roast pork and mushrooms, dried shrimps, and hot, green chili peppers.

*HEONG* — Fragrant. The term really refers to a pleasant olfactory reaction, more than a taste sensation, but it is more than that. Its elusive quality can be traced only by an example, for to the Chinese it is a flavor. To illustrate: A classically simple dish such as hearts of Chinese chard, properly toss-cooked with only oil and salt has *wok hay* or "pan aroma" and therefore is a gourmet's delight. This means that the vegetable is fresh and green, the pan (or *wok*) is sizzling hot, and the proportions of oil and salt judicious. The finished dish of vegetables is presented still green. It has the *wok hay* fragrance. This same principle applies to other dishes, especially of the toss-cooked variety.

*GUM* — Golden, as in citrus peel. The Chinese have an olive-shaped fruit called kumquat. *Kum* or *Gum* means gold. Reference to this flavor means a taste similar to the kumquat. Therefore, one enjoys a "golden" moment upon partaking of it. As with *foo,* this too might be considered a characteristically Chinese flavor. The aftertaste of artichokes gives the identical cool, acrid-sweet sensation to the taste buds. In your Chinese food adventures, one of the highlights of flavor exploration will come when you try the "thousand-year-old" preserved eggs. This flavor, too, is Golden.

Technically, there are more than the eight flavors, because many Chinese dishes culminate in a blend of several flavors. In planning a Chinese-style banquet the host will select a menu featuring contrasting courses including as many of the eight different flavors as possible to delight the palate of his guests. Whether being entertained at home or in a carefully selected restaurant, the guests will expect to be treated as gourmets. In typical Chinese fashion, they will discuss candidly the merits or demerits of the offerings and their flavors. Is the food too salty? Too bland? Too sour?

In America we have the saying "the proof is in the pudding." The Chinese also have a proverb "The mouth is an unlimited measure." Do you know what a Chinese gourmet would order first in a restaurant he has never tested before? First, *Yow Yim Choy Sum,* the Chinese chard hearts, toss-cooked, as we described.

Here is a classical example of all of man's five senses being brought into play by a deceptively simple dish of food. But only because that man is really, truly, a gourmet!

As soon as the waiter sets the dish of green chard on the table, our gourmet's five senses respond immediately: SIGHT — the chard hearts dish must look appetizingly green and firm; SMELL — it must carry the fresh fragrance of the "pan aroma" or *wok hay;* TASTE — the chard must be, of course, neither too salty nor too bland and must retain the "sweetness" of the natural vegetable; TOUCH — it must be steaming hot, as the Chinese say *yeet, lot, lot;* HEARING — the sound of crispness and crunchiness must be heard when biting into a piece of the chard.

The degree of success by which the dish of *Yow Yim Choy Sum* passes the test of the five senses is a fastidious example of the criterion upon which our gourmet will judge the skill of the chef in cooking other dishes. If the chef passes his test, the gourmet will then confidently consider the other dishes, be they seafood, meat or poultry.

The epicure might order for the pleasure of his guests an array of dishes such as this, keeping in mind the need for a variety of cooking methods in order to present a variety of textures as well as of tastes: *quick-boiled* abalone soup; *red-fried* soy squab; *stewed* beef flank; *steamed* chicken; *toss-cooked* vegetables; *poached* rock cod; *dry-fried* prawns en shell.

It is said that if a strange new species of the botanical, animal or marine world should be discovered by three friends, one an American, one a German, and the other a Chinese, here is what would happen:

The American would publicize, promote and sell it.

The German would classify and analyze it scientifically.

The Chinese would touch and smell and taste it, and bemusedly ask himself: "Should this be fried, boiled or roasted?"

Perhaps this story is not as apocryphal as it seems, because the refinement of five thousand years of Chinese cooking experience has resulted in the perfection of more than a dozen basic methods of preparing food.

Actually, these many methods of Chinese cooking can be applied to just one item — such as chicken — and result in a variety of tastes and textures.

### American and Chinese Food – How Do They Differ?

Originally we were going to title this section "The Secrets of Cantonese Cookery." But actually every page of this book is a continuing thesis on separate facets of a vast subject and the "secrets" are on every page. This book has been written for both American and Chinese-American housewives. We hope that a discussion of the environmental and social background of the Chinese, plus some specific comparisions of the differences of preparation and taste between Chinese and American dishes made from the same basic ingredients, will bring about a clearer understanding of the WHY of the differences.

It is acknowledged that culinary skills are considered one of the Chinese arts. From birth to the grave, the ceremonial significance of food plays an important part in the Chinese social pattern. A one-month-old baby is honored with a "Feast of the Full Moon." A deceased person is honored by his family and friends with a simple dinner partaken by the mourners following the interment rituals.

Chinese of all classes — from peasant to merchant prince — constantly seek and delve into the secrets of Chinese cooking. They appreciate and stress the proper preparation of food, from simple, plain, bland steamed rice to the fanciest of entrees. For many reasons, we firmly believe that every average Chinese eventually becomes an experienced cook — securing, at least the requisite knowledge and background, if lacking a complete mastery of the art. So it is not strange to hear then, that in certain districts of China, even the wealthiest of men master the kitchen as a hobby, and vie for honors on the nuances of flavor of a rich shark's fin soup, or a delectable glutinous rice chicken.

The former American diplomat and journalist, Nicholas Roosevelt, who wrote two cookbooks while isolated in the craggy Big Sur country of California, has said that living in self-reliance includes the ability to cook. He continued that "if you have to cook, it follows logically that you should learn to cook well."

The agrarian character of Chinese life, with a majority of the population living in small villages with open market places but no groceries and delicatessens, was a perfect setting for the principle forwarded by Nicholas Roosevelt. Most of the village people were poor. Even if they could afford it, there were no such conveniences as restaurants. If they became hungry, they had to cook. Our own parents came from such small villages in the province of Canton in southern China. They could afford only a few condiments such as a few ounces of peanut oil at a time, precious salt and soy sauce.

Boys and girls alike began their culinary training early in life by bringing water from the wells. They were all taught to wash rice, and then to cook it properly. Children were severely reprimanded if they cooked the rice either too hard or too soft. The penalty for a burned potful of rice was a stiff whacking, for such rice was not only unpalatable, but also a waste which "not even a sow should be forced to eat." Even today in America, most Chinese-American girls must know how to cook a presentable pot of rice.

This training in cooking extended to the men as well. The last empress of China, Tz'u Hsi, once commended the skill of an official's cook over a simple bowl of noodles and fried pork strips casually partaken somewhere on a rural tour. She commissioned the cook an official of the sixth rank and appointed him chef in the imperial kitchen. The first Chinese immigrants who came to *Gum Shan,* or the Golden Mountain as they referred to America, were mostly of the peasantry. Like the underprivileged the world over, they came to America for a better way of life. For fifty years following the Gold Rush of 1849, the many thousands of Chinese who came were mostly men. They did their own cooking.

During the Golden Era of bon vivant San Francisco, the Bonanza Kings of the West employed and taught Chinese how to prepare French and other continental dishes as well as the regular American fare. This experience proved that the Chinese, being natural cooks, could handle the food of any nationality with equal artistry. Thus came into being a character beloved in Western Americana, the familiar Chinese houseboy of fact and fiction, who was not only chef par excellence, but also loyal family friend, companion and counselor and household major-domo of some of California's finest families.

A peek into the kitchens of San Francisco's best restaurants today, regardless of the nationality of their cuisine, will reveal, still, many Chinese under a chef's white toque.

We have already touched briefly on some of the different kitchen techniques employed in preparing Chinese and non-Chinese food. To the slogan-minded, we might say: "Chinese food is fun." Bruce Bliven, the famed editor, wrote "in China for countless hundreds of years, pickled pigs' feet have been a traditional diet for the woman who has just had a baby. No modern research laboratory could devise a better one. The dark rice vinegar in which the pigs' feet are cooked releases some of the calcium in the bones; thus the mother replaces the calcium she gave to her baby during pregnancy. . . ." Certainly we are not medical men nor nutritionists. But tastewise, smacking one's lips over a piquant dish of hot vinegared pigs' feet definitely is more pleasurable than just swallowing a calcium pill.

How many times have you heard the expression, "Two hours after enjoying a Chinese dinner — I'm hungry again!"

The fact is, the non-Chinese partakes more of the entrees at a Chinese dinner than he does of rice. But a Chinese always takes more rice with his various dishes because it is his solid staple. With insufficient starch, no wonder a person becomes hungry in short order. Try eating a steak without your potato and/or bread accompaniment, and you will become hungry much sooner!

## Culinary Compass

The *wok,* which is the basic Chinese cooking utensil, is used versatilely as pot, pan, steamer, frying pan, deep fat fryer and double boiler. Like Chinese calligraphy, the *wok* and chopsticks are universally found all over China. In calligraphy, the same characters mean the same wherever read, but the pronunciations are different and there are many dialect variations between North and South, and East and West.

So what is cooked in the *wok,* with differences of condiments and techniques, can result in a dish in the styles of different provinces. Regardless of where the culinary compass points, however, it is *all* Chinese food. A foreigner visiting this country is confronted with such diverse regional standbys as Maine lobster, Southern fried chicken, Texas chili and Boston baked beans. Yet *all* are American dishes. The same principle applies to Chinese food.

We have been asked this question many times: "What is the difference between Chinese food, Cantonese food and Mandarin food?"

In the United States, the best-known Chinese cuisine is Cantonese-style. We would like to state that there is no such thing as "Mandarin food." Standard dictionary references describe the word "Mandarin" as a Chinese official. Perhaps the term "Mandarin" is misinterpreted as meaning Northern (North China) style.

The Chinese know and enjoy four regional categories of cuisines — each outstanding for both its flavor characteristics and its methods of preparation — and each represented by the city or province most intimately identified with it. These are: Eastern (Shanghai); Western (Szechuan); Northern (Peking) and Southern (Canton). Offshoots of these recognized regional schools of cooking have their localized innovations, of course, but these are the major classifications.

EASTERN Style: This embraces the entire delta area around Shanghai. Soy sauce is used more liberally in the cooking. As in the Southern style, the food is lighter than the Western and Northern cuisines. Many dishes are smother-cooked. Paradoxically, while much soy sauce is used, sugar is generously combined with it. The Ningpo area excels in seafood, and the Shanghai treatment of eels is a fascinating blend of explosive hot oil cooking and red hot spices. The province of Fukien, on the eastern coastline south of Shanghai, might be included with its high specialization in seafoods, and many soupy dishes. Some say Fukien cooking is a school in itself.

WESTERN Style: The food of West China is peppery hot. Many Americans may remember Chungking as the World War II capital of Free China, and the hot summers there. Hot climates seem to initiate highly seasoned cuisines, and the province of Szechuan is no exception. Chicken toss-cooked with hot peppers is a famous dish of this area. Also, parchment-wrapped chicken originated there.

Another western China province, Yunnan, produces a mouth-watering cured turnip of pungent potency.

NORTHERN Style: Who has not heard of the aristocratic Peking duck? This is the justly world-famous Northern dish, albeit really a part of the Shantung province school of cooking. Wine sauces are characteristic of Northern cooking. Spring rolls, a favorite of Chinese restaurants in America, originated here and probably are among the world's oldest hors d'oeuvres.

SOUTHERN Style: The Chinese are in harmonious accord that the Southern, or Cantonese, technique of cooking is the best and features a greater range of versatility than all the others. This is indeed fortunate for Americans, because Cantonese cuisine is predominant in most Chinese restaurants in the United States. While it is claimed that the Chinese "live to eat" one can double that claim for the Cantonese. Blessed by geography with fertility, a kind climate, rivers and a seacoast, the Cantonese had all the natural advantages with which to experiment on all manner of ingredients and cooking methods. A characteristic of Cantonese cooking is the magic of enticing and blending the natural flavors of the ingredients without a heavy dressing of sauces and seasonings. Perhaps the crowning achievement of cooking skill and method originated by the Cantonese is their *Chow* or toss-cooking style of handling finely sliced ingredients.

This toss-cooking method is admired by American cooks and housewives, for this technique preserves the natural fresh flavor, texture and color of meats and vegetables. This is the outstanding characteristic of Cantonese cooking. It is one which earns for Cantonese cuisine its rightful role of immortality among the world's great culinary arts.

Each region of China has its famous specialties, each has its own distinctive taste qualities. But all have a universal pattern of serving as the occasion dictates — village-style, dinner-style, banquet-style or superbanquet-style. Every point of the Chinese culinary compass also celebrates the same holidays and festivals, in which food always plays a part.

## Recipes' Pattern

From the literally thousands of Chinese recipes — whether concocted by an emperor's imperial chef or a peasant with a sense of expediency and imagination — we have chosen a practical number for you to try, to enjoy, to treasure. In making our choices, first and foremost the recipes had to be authentically Chinese. Whether they are centuries-old secrets or something relished by a Chinese-American substituting local ingredients, all are dishes accepted by the Chinese themselves.

With not only the American housewife in mind, but also the Chinese-American homemakers who today are spread throughout the United States, we have made our selections so that approximately *seventy-five percent* of the recipes can be prepared with common ingredients available everywhere. These recipes are not really hard to master. They require only a minimum of Chinese native condiments and ingredients. Some indeed, owe their transition from American to Chinese creations not through special ingredients but strictly through the methods of preparation, cooking and serving.

Especially in vegetables and meat dishes, when you reach a certain level of skill, like the Chinese-American housewife, you too, can improvise from the basic recipes to suit seasonable products, availability, etc.

Then we divert to the twenty-five percent portion composed of truly exotic dishes, such as the "Ceremony of the Fish." We can safely say that not one American in ten thousand has even heard of, much less tasted, this rare ceremonial creation. These recipes are definitely more difficult to execute. There are several reasons, in the interest of promoting a greater American cognizance of Chinese foods, why we decided to apportion twenty-five percent of our recipes to the "hard-to-do" category with native Chinese condiments and ingredients.

The advanced cook, who has ranged the lower peaks of Chinese culinary arts, can now test the gastronomical Everest. Several Chinese cookbooks have made a point of offering "easily prepared" dishes only. (Once you have reached and conquered all the "easy" lower peaks, the adventure is dulled.)

Even if you never try the more difficult recipes you will have absorbed a background and understanding of them, enough to know how to order them in Chinese restaurants with a sense of confidence. This is a satisfaction to anyone's ego.

Speaking of ordering and ego, this is a good time to explain why we are going to refer to condiments, sauces, ingredients and recipes bilingually.

First, you will get the English terms, and know what the basic, main ingredients are. We then include the English phonetics of the

Chinese recipe. Should you want to discuss Cantonese cuisine with a Chinese friend, or shop for ingredients you will be easily understood.

## Gourmets of the Golden Hills

The golden enchantment of California in 1849 brought Chinese as well as men from other parts of the globe to the Golden State. With a fine sense of poetry and realism, the Chinese in their native tongue spontaneously referred to their new home as *Gum Shan,* or Golden Hills. For more than a century San Francisco Chinatown has been the center of the world of *Gum Shan.*

San Francisco is also the Chinese food center of America. There are many reasons for this fact. It is logical that the best Chinese food and cooking should be found wherever there is a large concentration of Chinese, not only in America, but anywhere in the world.

San Francisco, for the Western hemisphere, is truly the paradise of the Chinese epicure. The Chinese population of this city by the Golden Gate is the size of a modest American city — 55,000 persons. Half of this number lives in Chinatown, a "city within a city" of many moods and intrigues, including even a temple rooted in its founding location of over a century ago. Within its boundaries, Chinatown serves every need and desire of the human being, from stomach to soul, from birth to burial. Like eternal Rome, Chinatown is the center of its world. Chinese from all over America make a pilgrimage to *Dai Fow,* which means emphatically The Big City, or San Francisco (Chinatown).

Here are located, either on the main thoroughfare Grant Avenue or on Waverly Place, the "Street of Balconies," most of the national headquarters of the family associations, founded by the Cantonese emigrants who came here first to mine gold, then to build the railroads, to work the farms and to contribute greatly to the growth of Western America. These are the Chans, the Wongs, the Lees, and the Quans, and others who now live all over the United States — perhaps in New York or in Cucamonga, California — but wherever they are, most have friends or relatives, or official family ties in San Francisco. Some 90 percent are Cantonese, emigrated from the province of Canton.

All civic, cultural, educational, religious, social and business activities of the Chinese gravitate around San Francisco Chinatown. In early summer the glutinous tri-coned stuffed puddings mean Dragon Boat Festival time. The partaking of moon cakes is Moon

Festival time and the wonderful climax of the year — Chinese New
Year's — means gourmet feasts for everyone. Every holiday is a
feast day.

The Cantonese love to eat. The holidays furnish a good excuse
to do so.

They are upholding a great tradition bestowed upon them in an
old folk saying which expresses the apex of Chinese happiness:
"To be married in Soochow,
To be clothed in Hangchow,
To be dined in Kwangchow." (the ancient name for Canton)
The city of Soochow is famous for beautiful women. Hangchow's
silks tailor into the most exquisite clothing. The chefs and cuisine of
Kwangchow, are considered the finest in *all* China.

The people of San Francisco Chinatown zealously guard this
heritage. From the cock's crow at dawn through dusk and deepest
night and dawn again, always there is some Chinese eating place
open for your gustatory pleasure every minute of the day and the
night. A few places do have some Shanghai, Peking and Szechuan
dishes. And of course, some of the famous non-Cantonese dishes,
such as Peking duck or Szechuan's parchment-wrapped chicken,
centuries ago were incorporated into the Cantonese cuisine. But
within these Cantonese-style restaurants, large and small, you will
find almost any dish which is served in Hong Kong, and at all hours.
This fact inspired us to entitle our chapter on Chinese tidbits
"Morning, Noon and Night."

Strolling along Grant Avenue (still called by the old denizens of
the district *Dupont Gai* — its pre-earthquake of 1906 name!) you
will observe on weekend or holiday evenings perhaps 300 or 400
Chinese pouring out of any of the larger restaurants, having enjoyed
a ten-course banquet as part of a family association convention, a
wedding celebration, or a month-old-baby party. Daily, smaller
parties of from 10 to 40 persons are routine. After dances and dates,
you will see, late at night, Chinese couples going for snacks. At
dawn when most of the city still sleeps, Chinatown is stirring. Its
*jook* or rice gruel house is busy with early workers stopping in for a
hot, nourishing bowl of *jook* laced with meat balls or sliced fish, and
a native-style non-sweet cruller to chew. In the same cracker-box
*jook* house late carousers may be enjoying the same dishes as anti-
dotes for a too-lively evening.

At high noon, Chinatown exchanges gossip and its businessmen
transact their affairs pleasantly at the several teahouses, sipping rare

choice teas, and nibbling at *deem sum* or "touch of the heart" meat balls, and other assorted tidbits such as taro root fried turnovers and red bean curd stewed chicken feet.

Strolling along Grant Avenue in the early morning, you will see for yourself another chapter of the Chinatown gourmet story. The sidewalk fronts of import-export houses such as Wo Kee Company, whose sign proudly states "Established since 1856," proclaim themselves to be some of the few business firms in California more than a century old. Trucks are unloading crates from Hong Kong filled with dried scallops, lily flowers, dragon's eyes and other exotic fare. Trucks from the hot valley farms are loaded with two dozen varieties of native Chinese vegetables such as winter melons larger than basketballs, little fuzzy squash, foot-long beans, and green bitter melons translucent as carved jade. Native groceries have hung at their windows glazed roasted ducks, huge crackly-skinned whole roast pigs, luscious roasted squabs and sausages bunched in bouquets. Delivery men dart about with bean curd cakes packed in bamboo containers, no different now than for centuries past. Bean sprout and noodle factories are busily turning out their day's quotas. San Francisco's Chinatown is America's major receiving point for all Chinese-type foodstuffs, be they from faraway Formosa, Hong Kong, Japan or Mexico, or from a nearby vegetable farm out in the country. Chinatown's produce and import houses are just as busy repacking and shipping out the very products they receive — to Chinese restaurants and shops all over the United States. Shipping stencils read: "Hop Sing Market — Dallas, Texas"; "Wing Fong Restaurant — Portland, Maine"; "Shaw Pang Market — Jackson, Mississippi"; "Wong's Cafe — Savannah, Georgia."

And you should not be surprised to see in a venerable Chinese restaurant, a festive banquet of several tables, covered to the borders with elaborate food, costing seventy dollars or more per table for ten persons, being hosted by a frugal, perhaps threadbare-looking gentleman. Clothes may make the man, but to the Chinese, who take eating seriously, "good food makes man the happiest." This is a Chinese expression of the importance of living, though it may seem to be an extravagance. But it is not, for, according to an old Cantonese proverb: "Money in pocket is not yours — but food in stomach is all yours."

Since San Francisco's Chinatown is the largest Chinese city outside of the Orient, and proudly claims that she possesses more celebrated Cantonese chefs than anywhere in the Americas, it is logical that the Gourmets of the Golden Hills would rendezvous here. For this is the gastronomical heaven where purists can find genuine Cantonese culinary masterpieces and superb Chinese food prepared with true ingredients and seasonings, to fully satisfy their critical palates.

But whether you live in San Francisco, somewhere else within the fifty states, or abroad, it is our goal to put some of Chinatown's cooking secrets within your reach. May no boundaries of miles restrict your interest, and may fresh, new, and exciting dining adventures with the Gourmets of the Golden Hills be opened to you through the portals of the *Eight Immortal Flavors*.

# Chinese Utensils and Techniques

## WAY OF THE WOK

---

Many years ago, we witnessed a meticulous Chinese gourmet — an older friend — gently chide his wife because she had left the ordinary, daily-use *wok* on the stove. The occasion was a special dinner honoring some very important guests. Our friend tested the tone of the regular *wok* with all the finesse and concern of a master swordsman testing his blade. He rejected the *wok* even though it was already placed on the hot stove burner awaiting his performance.

This gourmet asked for an old, fine-tempered *wok* which belonged to his mother. Then he began his virtuoso performance of cooking some simple Chinese greens just with peanut oil and salt. At the time we were somewhat puzzled but it was explained to us that the reason for requesting the old *wok* was because it exuded *wok hay* or cooking fragrance.

We began to appreciate — perhaps not to the degree as our old gourmet friend — but to realize, all the same, the importance of certain basic Chinese utensils in the cooking of Chinese foods. After all, PREPARATION and TIMING are two of the four principles which make a combination of ingredients distinctively Chinese. Proper, suitable utensils and correct cooking methods are the keys to those two principles.

We are not going to make a fetish of insisting that you must have a completely Chinese-tooled kitchen in order to cook Chinese dishes properly. In fact, with most of the utensils found in any reasonably equipped cook's domain, you can — with some experience and improvisation — turn out a tasty Chinese dinner. However, if you want to perform like, feel like, and cook like a Chinese gourmet-chef, then we recommend the following four Chinese utensils to assist you in your new cooking adventures.

*WOK:* This is the most versatile cooking vessel in a Chinese-type kitchen. In fact, the *wok* is the most practical cooking utensil ever invented by man. The best testimonial to this historic, centuries-old *wok* is its ever-increasing usage today. The *wok* is a concave pan, now made of thin iron or stainless steel ranging from 12 inches in diameter for family use to 24 inches in diameter for restaurant use. Its thinness and rounded bottom radiate a fast, evenly distributed heat. The "bowl" shape also makes for easy cleaning, plus forming the vital, large cooking area for the important Chinese technique of toss cooking. Both the shape and usage of the *wok* suggest a large hot salad bowl, because you toss the ingredients for the quick cooking method of "toss cook" or *Chow*. The *wok* indeed is versatile, for as we review the eleven basic Chinese cooking methods, the *wok* can be used to: deep fry *(Jow);* steam *(Jing);* smother cook *(Munn);* red cook *(Hoong Siew);* casserole steam *(Dun);* poach *(Jum);* toss cook *(Chow);* boil *(Bo);* light fry *(Jeen)*. Nine cooking uses out of eleven basic methods. What utensil rivals that score?

Two supplementary attachments for the *wok* are (1) a circular steel ring support for the bottom of the *wok,* fitted over the burner, to radiate the highest intensity heat for toss cooking; (2) a deep cover when used for steaming or long cooking processes. While the home gourmet-chef may indulge in possibly two *woks* of different sizes, for different uses, what about the average home cook? We recommend the 14-inch diameter size (top rim — measured from lip to lip) as being the most practical. A small 12-inch size orthodox *wok* has added an innovation — a handle as on a frying pan. *Woks* are obtainable at Chinese grocery and hardware stores.

Suppose you decide that for storage-room scarcity or other reasons you cannot have a *wok,* and still wish to cook the Chinese style — especially the basic toss-cook method. What utensil can you use for approximately the same purpose? A French-type iron skillet is almost ideal, because the inside is rounded.

*STEAMER:* Outside of Cape Cod's famous method of steam cooking clams and lobsters outdoors, cooking by steam is seldom practiced in the American home kitchen. In Chinese cookery, however, whether for a simple home meal or a super banquet, steaming is a principal technique of cooking.

Old-time Chinese restaurants use a "steaming cage" *(Jing Loong)* consisting of tiers of bamboo mesh-woven trays, porous in construction, to permit full penetration of steam generated by boiling water in a huge *wok* on which the trays rest. A large metal cover is lowered over the trays during the steaming process.

The Chinese-American housewife simply uses a large pot with a tight lid, and a one-pound coffee can, first perforated with a beer-can opener, then placed in the pot upside down in the water. The perforated can serves as an ideal trivet to elevate a deep dish and permits steam to contact it. For steaming food in shallow dishes, any standard trivet placed in a Dutch oven works very well.

*THE BIG KNIFE:* This is the most versatile and most indispensable of preparatory utensils in the Chinese kitchen. To be properly equipped, those who intend to do a lot of Chinese cooking should have two types of these cleavers. One is called the *Dai Doh* or Big Knife, designed for chopping through bones with powerful strokes, like splitting poultry into halves, quarters or smaller segments. With the *Dai Doh,* you can chop through shells of crabs and lobsters, mince all kinds of meat, scale large whole fish, and cut right through the bones to chunk them, flat pound and tenderize abalone or beef steaks, crush and pound garlic, ginger or onions, or use the thick back of the knife for mashing.

The other one is called a *Choy Doh* or "vegetable slicing knife," which is used for practically every type of slicing and cutting in the preparation of Chinese food. The *Choy Doh* is not a small knife either, having blade dimensions close to the *Dai Doh* — about 3½ inches wide and about 8 inches long. The back of the *Choy Doh* is thinner, about ⅛ of an inch tapering down to a thinner, sharper cutting edge. The round wooden handle, which is approximately 4 inches in length, can be used to crush Chinese condiments such as Black Beans *(Dow See)* and garlic *(Seen Tow)* into a paste. Pounding is called *Joong*. Also, the Vegetable Slicing Knife is much lighter than the Big Knife and handles with a fine sense of balance. You can use this versatile *Choy Doh* for paring all kinds of vegetables with a little practice, for slicing meats, poultry and fish paper-thin, and, using the flat of the blade, to scoop up the ingredients in one swift motion. More detailed tips on the use of the *Choy Doh* will follow in "Food Preparation" under CUTTING.

*CHOPSTICKS:* Most Caucasians are familiar with chopsticks as the eating utensils of the Chinese and other Oriental people. They may not know that a pair of chopsticks is also a very useful basic utensil in the Chinese kitchen. Chopsticks, as tableware, range in materials from the de luxe type of carved ivory or silver, to the inexpensive ones made from plastic or bamboo.

In the kitchen, bamboo chopsticks are used for whipping eggs, stirring, mixing, piercing or simply picking up food for tasting. These inexpensive bamboo chopsticks, universal among the Chinese (average cost 10 cents or less a pair) are a result of the evolution from their probable origin thousands of years ago — two crude twigs! Oftentimes the butt of many jokes, chopsticks are far more practical than expected, for they are like extended fingers or detached forceps with which you can pick up single small pieces of food. This cannot be accomplished with a fork without using both hands and a piece of bread as a "pusher." Which brings to mind this little story:

An American named John Smith constantly wondered why his new Chinese friend, Wong, never used a fork and always ate with chopsticks. Trying to be helpful, Smith suggested: "Wong, you should really try eating with a fork. Why do you always have to use those foolish-looking chopsticks?" Wong smiled with an appreciative understanding, and answered: "Today, with the dollar worth under forty cents, eating with chopsticks is the only way to make both ends meet!"

If you haven't learned to make both ends of the chopsticks meet, here's how:

## *ON USING CHOPSTICKS*

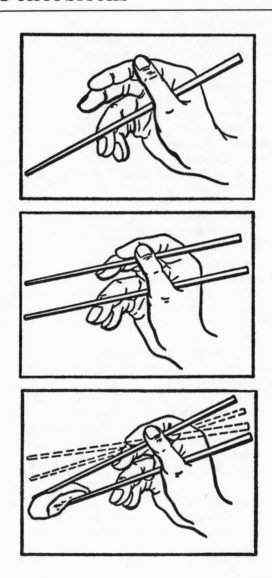

# FOOD PREPARATION

Unlike American dishes, Chinese food set on a table usually is ready to eat without further cutting. Therefore, preparation of the food absorbs more time. Here are some of the preparatory steps which make for characteristic Chinese cooking.

CHOOSING: We use this word both in the sense of shopping for fresh ingredients and handling of foods. When shopping, keep in mind that:

*Vegetables should be the most fresh and tender, especially leafy varieties for the toss-cooking method.*

*Fresh fowl must be used as much as possible. In recipes such as the Chaste Whole Simmered Chicken* (Bok Chit Gai) *it is imperative that a fresh pullet be bought. The same goes for duck and squab.*

*The Chinese custom is to serve fish whole. Fresh-caught fish is absolutely necessary, especially when steam cooked.*

CUTTING: The variety of cutting involved in Chinese dishes cannot help but focus the importance of the "Slicing Knife" or *Choy Doh*. The crux of the unique Chinese toss-cooking method is (1) cutting so that all ingredients are in uniformly small pieces, be they cubes, slices or shreds; (2) high heat, and subsequent short cooking time. So the longer time spent in cutting is balanced by the shorter cooking time.

Although the *Choy Doh* may be an entirely new kitchen tool to you, you can rest assured that in spite of its sinister appearance, the Slicing Knife is not hard to master. The two factors which will safeguard you are (1) the way you grasp the food to be cut with your holding hand and (2) how high you raise the blade of the knife with your cutting hand. Naturally, with a little practice the coordination and rhythm between the two hands will become instinctive.

First, on the hand holding the food, a vertical guard to the face of the knife is formed by the first two fingers with the fingertips tucked underneath (as in drawing). This guard, held at a right angle to the cutting board, allows the face of the knife to be guided by it during the up-down cutting movements.

Second, always keep the knife during its cutting movements no higher than the height of the finger guard. This means from 1½ to 2½ inches, depending on the size of one's hand and the height of what is being cut. Since the Chinese *Choy Doh* averages 3½ inches high in cutting position, there is a margin of safety. You will find that light, precise cutting strokes, with the blade leaning lightly against the guard, will be the best technique.

# ON USING THE CHINESE BIG KNIFE

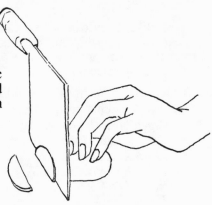

A: This is STRAIGHT-SLICING, a basic vertical cutting stroke for meats and vegetables. Note how raised fingers form a guard-guide for fast cutting.

B: DIAGONAL-SLICING is for coarser, tough-grained vegetables.

C: OBLIQUE-SLICING naturally forms more facets, but the knife still maintains vertical guard guide.

After you know how to handle the Slicing Knife, the following are some of its capabilities:

*Cube:* To cut into 1-inch or larger squares as a convenient size for Pineapple Pork, Abalone or Chicken.

*Crush:* To flatten with the broad side of the knife, usually garlic or ginger for marinades. Another form of crushing is to pound ingredients with the knife handle (this is a truly native style) in a thick bowl.

*Dice:* To cut into sizes from 1/16 to ½ inch, such as the ingredients of the familiar dish, Almond Chicken.

*Mince:* A fine chopping, usually of meats such as pork, in preparation for a steamed patty, such as a Salted Fish and Pork. Chinese do not like to use a meat grinder because it presses out some of the juices. In mincing, try to adopt a rhythm while handling the knife or knives and you will find the job no chore at all.

*Shred:* To cut into thin strips, such as barbecued pork, ham, chicken, or small green onions used for garnish.

*Slash:* To score lightly the skin of any large piece of meat or a large whole fish to permit the seasonings to permeate.

*Straight-Slicing* is suitable for meats and vegetables. The tenderness of the ingredient determines whether it should be straight-sliced or not. On meats, always cut across the grain, and into ⅛-inch thickness for toss cooking. A hint on mushrooms: Remove tough bottom stem, cut mushroom in half, then slice toward rounded edge.

*Diagonal-Slicing* is good for tougher, coarser-grained and fibrous vegetables such as asparagus, celery and cabbage. This method exposes a larger area of the grain and tenderizes quicker from the cooking heat. The difference between the straight and diagonal-slicing is to hold the "finger guard" at a 45-degree angle so the knife is guided diagonally. For more decorative effect use oblique-slicing.

And finally, *Breaking,* a seldom-mentioned method in which the flowerets of cauliflower or broccoli are broken up by hand in small pieces after the tough segments are cut by the big knife. The Chinese like to do this because the cooked pieces have a natural look to them.

READYING: Because of the lightning speed of toss cooking it is well to keep in mind that "preparation is nine-tenths of culinary inspiration." Basically, for any good cook — regardless of the national cuisine — the principles of good planning, thorough pre-preparation, neatness and systematic arrangement will decrease the confusion and increase the tastiness of the results.

A necessary safe rule for Chinese cooking is to have everything ready before any cooking begins. Meaning:

All ingredients should be washed, drained and pre-cut.

Dried ingredients (of which there are many in Chinese cookery) soaked.

All sauces, condiments and blends grouped together near the stove for quick handling.

Pre-cooking, such as parboiling, pre-frying or marinading accomplished.

A good rule for a beginner in Chinese cooking is to try one recipe at a time. In any case, it is wise never to try to cook more than two toss-cooked dishes at any one time.

Chinese food is best enjoyed when it is served hot. Here's a hint on how to serve two toss-cooked dishes and still have everything on the table ready and hot. For the average four-burner stove, suppose you have rice and soup already cooked, and a dish being steamed. Remove the rice or soup (they will stay hot, lidded) and use the two remaining burners for the toss cooking.

## CHINESE COOKING METHODS

Following are the basic methods of cooking which should enable you to turn out a representative array of Chinese dishes:

CASSEROLE STEAMING *(Dun)* The classic example of this method is the Winter Melon Cup, wherein the melon itself serves as the casserole. For concentrated Chinese-style Beef Broth concentrate, a deep, covered earthenware pot is used, and by a slow, simmering steaming of several hours the essence is extracted.

POACHING *(Jum)* You are familiar with poached eggs, which require very little time. But what about chicken or fish? Most likely this Chinese method is new to you, but it is worth trying. Good cooks enjoy showing off their skills, which this longer process requires in order to bring out the beautiful simplicity of quality undisguised. One of the favorites of Chinese gourmets is, for instance, Poached Whole Chicken.

DEEP FRYING *(Jow)* Similar to the American method, frequently using a batter and immersing the food in very hot oil. Most Chinese deep-fried dishes differ, however, in that most of them require more marinating, such as in *Chung Kwong* Squab and Hong Kong Lemon Chicken.

STEAMING *(Jing)* A favorite and practical Chinese home cooking method. Your very first taste of fish, steamed — retaining its delicate texture and natural flavors — will be a revelation. Steamed pork patties keep their own juices intact. Steamed Eggs with Minced Clams *(Sa Bok Jing Don)* make a smooth dish like custard but with more zing. Or steamed

Wrapped Meat Balls and Shrimp Turnovers (*Deem Sum*), the world's original hot hors d'oeuvres!

Steaming time varies from 15 minutes (for small sand dabs) to 30 minutes (for meat patties), depending upon the ingredients. For fish, water should be steaming when fish is placed in vessel, so that controlled cooking of the fish begins immediately. Steamed fish should never be overcooked, otherwise the texture is coarsened.

SMOTHER COOKING *(Munn)* Generally this process involves first a browning or braising of the main item, such as in Smothered Rock Cod. Then the low simmering process in which the resulting rich sauce becomes one of the major components of this dish. Smother-cooked meat dishes, simmered several hours, infuse the spices and other flavorings with the juices into meats, tenderizing at the same time.

RED COOKING *(Hoong Siew)* This, in a sense, is oftentimes a preparatory step rather than a method, since the final step is achieved by smother cooking, or steaming. Generally, soy sauce and other spices are used as a marinade. *Hoong* means red, and the sauce is what gives the reddish-brown tone to Red Cooked Bean Cake *(Hoong Siew Dow Foo)*. Red Cooked Soy Squab *(Hoong Siew Bok Opp)*, however, is a direct deep-fry dish.

QUICK BOILING *(Gwun)* This applies to quickly prepared soups. The quick, intense boiling such as in Fuzzy Squash Soup *(Mo Gwa Tong)* effects the same color, texture, shape, and nutrient retention as in toss cooking.

BOILING *(Bo)* Such as in the long-cooked Lotus Root Soup *(Leen Gnow Tong)* which renders a more full-bodied broth.

LIGHT FRYING *(Jeen)* Using a small amount of oil as in Dry-Fried Prawns *(Gawn Jeen Hah)* and Precious Flower Egg *(Gwai Fah Don)*.

BARBECUE *(Siew)* Barbecued Pork *(Cha Siew)* or Barbecued Spareribs *(Siew Pai Gwut)* can be prepared in your own oven or outdoor barbecue pit with good results. On the other hand, Whole Roast Pig *(Siew Gee)* or Whole Peking Duck *(Kwa Law Opp)* require a special brick or concrete cylindrical pit, or a heavily insulated restaurant-type barbecue box fired with perforated gas or butane pipes.

TOSS COOKING *(Chow)* Chinese cuisine has been acknowledged as among the world's greatest and their original toss-cooking technique is an outstanding characteristic as a result of their invention of the *wok* centuries ago. The concept of toss cooking is entirely different from anything practiced in American or European kitchens. Perhaps the closest to toss cooking is sautéing. Many writers refer to this Chinese method as "Stir-fry." We prefer the term "Toss cooking," which is more descriptively accurate. We suggest that the *wok* is like a large, *hot* salad bowl, blending ingredients over intense heat.

The perfect toss-cooked dish of vegetables and meat or seafood should retain the natural flavors, the natural textures, and the natural food colors. Here are a few hints on how to achieve that perfection:

*Use either a Chinese* wok *or a French-type cast iron skillet.*

*Use good quality vegetable oil (except olive oil) to oil the pan. Olive oil is too rich for Chinese cooking. Domestic corn, peanut or cottonseed oils will qualify.*

*Oil should be sizzling hot, but not heated to smoking, before ingredients are tossed in.*

*Cutting or slicing the ingredients into small shapes is mandatory in order to achieve the flash exposure of intense heat needed to preserve the intrinsic values of the ingredients.*

And readers, don't be afraid of the loud sizzling noise and hissing of steam created at the moment the ingredients meet the sizzling oil for the first time! This is the tip-off that your pan is properly heated, and is gustatory music to the ears of experienced Chinese cooks, who all know that *wok hay* or "pan flavor" is all important to conduct a "symphony" in cookery.

Toss cooking, like the weather, is a subject whose apparent simplicity belies its complexities. How to evaluate the heat is a prime factor in toss cooking. It is the key. So how can you tell? Even pretty good amateur chefs of Chinese cooking have asked: "Why don't my greens come out both crisp *and* cooked clear through, especially when the greens are thick and chunky, as served in a Chinese restaurant?"

The answer is: The average home range gas burner has a gas volume of 12,000 BTU (each BTU is a measurement unit of the amount of heat required to raise one pound of water 1° F.). The restaurant commercial burner using a Chinese *wok* for toss cooking is a 3-burner unit, with an average volume of 36,000 BTU. Even though the commercial *wok* also is larger, you can see that nevertheless the heat intensity still is several times greater!

Also, the average home installation cannot use the 3-burner unit anyway, because the gas pipe is only one-half inch diameter. The commercial kitchen gas pipe is from one and one-half to two inches thick.

So you see, even with a basic "high heat" guidance on the toss cooking recipes, the *degree* of variance can create different results. Probably more so than with the cooking of any other nationality, the Heat Variation Factor — the Chinese cooking — is the most important element for the successful end result.

Even with utensils of similar style and shape, the heat variation depends upon heat conductivity of the materials from which they are made. For instance, a copper-lined skillet bottom — while it distributes heat evenly — does not conduct heat rapidly and intensely, whereas cast iron does.

For toss cooking, gas is the most efficient fuel. The heat is intense while burning, and the burners cool off fast to avoid an afterglow which may overcook the food.

The use of electric ranges is increasing throughout the country, and its adaptation to toss cooking certainly must be considered. The latest types of electric range burners are satisfactory. But the older models were slow to achieve high heat and then retained the heat after being turned off. In several camping trips to ''get away from the office phone'' in the process of writing this book, we experimented with butane heat. From our personal experience, we must reluctantly report that butane heat simply isn't satisfactory.

Many of the recipes in this book have come from the personal files of Kan's restaurant's chefs. It was necessary to adapt from the larger restaurant portions and the stronger commercial burners, to home-use conditions. From the heat and cooking standpoint, naturally in the adaptation to home use more time was required.

One final observation on toss cooking based on our own experience and that of other Chinese cooks: Our recipes do give a specific number of minutes for which to cook specific items. But remember that with your own stove and your own utensils, you may find that in trying a certain recipe several times the cooking time may be increased or decreased slightly in order to achieve the perfect result. As even in automobiles of the identical year and model, differences in performance will appear for which the driver must compensate.

And in toss cooking this Heat Variation Factor is even more intimate and intense.

A word about our recipes. As most cookbook readers know, it is almost impossible to furnish precise amounts of ingredients in any recipe to achieve a taste which will please everyone. We are no exception.

Basically, good cooking is the result of good imagination, and no two persons will prepare a recipe exactly alike. But that is why cooking is such a fascinating and controversial subject, challenging the skill of both professional and amateur chefs.

In Chinese cookery, especially the method of *Chow* or toss cooking, success depends upon several combined factors, starting first with:

*Type of utensil used, thick or thin, composition of metal.*

*Gas or electric stove, new or old types, and size of burners.*

The second factor is the amount of liquid ingredients such as soup stock or water and the amount of cornstarch. Different main ingredients such as meats and vegetables vary in texture; some are more tender than others; therefore you may possibly have to add or reduce the amounts of liquids recommended, but only after you have experimented a few times.

We have stressed the importance of a dish of vegetables being "dry" and not running over with sauce and this applies to other dishes as well.

After the initial purpose of using a good chicken stock for rapidly "softening" the raw ingredients and to blend the juices of all the ingredients, just enough cornstarch paste is added to thicken the excess stock to bring it to a consistency slightly heavy enough to coat the food, but evenly. If you should find that there is too much stock, ladle some out of the pan. Many expert home cooks do not use thickener at all because experience has taught them how much liquid certain combinations of ingredients will need. The third factor is the amount of seasoning, but this is relatively simple, requiring just good common sense and your own taste buds. Again, it is a matter of adding or reducing the amounts slightly to your own taste.

CHINESE WOK AND COVER

# *N*ative Condiments, Sauces, and Ingredients

## GINGKOS IN YOUR KITCHEN

What is a gingko? It is a nut, one half inch thick and white. It grows on a large ornamental tree called the gingko which attains heights of 100 feet. A native of China, since ancient times it has been considered a sacred plant. The gingko has existed unchanged for millions of years. Ingredients such as the gingko are not strange to the Chinese, who through the many centuries have experimented with all manner of living things in their applications as food.

Many of the native condiments, sauces and ingredients we will use in the recipes, or mention throughout the book may be strange to you as to appearance, taste and usage.

Once you start poking around in native Chinese groceries you will be amazed at the tremendous number of condiments and ingredients which are dried. Today foods dehydrated for reconstitution are a miracle of the American supermarket. To the Chinese the basic principle has been old hat. For a millennial period before modern refrigeration, what better method could have been devised for food preservation?

You can buy foods sun-dried from things which grunt, or fly, or swim, or just grow. Pork sausages. Cured ducks. Salted fish. Lily pods. Modern dehydrated foods manufactured with the basic idea of convenience sometimes lose something in flavor. This is not the case with all Chinese foodstuffs. Nature's leisurely way of sun-drying actually often enhances, and subtly creates new nuances of flavor. A favorite slow-simmer soup, using *bok choy gon,* the Chinese chard, dried, is a superb example of a taste sensation distinctly different from the fresh greens.

Sauces is another category where an infinite variety exists, from the familiar all-purpose soy sauce to the not-so-familiar oyster sauce, or *Min See Jeong,* a bean sauce. All of them are flavoring agents which change your regular everyday foodstuffs magically from the American taste to the Chinese taste at your bidding.

These become the catalytic magic which transforms ordinary foods such as sliced beef and asparagus into a gourmet's delight simply by the seasoning of a Chinese concoction of salted black beans mashed with garlic. This simple home dish of asparagus beef, introduced to the American dining public by Kan's restaurant of San Francisco some years ago, drew such accolades that it was proposed to have the California State Fair honor it!

Such is the magic of a basic Chinese condiment. It is the string which holds together the ingredients to form a beautiful epicurean necklace.

In guiding you toward the purchase of native condiments and ingredients, we bear in mind the fact that normally you will not always have a complete stock of them. Most of our recipes can be cooked with a minimum of condiments. A classical Chinese marinade *See Yow Geong Jup-Jow,* literally meaning "soy sauce-fresh ginger juice-gin" is an example whereby one single blend serves to flavor many, many dishes and is the base for many recipes. Every Chinese knows the combination. Its adaptability makes it truly the great Synergistic Sauce.

As you progress — and learn and like more Chinese dishes — you probably will want to experiment with as many Chinese condiments and sauces as possible.

Here is a comprehensive list of items which will be tagged briefly as to name, description, flavor, basic uses and soaking time. This way, when you first confront them in a Chinese grocery, it will not be a complete Chinese puzzle. If you copy the phonetic spelling as given herein, any Chinese storekeeper will know what you want. Determine the amount of usage of any particular item, although most of them will keep rather well since they are either preserved, salted, dried, tinned or bottled.

ABALONE *(Bow Yee)* A mollusk available either dried or canned. The canned variety is cooked and much easier to handle. It adds ocean tang to soups and toss-cooking combinations. Dried abalones are raw and must be soaked overnight before cooking.

BAMBOO SHOOTS *(Jook Soon)* Tender shoots are cut from the bamboo bush and canned in chunks. Used as a vegetable in soups and toss-cooking blends, they contribute a crispy texture.

BEAN CURD *(Tow Fu)* One of the most useful of Chinese ingredients, it is the precipitated protein matter of soybeans pressed into cakes. Bean curd is white, firm and smooth and usually shaped in a ½-inch by 3-inch square. A looser textured variety is pressed in a large 12-inch square cake and cut, as needed, into small pieces. Aside from a faint beanish touch of flavor, it is bland and a great mixer for other highly flavored foods and can be prepared as an accompaniment in all methods — boiled, steamed, toss-cooked, fried, etc. It is even very delicious in its fresh state with spicy condiments and is known as "the meat without bones."

BEAN THREADS *(Fun See)* Thick, threadlike, translucent noodles made from beans which must be pre-soaked. It resembles vermicelli and is used in a vegetarian dish called *Jai,* or with fuzzy squash toss-cooked.

BIRD'S NEST *(Yeen Woh)* Certainly one of the most intriguing and mysterious of Chinese ingredients, both because of its name and its origin. At a glance, bird's nest looks like clusters of fine coconut shreds held together with a deep beige-colored sugar glaze. The cellophane-topped box which holds the bird's nest declares it to be ''the product of Malaya, Siam, Sumatra and Borneo.'' Indeed it is, being plucked from the nests of esculent swifts perched on cliffs in these faraway places. The ''bird's nest'' is a gelatinous material produced from a special type of seaweed obtained by the swifts. Harvested, dried and purified, it must be soaked and again cleaned before use. Bird's Nest is considered very nutritious and is a ''must'' for formal Chinese dinners in a soup form.

BLACK BEAN, DRIED *(Woo Dow)* Pea-sized oval beans used in many slow-simmer soups.

CHINESE BACON *(Lop May)* A cured side pork, used similarly to the native sausage *Lop Cheong*.

CHINESE SAUSAGE *(Lop Cheong)* A cured, richly flavored pork sausage, hung in stringed bunches in groceries. Cook it by steaming whole over rice till the fat is translucent. Or, parboiled and sliced it is used in combination with other meats and vegetables.

CLOUD FUNGUS *(Won Yee)* A type of cultivated fungus which in the dried state is grayish brown, one inch long. After soaking it turns into an opaque brown and is shaped like an ear. Gelatinous in appearance then, it retains a desirable crunchy texture. It is most popular in toss-cooked combination dishes.

CUTTLEFISH *(Muck Yee)* Thicker and larger than squid, this dried seafood is used mostly for slow simmer soups as a blending agent with Lotus Root. Soak overnight and remove cuttlebone, which is used as a canary food.

DRAGON'S EYES *(Loong Gnon)* A Chinese fruit of the same family as the lychee, but smaller, being only ¾ inch round. Tough, smooth, cinnamon colored shell, with pulpy grape-like fruit inside and a large, dark seed. The canned form is served for dessert. Dried, the shelled pulp is used in slow-simmer herb soups.

DUCK EGGS, SALTED *(Hom Don)* Cured in brine for 40 days, the egg after boiling has a spritely, salty tang. Be sure to wash and rub off the black clay packing. The eggs are boiled and eaten with rice, or broken raw into minced pork meat patty and steamed together.

DUCK LIVER, CURED *(Opp Geok Bow)* Hard, dark brown duck liver, wrapped in cured ducks' feet. It must be soaked 2 hours or more. With an intense meaty-concentrate flavor, like thick bovril, it is generally chopped with steamed minced pork dishes.

BLACK MUSHROOMS *(Doong Goo)* A thick Chinese mushroom used whole. They average from ½ to 2 inches in diameter, dried, and expand somewhat when soaked. Brownish, black capped, their flavor is woodsy and rich, with a meat overtone.

BUTTON MUSHROOMS *(Mo Goo)* A tinned French mushroom variety, sliced or whole, used in both soups and toss-cooked dishes.

FLOWER MUSHROOMS *(Fah Goo)* Another variety of the black Chinese mushroom, but thicker and somewhat flower shaped. This species is scarcer, and is thus classified as de luxe. Naturally, it is more costly, and reserved for use in expensive banquet dishes.

GRASS MUSHROOMS *(Cho Goo)* A fragrant, thin, leafy type of mushroom with a texture crisper and different from the black mushroom. It is more like an Italian mushroom and is best used in dishes such as steamed chicken.

FISH, SALTED *(Hom Yee)* The Chinese salt-cure and dry many varieties of fish. Some are simply hung up after drying, others are kept in oil. Like cured duck eggs, salted fish can either be enjoyed singly, or be blended with meats. Seaside, a suburb of Monterey in California, is a large processing center for dried flounder *(Dai Day)* which is shipped all over the United States.

GINGKO NUT *(Bok Gaw)* A beige-colored, tough-shelled nut, with ivory colored meat, it is also available shelled in tins. Gingko Nuts are used for soups and smother-cooked dishes.

GLUTINOUS RICE *(Naw Mai)* Round and pearly in appearance unlike the regular Patna long-grain rice which the Chinese eat for their daily grain. This rice is used for special dishes such as glutinous rice chicken, or the pyramid-shaped tamale, *Joong.* It is grown in the Central Valley of California, has a "tacky" texture and feel, and is used in ceremonial dishes.

HAIR SEAWEED *(Fot Choy)* A fine, hair-like dried seaweed, black, which is popular in festive dishes such as the Buddhist vegetarian *Jai.* Phonetically in the Chinese language the words *Fot Choy* sound similar to the words "good fortune" or "prosperity," and so it is symbolic as well as texturally delightful.

LILY FLOWER, DRIED *(Gum Jum)* Two to three inches long and a golden brown color, it is aptly called by the Chinese "Golden Needle," or *Gum Jum.* Possessing a light beef broth flavor, this exotic ingredient is used as a garnish-flavorer with fish, poultry or in toss cooking.

TIGER LILY PETALS *(Bok Hop)* A dried white fleshy petal, related to the Lily Root, this ingredient is used in soups and smother-cooked dishes.

LOTUS SEEDS *(Leen Gee)*  Available dried or canned. With a dark skin husk, these half-inch ovals are used for soups and smother-cooked dishes. A symbol of fertility, Lotus Seeds are used extensively in festival dishes, because the words mean "a successive birth of sons." They also are candied for sweetmeats.

MELON SEEDS *(Gwa Gee)*  Both black and red color, the last being more expensive. They are eaten like pumpkin seeds, or the meats are used in Moon Cakes.

OILS *(Yow)*  Vegetable oils have proven to be best for the high-heat type of Chinese cooking, as exemplified by the toss-cooking method. Standard brand vegetable oils (corn or peanut) are all very satisfactory. They hold a high temperature without smoking up. The Chinese also have a kitchen trick of "cooking" some raw oil, and having it on hand to use sparingly over dishes such as steamed salted and fresh fish to "flavor-smooth" it.

OYSTERS, DRIED *(Ho See)*  Reddish brown in color, the sun-drying process seems to impart more depth and body to the essential oyster flavor. Soak them first in cold water until the oysters expand, then soak them again in warm water, and remove sand. Use them in soups, or minced meat dishes.

PICKLED GINGER *(Seen Geong)*  Usually served in slices with Thousand Year-Old Eggs, ginger is also eaten with ceremonial Red Egg in a presentation for the customary Chinese infant's month-old party; available in jars.

PICKLED MUSTARD GREENS *(Hom Choy)*  The large foot-long mustard greens, pickled and cured, have a greenish dark-yellow color. Sold in bulk from brine barrels, you can buy them by piece or by weight. Sliced diagonally, very appetizing toss-cooked with beef. The stalks are crisp.

PICKLED SCALLIONS *(Kew Tow)*  Quartered and eaten as a complement to Thousand Year-Old Eggs, slivered as a flavor (and crisp texture) accent for sweet-and-sour fish creations. These, too, are available in jars.

RICE STICKS *(Mai Fun)*  An opaque rice noodle, thin as string, and wound in a five-inch-long pack. Deep fry them and use as garnish topping, or use as a regular noodle, preferably toss cooked.

RED DATES *(Hoong Joe)*  Little dried jujubes, with glossy red skin. They impart a sweetness, lighter than that of prunes, as a flavor for soups. Or use as garnish and flavor for the steaming of fish, and in desserts.

SEAWEED, DRIED *(Gee Choy)*  Literally named "paper vegetable," so thin and light is its black-purple, dehydrated form. It expands double when soaked and gives the tang of the sea in soups. *Gee Choy* is sold in small packets.

SHRIMP, DRIED — LARGE *(Hah Gawn)*  For flavoring in soups and cooking with meats and vegetables.

果白

**GINGKO NUTS**
*(Bok Gaw)*

皮菓

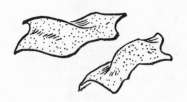

**TANGERINE PEELS**
*(Gaw Pay)*

棗紅

**RED DATES**
*(Hoong Jo)*

柱瑤江

**DRIED SCALLOPS**
*(Gong Yee Chee)*

耳雲

**CLOUD EAR FUNGI**
*(Wun Yee)*

角欖

**DRIED OLIVES**
*(Lom Gok)*

魚鮑

**DRIED ABALONE**
*(Bow Yee)*

魚魷

**CUTTLEFISH**
*(Muk Yee)*

針金

**DRIED LILY FLOWER**
*(Gum Jum)*

菇冬

**BLACK MUSHROOMS**
*(Doong Goo)*

角八

**STAR ANISE**
*(Bot Gok)*

竹崙

**SOY BEAN SKIN**
*(Foo Jook)*

腐豆

**BEAN CURD**
*(Dow Foo)*

豉蠔

**DRIED OYSTERS**
*(Ho See)*

薑生

**GINGER ROOT**
*(Sang Geong)*

子蓮

**LOTUS SEEDS**
*(Leen Jee)*

SHRIMP, DRIED — SMALL *(Hah Mi)* A tiny variety, literally called "rice-size shrimp" although they average one half inch long. They are also used for flavoring soups and are sometimes used to accent bland vegetables in toss-cooked dishes.

SOYBEAN SKIN *(Foo Jook)* Dried skin of soybean milk. Sold in packages, it is flat and thin, with a creamy-glaze appearance. Soak it before using in soups, or in smother-cooking recipes. You will enjoy its chewy texture, with its slightly nut-like flavor.

SOYBEAN SKIN, SWEET *(Teem Jook)* Similar but thicker than *Foo Jook,* its taste is slightly sweeter. It is used in smother-cooked recipes.

SQUID, DRIED *(Yow Yee)* Brown with whitish powder coating. Soak the squid overnight and use it for toss-cooked or steamed dishes.

THOUSAND-YEAR-OLD EGGS *(Pei Don)* Eggs cured really only 100 days, covered with a casing of lime and straw, which must be washed off. Shelled, the petrified egg has an amber-colored, firm, gelatinous-textured white. The yolk is dark and cheeselike. Basically an hors d'oeuvre, it is also used in The Three-Toned Egg recipe, etc.

VIRGINIA HAM *(Gum Wah Tuey)* Its definite flavor and firm texture make it an adequate substitute for the old-time "Golden Coin" ham of China, no longer available. It can be used as a good contrasting garnish.

WATER CHESTNUT FLOUR *(Ma Tai Fun)* A fine-textured powder ground from dried water chestnuts. When used in a batter, it produces a very crisp coating. This flour is also used for various desserts.

WOOD FUNGUS *(Mook Yee)* A dried fungus thicker than the Cloud Fungus *(Won Yee),* this is tougher in texture and more crisp. It is used for quasi-medicinal dishes such as *Gai Jow,* the New Mother's Best Friend Soup.

NATIVE HERBS *(Yok Choy)* A word should be said for the multitude of native Chinese herbs, of which many varieties are no longer available since they are indigenous to mainland China and therefore cannot be imported into the United States. Fanciers of Chinese food know that many herbs used in long-simmering soups are believed to have a quasi-medicinal benefit. The list is too long to enumerate here, but *Gay Gee,* for instance, a mandarin-red dried berry, is said to improve eyesight. Others claim similar benefits. But, fact or folklore, the Chinese have enjoyed these herbs both for flavor and the effect they are believed to produce. Their unavailability leaves a void in the authentic lore of Chinese culinary arts.

TECHNICAL INFORMATION ON HERBS FOR SOY CHICKEN

| | |
|---|---|
| *Gum Cho* — Licorice Root | *Sahn Lai* — Kaemferia Galanga |
| *Bot Gok* — Star Anise | *Sew Wai* — Anise Seed |

Place in cheesecloth and suspend in soy sauce that chicken is boiled in.

TERMS FOR FOUR FLAVOR SOUP HERBS AND THEIR "MEDICINAL" QUALITIES

*Wai San* – Yam Dicorea (Used to     *Leen Gee* — Lotus Nuts
   soothe dry throat membranes)     *Bok Hop* — Tiger Lily
*Nom Hung* — Southern Almonds

The entire combination is believed to clear lung congestion.

# CONDIMENTS

**BLACK BEANS, SALTED** *(Dow See)* Cured fermented small black beans, a staple possessing a distinctive flavor blend of saltiness, spiciness and pungency. Should be soaked briefly and washed before use. A common use is to mash beans with garlic, creating a seasoning popular for both seafood and meats.

**CHINESE VINEGAR** *(Chit Cho)* A native type which seems to be more mellow than American vinegar. Light amber color, it is used as a condiment, with a sliver of fresh ginger, for boiled crab and other similar uses. Another variety of native vinegar called *Hak Mi Cho* or dark rice type, is used more for smother cooking.

**COOKING WINES** *(Jow)* Since native Chinese alcoholic drinks are distilled from grains, rather than grapes, the term "wine" really is not technically correct, but bowing to popular usage, we shall refer to them as such. The ordinary Chinese rice wine, formerly imported in quantity, no longer is available. In America sherry is often used as a substitute in cooking. We prefer the use of gin, which is more akin to the Chinese rice wine. The use of gin in cooking tones down a fishy or gamy flavor.

**CURED OLIVE** *(Lom Gok)* Purplish-black, triangle-shaped half of Chinese olive, dried and cured. Its pungent flavor adds zest to certain fish and meat dishes of the steamed variety. Also, it can be eaten steamed simply with oil, slivers of ginger and a dash of sugar.

**FIVE FRAGRANT SPICES** *(Ng Heung Fun)* A cocoa-colored powder blend of five spices: Chinese star anise, cloves, fennel, anise pepper and cinnamon. This classical spice is unlike any American condiment, but it is also potent, so use it sparingly. Its very blend lends subtlety of flavor to meats and poultry in barbecue and smother cooking.

**GINGER ROOT** *(Sang Geong)* A staple Chinese ingredient which, in the fresh state, is a gnarled root with a light tannish, scaly skin. Fresh ginger has a spicy, refreshing quality which heightens the taste of foods. Chinese use this basic flavoring agent in meats, fish (where it is a subtle "de-fisher" without destroying the "sea sweetness" qualities), and also candy it. Young, tender tubers are best for toss cooking. Old ginger is more fibrous, but spicier and good for long, smother-cooked things like pig's trotters and vinegar.

KANTONESE SALT *(Wah Yeem)* A truly different salty seasoning. Used as a salt dip for deep-fried poultry, etc. Make at home by heating one cup of salt in a preheated skillet under moderate heat for five minutes, or until slightly brown. Stir constantly with spatula. Then let it cool, and add: one teaspoon of cinnamon powder, one teaspoon sugar, quarter teaspoon Five Fragrant Spices *(Ng Heung Fun)*, quarter teaspoon monosodium glutamate, and mix thoroughly.

MANDARIN ORANGE PEEL, DRIED *(Gaw Pay)* Brownish dried peels of mandarin orange segmented. When soaked, a citronish bittersweet "gold" flavor is imparted delicately to dishes such as *Sai Wo* Duck.

MONOSODIUM GLUTMATE *(Mei Jing)* It seems incredible that this flavor accent powder, a modern product packaged with a mass-production look, did have its origin centuries ago in old China. A charming story, which we like to believe, involved a contest in which several monks with gourmet tastes competed with each other to produce the most delicious batch of *Loh Hon Jai,* the standard monks' food consisting of various vegetarian ingredients. Because of their religious beliefs, absolutely no meat products could be introduced for flavor accents. All the entries were flavorful, but one — the winner's — was really outstanding! The winner had added one precious secret ingredient the others did not have — a powdered dried seaweed which later was discovered to be the first crude source of monosodium glutamate. It was not until 1908 that Dr. Kikunae Ikeda, the great Japanese scientist, successfully extracted Glutamic Acid from edible seaweed and from it crystallized monosodium glutamate and marketed it under the name of *AJI-NO-MOTO.* Then in 1921 Chinese scientist Poo-Nien Wu of Shanghai developed a process for extracting monosodium glutamate from wheat protein and was marketing his discovery, *VE-TSIN,* in China, Singapore, Malaya and the Philippines to the amount of 350,000 pounds a year. Other raw material sources are corn, soybean protein, and desugared beet molasses. Today, manufacturers in the United States produce billions of pounds of monosodium glutamate a year, but the latest development is the synthesizing of Glutamic Acid, which should bring the price of monosodium glutamate within the reach of all. Monosodium glutamate, described appropriately at times as "glasses for your tastebuds" — "essence of taste" and "the food flavor intensifier" — "the wonder powder," etc., is sold under many brand names on the grocery store shelves — but be sure to buy a reputable brand such as Ac'cent, which is almost 100 percent pure.

MUSTARD GREENS, CURED *(Muey Choy)* Tempered by sunning, brining, another sunning and then steaming through a week-long process, this ingredient is much used in home dishes such as minced pork patties combined with hot pepper.

PICKLED BAMBOO SHOOTS *(Seen Sun Yee)* Salty and sour thin membranes of tender bamboo shoots, the size of a piece of chewing gum. They come packed in tins, or they can be bought in bulk at the Chinese grocery. Of crisp texture, they form an excellent appetite stimulant in a recipe with sliced tender beef, steamed. The blended juice is great with rice.

RED GINGER *(Hoong Geong)* A pinkish-red cooked and cured ginger root, used mainly as a color accent garnish, sometimes as a flavor contrast, such as for *jook* (the Chinese rice gruel), or as a slivered garnish for many fish dishes. It may be purchased in tins or jars from any Chinese grocer.

ROCK SUGAR *(Bing Tong)* A Chinese variety which is golden colored, and used to give a glaze to foods such as soy sauce chicken.

SALTED CURED VEGETABLE *(Chung Choy)* A salty, still moist but cured stalk and leaf of cabbage, tightly wrapped in a ball about two inches in diameter. Of a deep brownish-green color, it is chopped and sprinkled on fish for flavoring, or mixed into minced or sliced pork. Sold by the piece. Keep jarred in a cool place.

SCALLOPS, DRIED *(Gong Yow Chee)* Another seafood flavoring ingredient, this one imparts a rich flavor to soups and minced meats. The half-inch thick discs are of a light amber color.

SESAME SEED OIL *(Gee Mah Yow)* Rich nut-fragrant oil, deep golden-toned, this is more like an essence. A few drops are enough to impart extra zip to soups or bland foods.

STAR ANISE *(Bot Gok)* An eight-pointed star-shaped fruit; dried, it is a deep burnt sienna shade and yields fragrant volatile oils. Star anise is used much in red-smother cooking wherein the flavors are slowly infused in the food. About one half inch in size.

SWEET TEA PICKLE *(Cha Gwa)* Amberish-colored sweet pickle, slender and three inches long. Crunchy. Sliced to accompany rice gruel *(jook)* or steamed with pork or beef.

BEAN CAKE FERMENTED *(Foo Yee)* Pressed bean curd cubes, about 1½ inches square, buff colored, packed in jars and fermented in alcohol. Similar to Liederkranz cheese in taste. A pungent condiment for cooking certain vegetables, pork and chicken. In homes it is used as a side dish, with a pinch of sugar and a few drops of vegetable oil, to go with rice.

# *SAUCES*

BEAN SAUCE *(Min See Jeong)* A brown salty bean paste packed in small tins or jars, it is useful as a flavoring agent in the steaming of fish, and for many bland vegetables, such as cauliflower, in the toss-cooking process.

OYSTER SAUCE *(Ho Yow)* One of the great sauces of a sophisticated national cuisine. *Ho Yow* literally means essence of oysters. A thick, brown sauce, with the rich full bouquet of the oyster — but, without any fishiness — it is used as a dip for the classic boiled chicken, or roast pork, and is used to season meats during the cooking process. Just a bit goes a long way. It is sold in bottles or tins.

PLUM SAUCE *(Seen Mouie Jeong)* A piquant dark brown, thick sauce in which pieces of roast duck, etc. are dipped for flavor accent.

RED SEASONING SAUCE *(Hoy Sin Jeong)* A piquant-sweet-spicy thick red sauce which has an overtone of a plum taste. But it is made of soybeans, garlic, salt and chili. A table condiment for Peking Duck, shellfish, etc. Packed in tins, it keeps well when tightly capped in the refrigerator.

SHRIMP PASTE *(Hom Hah)* A really strong salty-shrimpy paste of a mixed mauve-grey color, this comes in a chutney-type jar. It is similar to anchovy paste and is used in steaming to enhance roast pork, or chicken in home-type dinners to accompany steamed rice.

SPICED RED BEAN CURD *(Nom Yee)* A variation of bean cake fermented, but of slightly harder consistency. Brick-red in color, it has a pungent, aromatic flavor. Our favorite seasoning for slow, smother-cooked dishes like potatoes with duck, it can also be a side dish as a rice accompaniment.

SOY SAUCE *(See Yow)* For Chinese cooking, soy sauce is the great all-purpose and most indispensable of all sauces. It is a liquid, ranging in color from light brown to a dark reddish-brown and from a thinnish to a thick density — all depending on the grade and type. Soy sauce is used to flavor and color gravies and sauces and as a marinade. For the "red cooking" method, ingredients are incarnadined by the dark sauce. It may also be used as a table dip by itself, or mixed with mustard. Soy sauce is different from salt, has the taste of a beef essence, and is our all-purpose seasoning sauce.

Soy sauce is made by a fermentation process of the blend of cooked soybeans, roasted wheat and wheat flour, a yeast mold and salt. The best grades of Chinese soy sauce are still made by the old-fashioned, aged, natural fermentation process, rather than by the quickly made chemical hydrolysis method.

The type known as *Sang Chau,* light in color and density, is the premier kind for flavoring and dipping. It has the pure taste of an essence. Unless you ask for *Sang Chau* by name, you will get the darker soy sauce or *See Yow.*

Misted in antiquity, there is no definitive record of its origin, but soy sauce is a Chinese household necessity and has been for many centuries. Reference to the sauce has been made as early as the Chou Dynasty, some 200 years before Christ! Since that time literature about it has periodically appeared. Undoubtedly since its very origin soy sauce has been made in the home or as a village industry. As a manufactured product it started in 1688. With its long condimentary life, no wonder that, to the Chinese, soy sauce is the Sauce of Life.

# *S*oups

## *LO, THE LOVELY LOTUS*

---

Since primitive man simmered his first rude pot of soup, the alchemy of water cooked with various meats and vegetables has been transmuted into a thousand and one kinds of soups.

But have you ever tasted a lotus root soup?

To the Chinese the lotus is a symbol of perfection and purity. Everywhere in China when one sees limpid pools, one drinks in the beauty of the graceful cup-like blossoms, colored like a tinted dawn. The leaves are a verdant flotilla. To the eye also, the lotus is a beautiful sacred flower.

Hidden beneath the pool are the jointed brownish roots, the anchor from which the stems protrude. These roots have concentrically hollow spaces, and are very crisp to the bite. The Chinese do not waste anything, so naturally they found ways of eating the lotus roots. With their sophisticated culinary inventiveness, they have paired off this symbol of purity with cuttlefish, and the result is an extraordinarily rich, pure broth.

Or take a pigeon. Rather, catch a pigeon. Match it (dressed, of course) with a fuzzy squash — and you have another typical Chinese home soup. Both lotus and pigeons are, by the way, listed herein as soup recipes.

Or, perchance, would you care to tackle the fabulous shark's fin soup? Sensing your courage as a cook, we have included that recipe, too. But the bulk of our recipes are everyday soups to accompany home meals. They have the virtue of simplicity of preparation, usually including different varieties of vegetables for crisp texture and fresh flavor qualities. For this reason, every Chinese dinner usually has a soup of some kind included in the planning. And at a formal Chinese banquet, as many as three varieties of soup are served, beginning with shark's fin soup, continuing with bird's nest soup, and perhaps boasting a mustard green soup between courses. At elaborate dinners, the soups which are enjoyed between more solid courses also serve to neutralize and "clear" the palate, so that each succeeding one of the Eight Immortal Flavors can be fully savored.

Be it banquet offering or simple, quick-boiled soup, the basis of a full, flavorful blend is a good, rich soup stock. Beyond this, the ultimate character of texture and taste of the final soup depends on the particular blend of ingredients involved.

Frankly, for all the diversity that some writers have suggested between a Chinese and non-Chinese soup stock, the truth boils down (if we may use a kitchen pun here) to the fact that a patiently, well-made stock is essential; regardless of national label. It must be one which is infused by extraction with all the beneficial goodness from meat and bone, one in which there has been blended together all the natural flavors and sweetness from a long, tedious, slow cooking. It should also be one which has a neutral base on which to glorify other, subsequent flavors and blends. For this reason in Chinese soup stock we use only pork or chicken but not beef, which has a more pronounced flavor. Such soup stock is used by expert chefs as a necessary base for their liquid requirements in good cooking.

Chinese soups can be classified into light (or "quick") and heavy soups. Also they are sometimes labeled as quasi-medicinal, a classification not familiar in non-Chinese cuisine. In this latter category you will find, for instance, a recipe called "New Mother's Best Friend." Many soups of this nature usually feature some part of a creature of the forest — deer's tendons, for example, to symbolize the giving of speed; a bear's paw, to embody strength — which is blended with native Chinese herbs and simmered for many hours to extract all the potency therein.

The story is told about the mayor of a large city who went to his favorite Chinese restaurant, complaining to his favorite waiter of a cold. The Celestial servant claimed that the Chinese believed in the healing powers of mustard greens soup for such an ailment since it was *leong* or cool and soothing. The mayor partook of it, and next day felt greatly relieved.

Several days afterwards, and several rumors later, nearly everyone at city hall with a cold trekked to Chinatown. Chinese restaurants in that area got an unprecedented run on mustard greens soup. Pure coincidence? Who knows? At least mustard green is a healthy green, leafy and said to contain vitamins C and D.

Several Chinese light soups are in the mustard greens category. Any vegetable cooked quickly so that the nutritional values, texture and garden fresh taste and color are retained should be good for you. These Chinese soups are clear, not creamy, and can be prepared within the half-hour.

Many of the long-simmering soups call for some dried ingredients. This common utilization of dehydration is another characteristic of certain Chinese foods. Centuries ago, the Chinese discovered that many foods could be preserved by the practical but ancient methods of salting and drying in the sun and wind. Vegetables such as Chinese chard, lotus root, turnips, bitter melons, mushrooms, seaweed, etc. are used dried even when they are available fresh. Dehydrated seafood, such as cuttlefish, shark's fins, oysters, squid, abalone and scallops, is preferred because the use of dried ingredients more definitely changes the flavor characteristics of a soup and renders a more full-bodied taste. Evidently the process of solar benefits and long simmering does something extra.

For home serving, usually one soup is the rule. A full-bodied or substantial soup is desired for more than just its liquid content because ingredients such as pieces of meat, chicken, dried mushrooms, lotus root, and other vegetables offer something to "sink your teeth into."

As with the other Chinese dishes, each person can help himself; therefore all soups are served in a large tureen at the table.

## BASIC RECIPE FOR CHINESE SOUP STOCK

In a large covered soup pot, place:

> **1 chicken carcass**
> **½ lb. lean pork or 2 lbs. pork neck bones**
> **previously seasoned with:**
> **½ teaspoon salt**
> **½ teaspoon monosodium glutamate**

Add cold water to cover.

Cook at high heat until water boils, reduce to medium heat and cook slowly for two hours (so that flavor is fully extracted from meat). Add *boiling* water as needed.

Skim off fat, strain soup and cool to prevent souring.

*This one, cooked with pork, and the following, a chicken stock, are the two basic soup recipes, either of which you can choose for your own personal reasons.*

# BASIC RECIPE FOR CHINESE CHICKEN STOCK

In a covered soup pot, place:
**1 medium-sized dressed hen and giblets**
Add cold water to cover.
Cook at high heat until water boils, reduce to medium heat and cook slowly for two or three hours. Add *boiling* water as needed. When nearly cooked, add:

**2 stalks celery**
**2 chopped scallions**
**½ teaspoon salt**
**½ teaspoon monosodium glutamate**

Cook until vegetables are tender. Skim off fat, strain soup and cool to prevent souring. Discard vegetables.

*In a pinch, if you are really caught short, a canned chicken soup can substitute. The quality of freshness – so greatly stressed by the Chinese – can be equalized in the canned soup by the Chinese vegetable to be selected.*

# ABALONE SOUP
## (Bow Yee Tong)

In a small soup pot, place:   **6 cups basic or chicken stock**
Bring to a boil.
Add:   **¼ lb. sliced pork**
**1 can abalone, sliced, with**
**½ cup of the abalone liquor**
Continue cooking for 15 minutes, reduce to medium heat. Skim off fat.
Add:   **½ cup sliced water chestnuts**
**½ cup sliced canned mushrooms**
Bring soup to a boil again, and season with salt. Serves 6

*"A" is for abalone, and the beginning of the entire series of recipes, starting with the soups. The Chinese believe strongly in symbols. This initial recipe keynotes the whole series – for abalone soup is different from the entire range of American and European soups, yet it is as simple to make as a quick-boiled soup.*

# BIRD'S NEST SOUP
*(Yeen Woh Tong)*

Soak 4 hours in cold water:    ¼ **lb. imported pure bird's nest** *(Yeen Woh)*
Drain and rinse well with cold water.
Place the bird's nest in a pot with sufficient water to cover.
Add:    ½ **teaspoon baking soda**
Boil at high heat for 5 minutes. Drain and rinse with cold water. Return to pot.
Add:    7 **cups chicken stock to cover**
Boil at high heat for 15 minutes. Drain. Discard soup.
Place in soup pot:

- 6 **cups basic soup stock**
- **Bird's nest**
- ¼ **cup shredded white meat of uncooked chicken**
- ¼ **cup finely shredded cooked ham**
- 1 **teaspoon monosodium glutamate**
- **Salt to taste**

Bring to boil and cook at low heat for ½ hour.
Garnish with finely slivered green onions and grated cooked Virginia ham.
Serves 5

This is one of the classical Chinese soups, usually served at banquets, or home parties. As with many classics, this soup has the authentic mold of history stamped on it. During the 13th century, the invasion of Genghis Khan and his Mongol hordes hastened the twilight of the Sung dynasty. The young Emperor Ping and his faithful small band fled from stand to stand, making a final retreat to the tiny island of Yaishang in south China. A tight Mongol blockade made their food situation desperate. The emperor and his followers ate even the gelatinous matter found in the nests of swifts who stored it as food for their young. Despairing of ever defending his throne, the ruler and many of his court threw themselves into the sea. Thus is bird's nest soup a memorial to the tragedy of an emperor.

## CHINESE OKRA SOUP
*(See Gwa Tong)*

Trim off stringy edges from 2 medium sized Chinese okra. Wash and halve. Cut into ½-inch slices.

In a covered soup pot, place:     **5 cups basic or chicken soup stock**

Bring to a boil.

Add:                              **¼ cup sliced raw beef, pork, or chicken**

Cook at high heat for 15 minutes. Skim off fat.

Add:                              **Chinese okra**

Continue cooking at high heat for 10 minutes, or until okra is tender, season to taste with salt and monosodium glutamate. Break a raw egg and float on finished soup before serving (optional). Bits of okra and meat may be dipped in Chinese hot mustard and soy sauce during the soup course. Serves 5

*First of the Chinese vegetable soups. The relative speed of preparation of these soups preserves the refreshing garden greenness and texture – unexpected in a soup – and yet so routine in any Chinese vegetable dish. Try it with any type of meal.*

## MATRIMONY VINE SOUP
*(Gow Gay Tong)*

Have prepared:                    **6 bunches Matrimony Vine** *(Gow Gay)*

Remove and save all leaves and discard stems. Wash and drain.

In a soup pot, place:             **1 cup chopped lean uncooked pork**
                                  **6 cups chicken stock**

Cover and boil 15 to 20 minutes. Uncover and skim off fat.

Add:                              **Matrimony Vine leaves**
                                  **Salt to taste**
                                  **¼ teaspoon monosodium glutamate**

Stir and cook until soup reaches boiling point again (about 6 minutes).

Add gradually:                    **2 whipped eggs**

Remove from fire and stir gently until all ingredients are mixed. Serve at once. Serves 5

*Gow Gay, or Matrimony Vine, is ideal for making a quick boiled soup and one of the favorites among the* Ching, *or clear soup categories.*

## FOUR FLAVOR SOUP
*(Say May Tong)*

Purchase from Chinatown grocery or apothecary:

**½ cup lotus nuts** *(Leen Gee)*
**½ cup Tiger Lily** *(Bok Hop)*
**⅓ cup Southern Almonds** *(Nom Hung)*
**½ cup Yam Dioscorea** *(Wai San)*

Soak ingredients in cold water for ½ hour, rinse and drain.
In a large pot, place:　　**1 lb. uncooked lean pork**
**8 cups cold water**

Bring to a boil and skim.
Add:

**Salt to taste**
**½ teaspoon monosodium glutamate**
**Ingredients (first 4 above)**

Cover and continue to boil at medium high heat for 1½ hours. Serves 4

## FUZZY SQUASH AND PIGEON SOUP
*(Mo Gwa Bok Opp Tong)*

Peel two medium-sized fuzzy squash. Wash and halve.
In a large soup pot, place:　　**1 large dressed pigeon**
**8 cups Chinese chicken soup stock**

Bring to a boil. Reduce to medium heat, skim off fat.
Add:

**Prepared fuzzy squash**
**1-inch square of dried Mandarin orange peel**
**(previously softened in cold water)**

Cover and again bring to a boil. Reduce to medium heat, simmer for 2 hours. Before serving, salt to taste. Each serving should include some fuzzy squash.

The meat from the pigeon and fuzzy squash is also delicious when dipped in Chinese hot mustard and soy sauce between mouthfuls of soup. Serves 6.

*The role of a pigeon in a soup probably is unfamiliar to many. When you feel adventuresome, try this. Escoffier himself deplores the lack of attention to the pigeon, commenting that it "is worthy of the best tables." The Chinese, in giving much attention to the pigeon, have discovered a happy harmony between fuzzy squash and this neglected bird.*

## DICED WINTER MELON SOUP
*(Doong Gwa Nup Tong)*

In a covered soup pot, place:    **5 cups basic soup stock or chicken broth**
Bring to a boil.
Add:
    **½ pound diced winter melon**
    **¼ cup diced chicken**
    **4 diced water chestnuts**

Simmer 10 minutes, season to taste with salt and monosodium glutamate.
Serves 5


## EGG FLOWER SOUP
*(Don Fah Tong)*

In a covered soup pot, place:    **5 cups basic or chicken soup stock**
Bring to a boil.
Add:
    **1 cup frozen peas**
    **½ cup diced canned mushrooms**
    **¼ cup diced uncooked chicken**

Simmer 5 to 10 minutes.
Beat:    **2 eggs**
Add eggs and stir until eggs separate in shreds, season to taste with salt and
monosodium glutamate. Serves 5

*Frozen vegetables such as green peas are acceptable in both the modern
and the ancient Chinese menu. Hence these are ideal for quick soups.*


## GREEN PEA AND CHOPPED BEEF SOUP
*(Ngow Yuke Ching Dow Gung)*

In a small soup pot, place:    **5 cups chicken stock**
Add:    **¼ pound ground chuck**
Cook at high heat for 10 minutes, reduce to low heat and skim off fat.
Add:    **2 cups frozen peas**
Season to taste with salt and monosodium glutamate.
Cook until peas are tender. Garnish with shredded cooked ham before
serving. Serves 5

## FUZZY SQUASH SOUP
### (Mo Gwa Tong)

Peel 2 medium sized fuzzy squash. Wash and halve. Cut into ¼-inch slices.
In a covered soup pot, place:    **5 cups basic or chicken soup stock**
Bring to a boil.
Add:    **¼ cup sliced raw beef, pork, or chicken**
       **¼ cup sliced dried mushrooms (previously soaked and cleaned in water)**
Cook at high heat for 15 minutes. Skim off fat.
Add:    **Fuzzy squash**
Continue cooking at high heat for 10 minutes or until squash is tender. Season to taste with salt and monosodium glutamate. Break a raw egg and float on finished soup before serving (optional). Bits of squash and meat may be dipped in Chinese hot mustard and soy sauce during soup course. Serves 4

## OXTAIL PEANUT SOUP
### (Ngow Mei Fah Sung Tong)

In a large pot, place:    **2 oxtails cut up at joints**
Brown oxtails evenly at high heat. Stir frequently. Drain off fat.
Add:    **4 quarts warm water to cover oxtails**
       **½ cup shelled raw skinless peanuts**
       **1 inch square piece dried Mandarin orange peel (previously soaked in water until soft)**
       **5 whole dried Chinese dates**
       **3 thin slices ginger root**
Cook at high heat until soup is boiling. Reduce to low heat, and skim off fat.
Add:    **½ teaspoon monosodium glutamate**
Stir and add salt to taste.
Cook at low heat for 3 hours. Serves 4 or 5

*This oxtail, and the pig's tail recipe which follows, are two of the thicker, substantial soups – as compared with the vegetable types. Also a good example of the startling Chinese use of peanuts. Another "two-dish" item.*

## LOTUS ROOT SOUP
*(Leen Ngow Tong)*

In cold water to cover, soak overnight:

**1 dried cuttlefish** *(Muck Yee)*

Rinse several times in cold water. Peel off membranes and remove cuttlebone and tentacles. (Save the calciferous bone for your canary or for a bird owner.) Cut cuttlefish into 1-inch squares.

Peel two pounds lotus root. Wash and halve. Cut into ¼-inch slices.

In a large covered soup pot, place:

**2 pounds pork neck bones**

Cover with boiling water. Boil at high heat for five minutes, strain neck bones in colander and rinse under faucet with cold running water. Replace neck bones in empty pot and cover with about 4 quarts of cold water. Cook at high heat until water boils, reduce to medium heat. Skim off fat.

Add:

**Prepared cuttlefish**
**Prepared lotus root**
**½ tablespoon salt**
**2-inch piece of dried Mandarin orange peel**
  **(previously softened in cold water)**
**6 dried Chinese dates**

Cover and simmer at medium heat for 1 hour. Again skim off fat. Add boiling water to original water line and continue simmering for another 2 hours.

Before serving, add salt and monosodium glutamate to taste. Each serving of soup should include some cuttlefish and lotus root.

The meat from the neck bones, the cuttlefish and lotus root are delicious when dipped in Chinese hot mustard and soy sauce between mouthfuls of soup. Serves 6 to 8

*This is a favorite Chinese family soup. It is a "two-dish" affair with many solid ingredients for texture, and a satisfying, full-bodied rich broth.*

## MEATLESS WATERCRESS SOUP
*(Ching Sai Yong Choy Tong)*

Wash thoroughly 2 bunches young watercress. Cut into 4-inch lengths.

In a small soup pot, place:

**5 cups chicken stock**
**1 teaspoon monosodium glutamate**
**Salt to taste**
**Prepared watercress**

Cook at high heat for 1 hour. Serves 4

*Oddly enough, the combination of watercress and monosodium glutamate, a strictly vegetarian dish, provides a meaty flavor.*

# NEW MOTHER'S BEST FRIEND
*(Gai Jow)*

In a large soup pot, place:  1 large dressed hen, cut into 3-inch pieces
Cover with 4 quarts cold water.
Add to pot:  ½ cup washed cloud ear fungus *(Mook Yee)*
  (soaked overnight in cold water)
  2 slices ginger root
  9 washed Chinese mushrooms, halved (soaked overnight in cold water)
  9 washed Chinese dates
  ½ teaspoon monosodium glutamate
  Salt to taste

Cover pot, bring soup to a boil. Reduce to medium heat, skim off fat. Continue to cook at low simmer for 1 hour. Ladle some of the ingredients into each bowl with the finished soup and add 1 tablespoon or more gin to each serving. Serves 8 to 10

We must confess that we had to give an American name to this important soup. The Chinese simply call it chicken wine, the word *Jow* being the general term for all spirits. This *Gai Jow* is a centuries-old traditional soup administered to bolster the morale of mothers of new-born babies. It is said to restore both strength and spirit — a remedy for what is known as "new babies blues." You must admit the Chinese were pretty subtle to use a chicken saturated in spirits to further an occasion for celebrating. Moreover, the textural blend of crunchy cloud ear fungus and soft mushrooms, plus the gin, makes it a soup you should dare to try — even without the benefit of a new-born baby. It is customary for the paternal family to exercise the courtesy ceremony of distributing pots of this soup to friends and relatives, and also to serve it to guests who come bearing gifts to honor the new heir or heiress and to visit the mother.

## MUSTARD GREENS SOUP
*(Gai Choy Tong)*

In a soup pot, place:       **5 cups basic or chicken soup stock**
Bring to a boil.
Add:
- **1 pound washed Chinese mustard greens, cut into 2-inch lengths**
- **¼ cup sliced raw beef or pork**
- **2 thin slices fresh ginger root**
- **½ teaspoon monosodium glutamate**
- **Salt to taste**

Cook at low heat 10 to 15 minutes, skim off fat. Just before placing on table, break 1 raw egg over soup (optional). Serves 4

## GREEN PEA MUSHROOM SOUP
*(Ching Dow Mo Goo Tong)*

In a covered pot, place:    **5 cups basic or chicken soup stock**
Bring to a boil.
Add:
- **½ cup sliced button mushrooms**
- **1 cup frozen, or fresh, shelled green peas**

Simmer 10 minutes, until peas are tender, season to taste with salt and monosodium glutamate. Serves 4

## LETTUCE AND CHOPPED BEEF SOUP
*(Sang Choy Ngow Yuke Gung)*

In a small soup pot, place:   **5 cups chicken stock**
Add:                        **¼ lb. ground chuck**
Cook at high heat for 10 minutes, reduce to low heat and skim off fat.
Add :                      **½ head shredded lettuce**
Season to taste with salt and monosodium glutamate.
Cook until lettuce is tender, garnish with shredded cooked ham and diced scallions or chives before serving. Serves 4

In season, the substitution of thin-sliced cucumbers for lettuce is equally refreshing. With cucumber, omit scallions or chives.

## PIG'S TAIL AND PEANUTS SOUP
*(Gee Mei Fah Sung Tong)*

Parboil:

3 young medium-sized pig's tails cut in 1-inch pieces, blanched in boiling water

Place in a soup pot:
Bring to a boil.
Add:

3 quarts basic soup stock

Pig's tails
1 cup raw skinned peanut meats
1 inch square piece dried Mandarin orange peel (previously soaked in water)
½ teaspoon monosodium glutamate

Boil at medium heat for 1½ hours. Skim off fat, and salt to taste. Serves 4 or 5

## SAND DAB SOUP
*(Top Sah Tong)*

In a small soup pot, place:
Bring to a boil.
Add:

5 cups basic or chicken stock

¼ lb. dried beans threads (previously soaked and softened for 1 hour in water)
1 teaspoon finely shredded ginger root
1-inch square piece shredded Mandarin orange peel (previously soaked in water until soft)
2 shredded Chinese dates
3 thinly shredded dried mushrooms (previously soaked in water until soft)

Reduce to medium heat.
Add:

Filets of fresh sand dabs or filet of sole cut into 1x2-inch oblongs

Continue cooking for 5 minutes, season with salt and monosodium glutamate. Serves 4

*This recipe is an excellent example of the Chinese technique of neither overcooking nor coarsening the delicate texture of fish, and retaining the natural flavors. The bean threads and other ingredients make it somewhat of a fish chowder, Cantonese style.*

## SHARK'S FIN SOUP
*(Yee Chee Tong)*

In a large dishpan, place:          **4 large dehydrated shark's fins**
Cover with boiling water and soak overnight. Wash and rinse. Repeat process.
Transfer shark's fins to a large pot, boil with 1 whole fresh ginger root for 3 hours. When cool, remove and discard all skin, bones, flesh and liquid and save the cartilages, which are golden brown in color. Drain. Place the cartilages in a smaller pot with 1 whole ginger root and 1 whole onion. Cover with water and boil for 5 hours. Pour off water. Rinse and repeat the process. Save cartilages only. Drain.
In a soup pot, place:          **8 cups chicken soup stock**
Bring to a boil.
Add:          **Shark's fin cartilages**
**Shredded breast meat of chicken from soup stock**
Cook at medium heat for ½ hour, add salt and monosodium glutamate. Just before serving in a tureen, garnish soup with finely shredded Virginia ham and finely cut scallions. Serves 4 to 6

The cuisine of each nation has its own superlative dishes. The Chinese offer food creations so extensive that with seafood alone it is said that at least 365 variations can be prepared — one for each day of the year. From this multitude, possibly a handful of dishes stand supreme for the Chinese gastronome.
One of these is shark's fin — more prized than caviar in its recognition by international epicures. The offering of shark's fin is absolutely *de rigueur* for all formal Chinese dinners.
Why is shark's fin such a premium item of cuisine?
A lust for life — whose perpetuation is said to be aided by the partaking of this piscatorial delicacy — may be one reason. You see, the cartilages are the "muscles" which motivate the shark's fins, giving this fish its tremendous speed and maneuverability. The Chinese believe that this great energy is transferred and absorbed by human beings by the consuming of the cartilages. Unromantically, dieticians believe that the benefits really spring from the high protein content of the product.
This fin — or really cartilage when prepared — is served in many styles of soups and entrees. The top quality, and therefore most expensive product, is transformed into translucent strands as thick as knitting needles and measuring about five inches long. In a restaurant, a serving of these golden cartilages as an entree can cost from twenty to fifty dollars. The average quality shark's fin, however, is from two to three inches long, and the cost lowers to about one quarter of the premium price. The least expensive

grade consists of remnants, about one inch in length. However, even these are considered a luxury.

For this reason etiquette calls for picking up the initial bites of the cartilages with chopsticks — regardless of the grade served — to convey the idea that any shark's fin is fine enough to be picked up individually and to be relished for its truly superb texture. The centuries-old ritualistic courtesy of the Chinese marks this gesture as a compliment to one's host. Lastly — and equally traditional perhaps — is the serving of shark's fin at wedding banquets. The Chinese believe that the cartilages confer many bodily benefits, including the qualities of strength and virility. And, especially for a nuptial occasion, who would wish to dispute this belief?

## SEAWEED SOUP
### (Gee Choy Tong)

In a small soup pot, place:     **5 cups basic or chicken stock**
Bring to a boil.
Add:     **4 diced raw prawns**
     **¼ lb. ground chuck or chopped pork**
     **4 chopped water chestnuts**
Reduce to medium heat and cook for 15 minutes.
Add:     **3 sheets dried Japanese seaweed broken into small pieces**
Continue cooking for 5 more minutes. Season with salt and monosodium glutamate. Serves 4

*Riches from the sea abound in this soup. Brimful of beneficial iodine, seaweed is a basic source of monosodium glutamate. Eat seaweed? And why not – because you'll be surprised by its unique blend of fresh ocean flavor with a natural "sweetness." It's a soup which is sophisticated, gastronomically speaking, and healthy, too. Once you develop a liking for it, seaweed will be one of your favorites.*

## SPINACH SOUP
*(Boh Choy Tong)*

In a soup pot, place:　　　　　**5 cups basic or chicken soup stock**
Bring to a boil.
Add:　　　　　　　　　　　　**4 pieces garlic**
　　　　　　　　　　　　　　**1 pkg. frozen chopped spinach**
　　　　　　　　　　　　　　**¼ lb. ground chuck**
Stir well, cook at low heat for 10 minutes and season to taste with salt and monosodium glutamate. Serves 4

## WATERCRESS BEEF SOUP
*(Sai Yong Choy Yuke Gung)*

In a small soup pot, place:　　**5 cups boiling water**
　　　　　　　　　　　　　　**½ teaspoon monosodium glutamate**
　　　　　　　　　　　　　　**2 or 3 bones from prime rib roast**
　　　　　　　　　　　　　　**2 small bunches watercress washed**
　　　　　　　　　　　　　　　　　**thoroughly, cut into 4-inch lengths**
　　　　　　　　　　　　　　**Salt to taste**
Boil at high heat for 30 minutes, skim off fat before serving. Serves 4

## WINTER MELON CUP
*(Doong Gwa Joong)*

Wash and scrub, then slice the top (3 inches deep) off a 10-pound Chinese winter melon. Scoop out seeds and pulp.
In the winter melon, place:　　**¼ cup diced bamboo shoots (canned)**
　　　　　　　　　　　　　　**¼ cup diced button mushrooms**
　　　　　　　　　　　　　　**¼ cup washed dried lotus nuts**
　　　　　　　　　　　　　　**6 oz. diced raw chicken**
Pour into winter melon:　　　**Chinese chicken stock to ¾ full**
Place entire winter melon into a deep dish to support it. Place the dish in a large pot or *wok*, with three inches or more of hot water to generate steam. The pot must be wide enough so that winter melon and supporting dish can be removed later. Steam whole winter melon in covered pot for 3 hours or more. Add hot water to pot frequently to retain steaming action, depending on age of melon (young: 1-2 hours; old 3-4 hours).
Add:　　　　　　　　　　　　**½ cup frozen green peas**
　　　　　　　　　　　　　　**Salt and monosodium glutamate to taste**

During last ½ hour, add enough chicken stock to fill the pot about ¾ full. Remove winter melon and dish together, and place on table. The melon serves as a tureen. Each dish of soup should be ladled out with some of the ingredients and a bit of the melon. Serves 6

*We end the soup recipes on a note of elegance by presenting you a winter melon cup, whose exotic appearance diverts you from the clever technique of the melon's being cooked in its own large natural tureen. A winter melon cup ranks high enough to be served as a Chinese banquet soup. Any home cook can be proud of serving this imposing soup to her guests.*

*This soup is another example of the Chinese steaming process wherein the integrated flavors of the many ingredients and the juices of the melon are completely and preciously retained.*

# Rice

## THE ETERNAL CHINESE QUESTION

Have you had your rice today?

This is the classical, polite question which Chinese people the world over ask when they mean to inquire:

"How are you today?"

Such is their basic reliance on rice as the staff of life, for as far back as the dawn of history the Chinese started to cultivate this grain with primitive stonebladed hoes. Rice is to the Chinese what bread is to the American. And more. To the Chinese, rice is the symbol of life itself, with all the pride and prejudice which is a part of life.

So whether the greeted one has tasted rice just a few hours ago, or has starved for days, the classical reply still would be, "Yes, I have partaken of sufficiency, thank you."

The vital importance of rice has created many stories and beliefs around it. In Chinese literature, a bowl of rice symbolizes all food. When a bowl of rice is upset, ill fortune is sure to follow. And when a person spills it deliberately, a prime insult has been effected. It is no wonder that the serving of burnt or improperly cooked rice to a guest is considered extremely bad etiquette, no less than the offering of burnt toast.

A man whose business or job has been squeezed from him has "his rice bowl snatched away." One who loses his job has "his rice bowl broken." A corrupt public official is mocked as "a rice barrel." On public issues the Chinese pose the "rice bowl question." Children are indoctrinated with the legend that for each grain of wasted rice left in their rice bowls, a pockmark will appear on the face of their future husband or wife!

The time-honored practice of throwing rice at brides has a Chinese version, too. Once upon a time, in ancient China a beautiful bride was shadowed by a powerful golden pheasant which a rejected suitor ordered for the purpose of slaying her. Trapped on her bridal day, she had the servants throw rice away from her doorstep before she appeared. While the greedy pheasant gobbled at the rice on the ground, the bride nimbly slipped into her bridal chair, and safely escaped to her wedding.

Though a basic food like bread, rice is infinitely more versatile as a table offering. Rice can be served steamed, fried, casseroled, toasted, bundled into a tamale, and made into a thin soup or gruel called *Jook*. A bowl of plain steamed white rice looks deceptively simple, doesn't it? But the Chinese, ingrained with half a hundred centuries of rice experience, have developed a sharply trained palate concerning this grain. With one glance and one morsel, they know exactly whether or not it has attained the perfect form it should have.

An inherent blandness does not hide the fact that rice does possess an aroma. It is a light, mellowed fragrance not unlike fresh bread, but rounder in feeling due to the moisture of the steam. Some say it should look snow-white, which seems slightly crystalline. Perhaps a more accurate description is that rice should be milk-white, ripe and inviting, though firm. Only raw rice has a hard, polished look. Each cooked grain must have a plumpness. Another criterion for perfect cooked rice is that it cannot be mushy. It must have body. Each grain of rice must be proudly separated from its companion.

This is a good point to mention glutinous rice *(Naw Mai)*, a specialty rice which the Chinese use for holiday ceremonial dishes, and whose inherent cooking value is that of being "non-separated" or plain sticky.

This rice is the base for the tamale-shaped *joong*, in which the rice blandness is cunningly contrasted by fillings of ham and brine-cured eggs. *Joong* is the festive snack dish enjoyed during the Dragon Boat Festival which is celebrated each June. Glutinous rice has a "tacky" texture and feel, and experiments have been made for its use as a commercial food flour to create a smooth holding sauce for creamed foods.

Only one small area in the Central Valley of California grows this rice, but because of its traditional use for holiday ceremonial dishes, undoubtedly it will continue to be available.

Chinese food, so varied that a well-planned dinner for eight persons should have eight gourmet flavors instilled in the various dishes, finds that the blandness of rice is the perfect preceptor for the taste buds. Its very blandness blends into the flavor of whatever food is taken with it. Rice clears the palate after it is partaken, so that the diner is prepared to contemplate and savor the full flavor of the following course.

At fashionable formal banquets, however, rice is never served with the chef's various elaborate concoctions. The considerate host is supposed to offer you only the finest — not fill you with an everyday staple such as rice! However, at these feasts, a small, almost ceremonial amount of rice is offered at the end of the meal to signify that the festive event has come to an end, and that all imbibing of liquors and wines should cease.

When to eat rice, and why, is a subject we would like to discuss here because many Americans who enjoy dining at a Chinese restaurant say "wonderful — but an hour later we are hungry again."

Why? The average Chinese dinner, served with many entrees including seafood, meat and fowl — rather than a main entree of a meat dish such as steak or roast — really needs a base of rice during the meal. For the multi-entree Chinese meal, rice also serves as the perfect blender of flavors. Generally, however, the Americans tend to order and dine in banquet style. That is, with little or no rice, regardless of whether they are ordering a simple or elaborate dinner.

When enjoying Chinese food, do as the Chinese do. The advice is rice. A graphic illustration would be to explain a vernacular Chinese phrase used daily — *Soong Fon* — meaning literally that the entrees "accompany or supplement the rice."

So follow the Chinese family dining practice of enjoying your bowl of rice with the various courses. You will never be "hungry an hour later!"

Rice has been a staple food of the Chinese since time immemorial. Prior to 1914, rice from China entered the United States duty free. Through the years and through several wars, it has reached the situation where all rice consumed by the Chinese is grown in the United States. The majority of the Chinese in America live in California — and today, most of the rice they eat is grown in Texas. The Lone Star state produces a long grain Patna-type rice which cooks into separate grains and is most akin to the old native type.

This, then, is the Chinese "bowl of rice" around which life itself revolves. Here is a centuries-honored method of cooking it!

# STEAMED RICE À LA KAN
### (Bok Fon)

Wash thoroughly in 4 or 5 waters, rubbing between the hands until water is no longer milky:    **2 cups rice**

Drain washed rice, add fresh water which will measure 1 inch above rice or to the first joint in first finger, or about

**3 cups water**

IMPORTANT: Use a tall deep pan with a heavy bottom and tight-fitting lid. Revere Ware or any copper-bottomed ware is fine. Cover pot tightly and bring to a rolling boil. When visible water has evaporated, turn heat as low as possible and cook rice 15 minutes longer. The excess water which the rice absorbed during the vigorous boiling will now evaporate, leaving rice tender and each grain separate. Fluff with chopsticks or fork in the cooking utensil before serving. Serves 4 to 6

*Rice may be kept hot for delayed serving by placing an asbestos pad under the pot and keeping the pot covered.*

# GLUTINOUS RICE WITH CHINESE SAUSAGE
### (Naw Mai Lop Cheong Fon)

Have prepared:    **3 cups Glutinous rice, washed and drained**
**2 cups Chinese sausage** *(Lop Cheong)*, **diced**
**½ cup dried Chinese mushrooms, sliced thin (previously softened in water)**

In a heavy pot, place:    **Glutinous rice**
**2½ cups boiling water**
**½ teaspoon salt**

Cover and cook at high heat until water boils. Uncover.

Add to top of rice:    **Diced Chinese sausage and mushrooms**
**½ cup dry shrimp**

Cover and cook, reduce to very low heat, and continue cooking another 20 minutes. Uncover. Remove pot from stove and stir and mix all ingredients thoroughly. Serves 6

## BEEF RICE CASSEROLE
*(Ngow Yuke Fon)*

Have prepared:
    **1 pound raw tender beef (top round), sliced in ⅛-inch strips**
    **3 green onion tops, cut 1 inch long**
    **3 cups cooked rice (keep hot)**

In a preheated *wok* or skillet, place:
    **2 tablespoons vegetable oil**

Bring oil to sizzling point and add:
    **Sliced beef**

Brown rapidly for 1 minute, no more, and reserve.

To the same utensil, add:
    **Sliced green onions**
    **½ teaspoon salt**
    **2 tablespoons Oyster Sauce *(Ho Yow)***
    **¼ teaspoon sugar**
    **1 cup hot chicken broth**

Turn and mix at high heat for 1 minute.

Add:
    **Pre-browned beef**

Add gradually:
    **1 tablespoon cornstarch. Make paste with 1 tablespoon water.**

Turn and mix all ingredients rapidly, 2 to 3 minutes, until gravy thickens. Pour hot beef combination with gravy over rice in casserole. Serves 4

## FRIED RICE
*(Chow Fon)*

Have prepared:
    **4 cups cold cooked long grain rice**
    **½ cup diced barbecued pork *(Cha Siew)* (Ham may be substituted)**
    **¼ cup diced green onion**

In a preheated *wok* or skillet, place:
    **2 tablespoons vegetable oil**

Turn to high heat, toss pork and onion for 1 minute, then add rice, along with:
    **½ teaspoon salt**
    **¼ teaspoon monosodium glutamate**
    **1½ tablespoons soy sauce**

Press rice gently into pan and fry for a few seconds, repeating the process until the rice is hot clear through. Turn and mix rapidly for 5 minutes. Add a few drops of oil if necessary to prevent burning.

Add:                              **2 eggs (thoroughly beaten)**
Mix and toss until eggs are done, about 1 minute. Serves 4 to 6

## *CHICKEN RICE CASSEROLE*
### *(Gai Kow Fon)*

Have prepared:                   **1½ pounds boned uncooked chicken, sliced
                                      into ¾-inch pieces**
                                 **½ pound sliced bamboo shoots**
                                 **1 small can sliced button mushrooms**
                                 **½ pound fresh snow peas, washed, strings
                                      removed**
                                 **3 cups cooked rice (keep hot)**
In a preheated *wok* or skillet, place:
                                 **2 tablespoons vegetable oil**
                                 **¾ teaspoon salt**
Bring oil to sizzling point at high heat.
Add:                             **Sliced chicken**
Toss and turn rapidly for 1 minute.
Add:                             **Sliced bamboo shoots, mushrooms and
                                      snow peas**
                                 **1 cup hot chicken stock**
Cover and cook at medium heat for 3 minutes. Uncover.
Add:                             **1 teaspoon soy sauce**
                                 **¼ teaspoon sugar**
Turn and mix all ingredients thoroughly for 1 or 2 minutes until very hot.
Add gradually:                   **1 tablespoon cornstarch. Make paste with 1
                                      tablespoon water.**
Continue to cook at high heat, tossing and turning frequently, 2 to 3
minutes, until gravy thickens. Place hot rice in a casserole and pour chicken
combination and gravy over rice. Serves 4

# YEONG JOW FRIED RICE
*(Yeong Jow Chow Fon)*

Have prepared:
> ¼ **cup raw prawns or shrimp, diced**
> ¼ **cup barbecued pork or cooked ham, diced**
> ¼ **cup green onions, cut ⅛ inch thick**
> ¼ **cup green peas**
> 1 **cup shredded lettuce**
> 3 **cups cold cooked rice**

In a preheated *wok* or skillet, place:
> 2 **tablespoons vegetable oil**

Bring oil to sizzling point and add:
> **Diced prawns or shrimp**
> ½ **teaspoon salt**

Toss and turn for 2 or 3 minutes or until cooked.

Add:
> **Diced barbecued pork or ham, green onions,**
> **peas, lettuce and rice**
> 2 **tablespoons soy sauce**

Press rice gently into pan and fry for a few seconds, repeating the process until all the rice is hot clear through, then turn and mix rapidly for 5 to 7 minutes. Add a few drops of oil if necessary, to prevent burning. Serves 4

*This de luxe version of fried rice is named after a city in old China where it originated. The vegetables, meat and seafood, combined with rice, makes* Yeong Jow *fried rice an ideal one-dish meal.*

# $\mathcal{V}$egetables

## WHAT'S A FUZZY SQUASH?

A fuzzy squash *(Mo Gwa)* is covered with a fine protective fuzz. It is a typical Chinese vegetable. So is the lotus root, winter melon, and bitter melon, with its pebbled surface and translucence of carved green jade.

All these and other strange-appearing native Chinese vegetables can be found in a bewildering array, piled in front of the local grocery of any good-sized Chinatown. This botanical inheritance can be traced historically as far back as 2737 B.C. when Shen Nung, the father of the art of tilling the soil, personally experimented with various kinds of plant life to discover new edible foods. Since the dawn of Chinese civilization, agriculture has been the main occupation of its people and it still is. The cultivation of such a variety of vegetables is a natural development.

Vegetables dominate the area of the toss-cooking method so, naturally, we will discuss the use of regular American vegetables as well as the native Chinese species. Both in the introduction and the cooking techniques chapters we have repeatedly stressed the unique qualities to be discovered in the Chinese method of handling vegetables, so we need not duplicate that advice here.

Without going into unduly bothersome details, this principle should guide you in the use of American vegetables whenever Chinese vegetables are not available.

Use a similar type of vegetable. For instance, if native Chinese broccoli *(Gai Lon)* is not available, try the regular broccoli. Use Kentucky Wonders in place of the foot-long Chinese beans *(Dow Gok)*.

Actually, in each case, a slightly new and different dish has been created — yet, one similar in feeling and texture. For several generations, Chinese-American housewives have adapted themselves thus in the kitchen. As you begin to master Chinese cooking, you, too, will have the fun of experimenting.

To hammer home the point: That great American institution, spinach — in spite of its health-giving qualities and Popeye's endorsement — still is said to be hated by youngsters (only youngsters?). Treated Chinese style, if it's not loved, at least it won't be hated!

In the recipes following you will note that a good portion of them are not "pure" vegetables — that is to say, not just the vegetables alone, cooked and seasoned. You will note that many of the vegetables are combined with meat or seafood of some kind. Technically, they really are vegetable combinations. The reasons for this are several.

The abundance and variety of vegetables, plus the factor that a majority of the Chinese populace (as in many other countries) were without the luxury of unlimited supplies of meats, naturally shaped the cooking pattern to adjust to the economy. Also, millions of Chinese Buddhists and people of other religious sects, such as Confucianists and Taoists, abstained from beef. The buffalo is a useful worker in the fields, contributing greatly to the welfare of man, and it was deemed religiously cruel to eat its meat. Another Confucian precept was the usage of one-fourth meat to three-fourths vegetables. Thus meat scarcity and the quasi-religious aspects of Chinese life combined to evolve man's primal carnivorous habits into the very palatable "vegetables and meat or seafood" creations which today are being highlighted by many food writers as *the* great new thing on the American culinary and dietary scene.

Whether by design or accident, its proven taste appeal and nutrient-preserving factors should make the vegetable combination, toss-cooking technique, one to be examined carefully by the American housewife.

Here are some basic pointers for the cooking of vegetables in the Chinese manner:

*Buy only fresh, tender vegetables.*

*Never overcook when toss cooking. Let them retain their natural colors.*

*Pan and oil must be sizzling hot, so that vegetables will not become limp and lose their flavor characteristics. Use as little water or soup stock as possible.*

*Learn to half-cook your vegetables until it becomes a habit.*

Following is a glossary of all native Chinese vegetables obtainable in season in the United States, with a brief description of each.

BEAN SPROUTS *(Ngah Choy)* This is a sometimes maligned little vegetable, because it is common and cheap. So in some Chinese restaurants, its overuse as a "filler" has given it an off-prestige standing. But used judiciously in the home, it is very good in some toss cooking, and texturally it is delightful. The very name *Ngah Choy* literally means "vegetable for the teeth," implying a crunchy sensation.

Bean sprouts are tiny shoots which grow from the soybean. They are one of the trio of basic Chinese foodstuffs — bean sprouts, bean curd and soy sauce — derived from this wonder bean. The sprouts average two inches long, are opaque white and the bean head is yellow. Sprouts should be used the same day purchased. If they are to be stored overnight, they should be washed thoroughly, and the husks on the bean head plucked. Submerge the sprouts in water.

Bean sprouts are readily available in most metropolitan centers, and even non-Chinese supermarkets carry them. We prefer the fresh sprouts, but canned ones also are available.

Another variety of bean sprouts, germinated from a larger type bean is the *Dow Ngah*, or BIG BEAN SPROUT. This variety grows a little longer, with a larger golden head, and the sprout is crunchier, but has a more raw "beany" flavor. This variety is not used in Chinese restaurants.

BITTER MELON *(Foo Gwa)* In reality a member of the squash family, this, to the average American, is an exotic-looking vegetable. The size of a cucumber, it is also known as a balsam pear, although it grows on a vine. The bitter melon has a linear, pebbly surface, smooth, jade-like in texture and color. When split open, the inside pulpy sponge and red seeds must be removed before cooking. Possessing a cool, slightly bitter flavor, it blends well with meats, fish filets or chicken in toss cooking, because the total effect has a "zing." Bitter melons are abundant in summer.

BOTTLE GOURD *(Foo Lo Gwa)* A spring and summer vegetable used, sliced, for toss cooking in meat combinations.

CHINESE BROCCOLI *(Gai Lon)* Same color as mustard greens. Small-stalked, 12 to 14 inches long. Used in toss cooking and as a staple because, when properly cooked, it is crisp and flavorful.

CHINESE CELERY CABBAGE *(Siew Choy or Wong Nga Bok)* Predominantly long, wide white stalks, with crinkly light-green leaves on edges of stalks. Shaped like a head of celery, but chunkier, it is used either for toss cooking or quick soups.

CHINESE CHARD *(Bok Choy)* An all-year-around inexpensive staple toss-cook vegetable. Young stalks of a milk-white color are edged with loose green leaves. The vegetable has a yellow flower in the center. Traditionally, the winter crops are choicest.

CHINESE CHIVES *(Gow Choy)* Dark green, 6 inches long, flat and possessing a sharp pungency. Very good for emphasis on eggs, or toss-cooked sliced beef.

CHINESE OKRA *(Sing Gwa)* An almost blade-sharp, horizontally serrated vegetable, light green and the size of a cucumber. The sharp tough edge must be trimmed. It is usually cut in triangle chunk pieces for quick soups and sometimes toss cooked, too. Chinese Okra is a summer vegetable, with a refreshing, slightly sweet taste.

**BITTER MELON**
*(Foo Gwa)*

苦瓜

**SNOW PEAS**
*(Ho Lon Dow)*

荷蘭豆

**FUZZY SQUASH**
*(Mo Gwa)*

毛瓜

**WATER CHESTNUTS**
*(Mah Tai)*

馬蹄

**BAMBOO SHOOT**
*(Jook Soon)*

竹笋

**WINTER MELON**
*(Doong Gwa)*

冬瓜

**LOTUS ROOT**
*(Leen Gnow)*

蓮藕

**TARO ROOT**
*(Woo Tow)*

芋頭

**CHINESE CHIVES**
*(Gow Choy)*

韭菜

**LONG BEANS**
*(Dow Gok)*

荳角

**CHINESE TURNIPS**
*(Law Bok)*

蘿蔔

**CHINESE PARSLEY**
*(Yuen Sai)*

芫茜

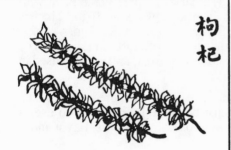

**MATRIMONY VINES**
*(Gow Gay)*

枸杞

**CHINESE OKRA**
*(See Gwa)*

絲瓜

**CHINESE CABBAGE**
*(Siew Choy)*

兆菜

**MUSTARD GREENS**
*(Gai Choy)*

芥菜

CHINESE PARSLEY *(Yuen Sai)* This Chinese parsley or coriander has willowy, flat, serrated leaves, is blue-green colored, and is more tender and more pungent than the American variety. Excellent for garnish alone, once you learn to like the flavor, you will want to use it in many recipes. It is available all year around.

CHINESE TURNIPS *(Law Bok)* Plentiful and best in winter, this long white turnip is used for long-simmer soups, smother-cook dishes, toss cooking, and in raw fish salad.

LONG BEANS *(Dow Gok)* The name describes this pencil-thick, light green bean. Usually cut in 2-inch lengths, it is a seasonal vegetable combination toss-cook item. Sometimes diced, it is a summer vegetable.

FUZZY SQUASH *(Mo Gwa)* Ovoid-shaped apple-green squash, average 4 inches long. Popular in soups and toss cooking, it has fine 1/16-inch fuzz.

LOTUS ROOT *(Leen Ngow)* The red-brown tuberous stem of the water lily plant, displayed at groceries in segments of about 10 inches long, 2 inches in diameter, and linked. Grown chiefly in Hawaii and Mexico, the season runs from July through February. It remains crisp in toss cooking, and is cooked soft in soups.

MUSTARD GREENS, CHINESE *(Gai Choy)* Another favorite of the Chinese, used commonly in soups. It is a darkish, apple-green plant with nodular, loose leaves and curved stalks. The large plants are 10 to 12 inches long. They have a cool, quinine taste. Skillful cooks can quick-toss-cook it magnificently in big chunks, and it comes out a beautiful jade color. The baby mustard greens are bunched in 4- to 6-inch sizes, and are also used in soups.

MATRIMONY VINE *(Gow Gay)* One-inch-long, dark-green leaves on a vine with sharp thorns. The leaves must be carefully removed to use in soup. This all-year-around vegetable has a cool, slightly bitter flavor and is a family-style favorite.

PIG WEED *(Hon Choy)* A small-leaved plant, with 1-inch-size clustered leaves on a stem, possessing a beef essence flavor in quick soups. The plant is 5 to 7 inches long, with pink or red root.

SNOW PEAS *(Ho Lon Dow)* These flat Chinese peas are also called Pea Pods or Sugar Peas. They are 3 to 4 inches long, by 1 inch wide. Break off tips and de-string them before quick-toss cooking. They are cheapest in the months of May through September, very expensive in other seasons.

TARO ROOT *(Woo Tow)* A staple in South China, somewhat like a potato. Harmonious in smother-cooked dishes, taro root is famous as an ingredient of a festive duck dish. It is also steamed with Chinese sausages and bacon.

WATER CHESTNUTS *(Mah Tai)* One-inch diameter, tough, dark-brown skinned bulb plant. Fresh ones must be peeled, but the crisp-textured vegetable with the light, sweetish flavor is also available peeled, whole or sliced, in cans.

WHITE CHINESE EGGPLANT *(Bok Ker)* The size of a cucumber, and therefore less pulpy and more tender than regular eggplant, this vegetable can be toss cooked, or steamed with a strong bean curd cheese *(Foo Yee)*.

WINTER MELON *(Doong Gwa)* More of a squash than a melon but, as the name implies, the best season is winter. However, it can be stored and is thus available almost all year around. The shape of a round watermelon up to 12 pounds or more, winter melons are sold whole or in any size chunk you wish. The skin is tough and bumpy, apple green, with dark green spots and a chalky white dust which scrapes off. The melon meat is of an ivory color, about 1½ inches thick, while the rest of the center is pulp. Used for whole Melon Cup Soups or diced and sliced, winter melon can also be toss-cooked or glazed for Melon Candy.

## CHINESE CHARD WITH OIL AND SALT
*(Yow Yim Bok Choy)*

Have prepared:
> 1½ pounds washed Chinese chard *(Bok Choy)*, cut into 2 x ½-inch pieces

In a preheated *wok* or skillet, place:
> 2 tablespoons vegetable oil
> 2 cloves crushed garlic
> ½ teaspoon salt

Turn to high heat, mix all ingredients rapidly for 2 minutes until garlic is browned.

Add:
> Sliced Chinese chard
> ½ teaspoon soy sauce
> ¼ teaspoon monosodium glutamate

Toss and mix for 1 minute, and add:
> ¼ cup chicken stock

Cover and cook at high heat for three minutes. Uncover and turn to medium heat.

Add:
> 1 tablespoon cornstarch. Make paste with 1 tablespoon water.

Toss and mix rapidly 2 or 3 minutes until gravy thickens. Serve as vegetable entree with hot steamed rice. Serves 4

*Chinese chard is probably the most common of all Chinese vegetables. It is not particularly distinctive in character and flavor. Yet – this "plain Jane" vegetable, toss-cooked this way is regarded by gourmets as a challenge to a chef's ability to make it glamorous! The end result should be a sparkling dish of* Bok Choy, *"dry" in appearance – not running over with liquid – barely half-cooked and hot and crunchy to the bite. We warn you that it will take experience before you achieve success – for much depends upon the utensil used, intensity of heat and correct timing. You may reduce the amount of chicken stock and use little or no cornstarch, depending on individual preference.*

## SPINACH WITH FOO YEE SAUCE
*(Baw Choy Foo Yee)*

In a preheated *wok* or skillet, place:
> 3 tablespoons vegetable oil

Turn to heat and add:
> 1 teaspoon salt
> 1 teaspoon minced garlic

Brown slightly, very rapidly and mix.

Add:
    **3 pounds washed green spinach leaves cut into halves**
    **2 preserved bean cakes** *(Foo Yee)* **mashed with 2 teaspoons juice from jar**

Turn and mix, cover and cook at medium heat for 3 minutes. Remove cover, turn to high heat, toss and mix for 3 more minutes. Serve with hot steamed rice. Serves 4

*Here is a good example of how almost any commonplace vegetable can be turned into an epicurean dish by simply adding preserved bean cake and a smidgen of garlic. Try it also with string beans, cabbage, cauliflower, broccoli or lettuce and you will discover why* Foo Yee *is oftentimes referred to as the miracle ingredient among Chinese condiments.*

## OIL AND SALT HOT LETTUCE
### (Yim Yow Sang Choy)

Have prepared:
    **1 large firm head of lettuce, washed. Separate leaves and tear into halves.**

In a preheated *wok* or skillet, place:
    **2 tablespoons vegetable oil**
    **½ teaspoon salt**

At high heat, bring oil to a sizzle.
Add:
    **Lettuce leaves**
    **⅓ teaspoon monosodium glutamate**

Toss and turn for 1 minute, then cover utensil and cook at medium heat for 2 minutes, or until lettuce is 80 percent cooked, but not wilted. Serves 4

*This is how the Cantonese glamorize an ordinary head of lettuce – through a quick-cooking technique, using oil, salt and monosodium glutamate instead of a sauce to enhance the vegetable. You may have to do some experimenting before achieving the crunchy, "not raw, not cooked, but hot clear through" technique, by a variation of mere seconds in cooking time.*

## *BITTER MELON WITH BEEF*
*(Foo Gwa Ngow Yuke)*

Have prepared:
> **1 pound Chinese bitter melon *(Foo Gwa)*. Cut each melon horizontally into halves and remove all seeds. Slice vertically into ¼-inch-thick pieces. Blanch in boiling water for 2 minutes and drain.**
> **½ pound sliced tender beef in ⅛-inch-thick strips**

In a mixing bowl, place:
> **¼ teaspoon salt**
> **¼ teaspoon soy sauce**
> **Dash of sugar**
> **1 teaspoon cornstarch**

Mix ingredients thoroughly and add:
> **Sliced beef**

Let stand for 5 minutes.

In a preheated *wok* or skillet, place:
> **1 tablespoon vegetable oil**
> **½ teaspoon salt**

Turn to high heat and add:
> **Marinated beef**

Toss-mix and brown rapidly about 1 minute, remove beef and place aside. (Beef should be rare in center.)

In the same utensil, place:   **2 tablespoons vegetable oil**

Turn to high heat until oil is very hot.

Add:
> **1 tablespoon mashed fermented black bean *(Dow See)* combined with 1 clove mashed garlic.**
> **Blanched bitter melon**
> **Dash of monosodium glutamate**
> **Dash of ground pepper**

Toss-cook at medium-high heat for 1 minute.

Add:   **¼ cup chicken stock**

Cover and cook for 2 minutes. Uncover.

Add:   **Pre-browned beef**

Toss-mix gently for 1 minute until all ingredients are blended.

Gradually add:
> **1 tablespoon cornstarch. Make paste with 1 tablespoon water**

Toss and mix continuously, making sure liquid is well blended with cornstarch paste. When gravy thickens sufficiently to lightly coat the bitter melon and beef (about 2 minutes), remove from fire and serve immediately with hot steamed rice. Serve 3 or 4

*Foo Gwa, or Bitter Melon, is one Chinese vegetable that you really have to develop a liking for because of its slightly bitter undertone. But once you acquire the taste, you will crave it often and truly enjoy its exhilarating, cool, quinine qualities.*

## CHINESE CHARD HEARTS WITH CHICKEN OR PRAWNS
### (Choy Sum Gai Kow Hah Kow)

Have prepared:
> 1 pound washed Chinese chard hearts, sliced 2 inches long and ½-inch wide
> 1 cup boneless chicken or prawns (uncooked)

The outer leaves are removed from Chinese chard *(Bok Choy),* very much like removing the outside stalks from celery to obtain celery hearts. The leaves are tender and edible and can be reserved for another recipe. (See Chinese Chard and Oil and Salt.)

In a preheated *wok* or skillet, place:
> 2 tablespoons vegetable oil
> ½ teaspoon salt
> 2 small cloves crushed garlic

Turn to high heat, until oil is very hot and garlic is slightly browned.

Add:
> Chicken or prawns

Toss and turn until 80 percent cooked.

Add:
> Chard hearts
> ½ teaspoon soy sauce
> ¼ teaspoon monosodium glutamate

Toss and mix rapidly for 1 minute.

Add:
> ¼ cup chicken stock

Cover and cook for 5 minutes at high heat. Uncover.

Add gradually:
> 1 teaspoon cornstarch. Make paste with 1 teaspoon water.

Toss and mix constantly until sauce is just thick enough to coat all ingredients. Remove from fire and serve with hot steamed rice. Serves 3

# WATER CHESTNUT TUMBLE IN LETTUCE CUPS
## *(Mah Tai Soong)*

Have prepared:
**Crisped leaves of 1 head firm white lettuce**
**1½ pounds canned or fresh, peeled water chestnuts, drained and diced very small**
**½ cup lean pork, parboiled and minced**

In a preheated *wok* or skillet, place:
**2 tablespoons vegetable oil**

Bring oil to sizzling point and add:

**Diced water chestnuts**
**Minced pork**
**½ teaspoon salt**
**1 teaspoon soy sauce**
**¼ teaspoon monosodium glutamate**
**Sprinkle of black pepper**

Toss and mix rapidly for 1 minute.
Add:
**1 cup chicken stock**
Cover and cook at high heat for 3 minutes. Uncover.
Add gradually:
**2 tablespoons cornstarch. Make paste with 2 tablespoons water.**

Toss and mix for 3 to 5 minutes until sauce thickens and is well blended with all the ingredients. Transfer *Mah Tai Soong* to compote or serving dish. How to serve it: Each guest takes a lettuce leaf and places two tablespoons of the *Soong* in it and eats it with his hands. Serves 3 or 4

*This is the dish for those who love the crisp, sweet water chestnut. Ideal as a summer dish,* Mah Tai Soong *is light and refreshing.*

# CABBAGE WITH DRIED SHRIMPS
*(Yeah Choy Chow Hah Mai)*

Have prepared:

½ **pound dried tiny shrimps** *(Hah Mai)*, **pre-soak ½ hour in cold water. Rinse and drain.**

1 **small head cabbage, sliced in ½-inch strips**

3 **cloves garlic, crushed**

In a preheated *wok* or skillet, place:

2 **tablespoons vegetable oil**

Bring oil to sizzling point at high heat.
Add:

**Crushed garlic**
**Washed dried shrimps**

Toss and turn about ½ minute.
Add:

**Sliced cabbage**

Toss cook at high heat 1 minute.
Add:

½ **teaspoon salt**

1 **teaspoon soy sauce**

1½ **cups hot chicken stock or water**

½ **teaspoon sugar**

¼ **teaspoon monosodium glutamate**

Toss and turn all ingredients thoroughly. Cover and cook at high heat 10 minutes. Uncover.

Add gradually:

1 **teaspoon cornstarch. Make paste with 1 teaspoon water.**

Continue to cook at high heat, tossing and turning (2 to 3 minutes) until sauce has thickened, and is completely blended with all other ingredients. Serves 4

## *LOTUS ROOT WITH BEEF*
*(Leen Ngow Chow Ngow Yuke)*

Have prepared:

**1 pound fresh lotus root *(Leen Ngow)*. Peel, wash, and drain, and vertically slice into ¼-inch pieces or thinner. Quarter the round, thin slices.**
**¾ cup celery sliced in the same manner**
**½ cup dried onion, thinly sliced**
**½ cup wood ears, *(Won Yee)* previously soaked and softened with water, rinsed and drained**

In a mixing bowl, place:

**1 cup thinly sliced beef**
**½ teaspoon soy sauce**
**¼ teaspoon sugar**
**1 teaspoon cornstarch**

Marinate beef thoroughly (5 minutes) in the salt, soy sauce, sugar and cornstarch mixture.

In a preheated *wok* or skillet, place:

**1 tablespoon vegetable oil**

Add:

**Marinated beef**

Bring to high heat, toss and mix rapidly for ½ minute and remove beef from pan.

Using the same utensil, again add:

**2 tablespoons vegetable oil and bring to high heat.**

Add:

**Sliced lotus root, celery, onions, wood ears**
**1 teaspoon salt**
**1 teaspoon soy sauce**
**¼ teaspoon sugar**

Toss and mix at high heat for two minutes.

Add: **½ cup chicken stock**

Cover and cook at medium heat for three minutes. Remove cover. Turn to high heat.

Add:

**Cooked beef**
**1 tablespoon cornstarch. Make paste with 1 tablespoon water.**

Toss cook all ingredients rapidly for 3 or 4 minutes. Serve very hot with steamed rice. Serves 4

Leen Ngow, *or Lotus Root, is generally used in soups because of its root-like texture which requires long cooking. When sliced thin and toss-cooked, however, the texture becomes crunchy.*

# MOCK LAMB (GOURMET VEGETABLES)
## (Gah Ming Yeong)

Have prepared:
> ½ cup finely sliced raw beef
> 1½ cups finely sliced bamboo shoots
> ½ cup finely sliced Chinese dried mushrooms (pre-soaked)
> 1 cup finely sliced celery
> ⅓ cup finely sliced dried onion

In deep fat fryer, cook in 350° oil:
> 1½ cups rice sticks (Mai Fun). Remove when crisp and light.

In a preheated *wok* or skillet, place:
> 2 tablespoons vegetable oil

Bring oil to sizzle at high heat and add sliced beef. Toss and turn rapidly for 1 or 2 minutes and remove from pan when half cooked.

In the same utensil, add:        1 teaspoon salt and all the sliced ingredients

Bring to medium-high heat. Toss and turn all ingredients for about 2 minutes.

Add:
> ½ cup chicken stock combined with
> ½ teaspoon monosodium glutamate

Cover and cook at medium heat for 3 minutes. Remove cover.

Add:
> 1 teaspoon soy sauce
> ½ teaspoon sugar
> Half-cooked sliced beef

Increase to high heat and continue to toss cook. When all ingredients are thoroughly blended, immediately add:
> 2 teaspoons cornstarch. Make paste with 2 teaspoons water.

Continue to toss cook until sauce has thickened (about 1 minute, no longer).

Place on serving dish, top with the crisped rice sticks. Serves 3 or 4

*This is the Cantonese adaptation of a North China dish. The mock lamb is beef, and fluffy rice sticks represent the "lamb's wool." This imaginative dish, because of its delightful combination of textures, is known as "Gourmet Vegetables."*

# DICED CHINESE LONG BEANS WITH BARBECUED PORK
*(Dow Gok Soong)*

Have prepared:
> **1 pound Chinese Long Beans** *(Dow Gok)*, **washed, drained, and diced into ¼-inch pieces**
> **½ cup diced barbecued pork** *(Cha Siew)* **(chicken, beef or ham may be substituted for barbecued pork)**

In a preheated *wok* or skillet, place:
> **2 tablespoons vegetable oil**
> **½ teaspoon salt**
> **½ teaspoon finely minced garlic**
> **½ teaspoon bean sauce** *(Min See Jeung)*

Bring to high heat until oil is very hot. Brown garlic slightly.

Add:
> **Diced barbecued pork or above-mentioned substitutes**

Toss and mix for 1 minute, then add:
> **Diced Chinese Long Beans**
> **1 teaspoon soy sauce**

Toss cook for 1 minute at medium heat.

Add:
> **½ cup chicken stock**

Cover and cook at high heat for 5 minutes. Remove cover.

Add:
> **2 teaspoons cornstarch. Make paste with 2 teaspoons water.**

Increase to high heat. Toss and mix until sauce is just thick enough to coat all ingredients. Serve with steamed rice. Serves 3

Dow Gok, *or Chinese Long Beans, may be prepared in many different styles, but this is one of our favorites. It is important to avoid overcooking Long Beans since they have a tendency to become mushy and lose their fresh taste.*

# CAULIFLOWER WITH BEEF

## (Choy Fah Chow Gnow Yuke)

Have prepared:

½ pound thinly sliced tender beef (about ⅛-inch thick)

2 pounds washed cauliflower. Break into flowerettes, slice stalks into ½-inch lengths. Parboil 2 minutes and drain.

In a mixing bowl, place:

½ teaspoon salt
½ teaspoon soy sauce
¼ teaspoon sugar

Mix ingredients and add:      Sliced beef
Marinate for 5 minutes.
In a preheated *wok* or large skillet add:

1 tablespoon vegetable oil

Turn to high heat and add:      Marinated sliced beef
Toss-mix and brown rapidly about 1 minute, remove beef, and place aside. (Beef should be rare in center.)
In the same utensil, place:

2 tablespoons vegetable oil
½ teaspoon salt

Turn to high heat and add:      Cauliflower

1 teaspoon soy sauce
½ teaspoon sugar

Toss and mix for 1 minute, then add:

½ cup chicken stock

Cover and cook for 5 minutes. Remove cover.
Add:      Pre-browned beef

1 tablespoon cornstarch. Make paste with 1 tablespoon water.

Toss and mix continously making sure liquid ingredients are well blended with cornstarch paste. When gravy thickens sufficiently to lightly coat the cauliflower and beef (about two minutes), remove from fire and serve immediately. Serves 4

*Here is how a Chinese cooking technique can transform a bland vegetable into a tasty, nutritious dish. Instead of being soft, uninteresting, with the flavor taken out by long boiling, it is only half-cooked through, yet the flavor of the beef and other seasoned ingredients blend to make a combination which will satisfy the most jaded palate.*

# TOMATO CURRY BEEF
*(Fon Ker Gah Lay Ngow Yuke)*

Have prepared:
    **3 large ripe tomatoes, cut into quarters**
    **1 small bell pepper, sliced into ¾-inch squares**
    **2 dried onions, sliced into ¾-inch wedges**
    **½ pound tender beef, cut into 2 x 1-inch pieces, ¼ inch thick**

In a preheated *wok* or skillet, place:
    **2 tablespoons vegetable oil**

Bring to high heat. Add:     **Sliced beef**

Brown slightly for ½ minute. Do not overcook. Remove beef.

In an oiled pre-heated *wok* or skillet, place:
    **Sliced onions, tomatoes and peppers**
    **¼ cup chicken stock**

Cover and cook at medium heat for 3 minutes. Uncover.

Add:
    **1 tablespoon top quality curry powder**
    **1 tablespoon sugar**
    **1 tablespoon tomato catsup**
    **1 tablespoon soy sauce**

Turn and mix all ingredients and continue to cook at medium heat for 1 minute. Add gradually:     **2 tablespoons cornstarch. Make paste with 2 tablespoons water.**

Turn and mix 2 minutes until sauce thickens and add sliced beef. Continue to turn and mix rapidly until all ingredients are thoroughly blended and become very hot. Serve at once with hot steamed rice. Serves 4

# BEAN CAKE SAUTÉED WITH MEAT
## (Dow Foo Yuke)

Have prepared:  **8 bean cakes** *(Dow Foo)*. **Slice each bean cake into 6 pieces.**
**½ cup uncooked pork or ham, sliced thin**
**¼ cup green onions, cut into ¾-inch lengths**

In a preheated *wok* or skillet, place:
**2 tablespoons vegetable oil**

Bring oil to sizzling point and add:
**Sliced pork or ham**

Brown meat at medium-high heat 5 minutes.

Add:  **Sliced bean cakes and green onions**
**1 tablespoon bean sauce** *(Min See Jeung)*

Turn and mix gently at medium-high heat for 10 minutes, making sure bean cakes are not broken up.

Add:  **½ teaspoon monosodium glutamate**
**½ teaspoon salt**
**½ cup chicken stock**

Continue to turn and mix gently at high heat for 5 minutes until very hot.

Gradually add:  **2 teaspoons cornstarch. Make paste with 2 teaspoons water.**

Turn and mix for a few seconds until sauce thickens sufficiently to coat ingredients. Serve immediately with steamed or fried rice. Serves 3 or 4

## FRESH ASPARAGUS CHICKEN WITH BLACK BEAN SAUCE
*(Lei Soon Gai Kow)*

Have prepared:

**1½ pounds fresh green asparagus, pared 1 inch below green part and sliced diagonally into ½-inch thick slices**

In a sauce pot, place:

**2 cups boiling water**

Add:

**Sliced asparagus**

Cover and cook at high heat for 2 minutes (no longer). Remove asparagus.

Also have prepared:

**1 cup uncooked white meat of chicken cut in ¾-inch squares**

**1 full tablespoon mashed fermented black beans *(Dow See),* combined with 1 clove mashed garlic and 1 tablespoon soy sauce, with a dash of monosodium glutamate.**

In a preheated *wok* or skillet, place:

**2 tablespoons vegetable oil**
**½ teaspoon salt**

Increase to high heat and add:

**Sliced asparagus**
**Boned chicken**
**Black bean sauce mixture**
**½ cup chicken stock**
**½ teaspoon sugar**

Toss and mix rapidly but gently for 1 minute. Cover and cook for another 2 minutes. Uncover.

Add gradually:

**1 tablespoon cornstarch. Make paste with 1 tablespoon water.**

Continue to cook at high heat, turning and mixing constantly (1 to 2 minutes) until sauce is just thick enough to coat asparagus and chicken. Remove from fire and serve with steamed rice. Serves 3 or 4

*Fresh asparagus is dramatized through this Chinese combination, with chicken and black bean sauce.*

# FUZZY SQUASH WITH BEAN THREADS, MUSHROOMS, PORK
## (Jeet Gwa Fun See Doong Goo Yuke)

Have prepared:

¼ pound bean threads *(Fun See),* previously softened in hot water for 10 minutes and then in cold water 30 minutes and drained.

½ cup dried Chinese black mushrooms *(Heong Soon),* previously soaked in water for 15 minutes, then shredded into very thin slices

½ pound uncooked lean pork, sliced very thin.

1 medium-sized fuzzy squash (½ to ¾ pound), peeled and sliced vertically, ¼-inch thick and halved.

In a preheated *wok* or skillet, place:

2 tablespoons vegetable oil
½ teaspoon salt

Increase to high heat until oil is very hot.
Add:                       Sliced pork
Toss and mix for 1 minute, then add:

Softened bean threads and sliced mushrooms
2 teaspoons soy sauce

Toss cook rapidly for 1 minute, then add:

1½ cups chicken stock

Cover and cook at high heat for 2 minutes. Uncover.
Add:                       Sliced fuzzy squash
Toss and mix all ingredients thoroughly, cover and cook at high heat another 2 minutes. Add more salt and soy sauce to taste. Serve with steamed rice. Serves 4

*Here is a simple dinner-style dish employing the use of two main "soft" textured ingredients – fuzzy squash and bean threads. Combined with "chewy" bits of mushrooms and meat, it acquires an almost indefinable character for which gourmets develop a yen, time and time again.*

# GREEN PEAS WITH CHOPPED BEEF
*(Ching Dow Yuke Soong)*

| | |
|---|---|
| Have prepared: | **3 cups defrosted frozen green peas or 3 cups fresh shelled peas. (If fresh peas are used, boil 8 to 10 minutes.)** |
| | **¼ cup diced celery** |
| | **½ pound raw chopped beef** |
| | **½ cup diced onion** |

In a preheated *wok* or skillet, place:

> **2 tablespoons vegetable oil**
> **½ teaspoon salt**

Bring to high heat, and add:

> **Raw chopped beef**
> **Green peas, celery and onions**

Toss and mix all ingredients rapidly and thoroughly.

Add:

> **1 teaspoon soy sauce**
> **½ cup chicken stock**
> **¼ teaspoon sugar**
> **¼ teaspoon monosodium glutamate**

Cover, and continue to cook at high heat for 5 minutes. Remove cover.

Add:

> **1 tablespoon cornstarch. Make paste with 1 tablespoon water.**

Toss and mix all ingredients rapidly 2 or 3 minutes until thoroughly blended with cornstarch paste. Serve with hot steamed rice. Serves 4

# BITTER MELON WITH CHICKEN
## (Foo Gwa Gai Kow)

Have prepared:

1½  pounds Chinese bitter melon *(Foo Gwa)*. Cut each melon horizontally into halves and remove all seeds. Slice vertically into ¼-inch thick pieces. Blanch in boiling water for 2 minutes and drain.

1  cup boned, uncooked chicken, cut into ½-inch pieces.

In a preheated *wok* or skillet, place:

2  tablespoons vegetable oil
½  teaspoon salt
1  tablespoon chopped garlic
2  tablespoons black bean sauce

Turn to high heat until garlic browns.

Add:

Blanched bitter melon
Sliced chicken
¼  teaspoon soy sauce
Dash of monosodium glutamate
Dash of ground pepper
½  teaspoon sugar

Toss cook at high heat for 1 minute.

Add:                ½ cup chicken stock

Cover and cook for 3 minutes. Uncover.

Gradually add:

1  tablespoon cornstarch. Make paste with 1 tablespoon water.

Toss and mix continuously until liquid is well blended with cornstarch paste. When gravy thickens sufficiently to light coat the bitter melon and chicken (about 2 minutes) remove from fire. Serve immediately with hot steamed rice. Serves 4

## *CHINESE TURNIPS WITH BEEF*
*(Law Bok Chow Ngow Yuke)*

Have prepared:

**2 pounds Chinese turnips *(Law Bok)*. Peel off skin with potato peeler and wash. Slice vertically into ¼-inch pieces and into quarters (about 1½ x 1½ inches). Cook in boiling water until half done, drain.**

**½ cup scallions. Use white sections cut into 1-inch lengths.**

**¾ pound sliced tender beef in ⅛-inch-thick strips**

In a mixing bowl, place:

**½ teaspoon soy sauce**
**¼ teaspoon sugar**
**¼ teaspoon cornstarch**

Mix ingredients thoroughly, add: **Sliced beef**
Marinate for 5 minutes.
In a preheated *wok* or skillet, place:

**2 tablespoons vegetable oil**

Increase to high heat and add: **Marinated beef**
Toss and brown for 1 minute, remove beef and place aside.
In the same utensil, place:

**2 tablespoons vegetable oil**
**3 small cloves garlic**

When garlic is brown, add:

**Blanched turnips**
**½ teaspoon soy sauce**
**Dash of monosodium glutamate**
**1 teaspoon bean sauce *(Min See Jeung)***
**½ teaspoon salt**

Toss cook at high heat for ½ minute.
Add: **1 cup chicken stock**
Cover and cook at high heat for 5 minutes. Uncover.
Add:

**Browned beef**
**Sliced scallions**

Toss-mix gently 1 minute until all ingredients are well blended.
Gradually add:

**1 tablespoon cornstarch. Make paste with 1 tablespoon water.**

Toss and turn continuously at high heat until liquid is well blended with cornstarch paste. When gravy thickens sufficiently to coat turnips and beef (about 2 minutes) remove from fire. Serve with hot steamed rice. Serves 3 or 4

# CHINESE CHARD HEARTS WITH BEEF

*(Choy Sum Chow Gnow Yuke)*

Have prepared:    **1 pound washed Chinese chard hearts, sliced 2 inches long and ½ inch wide**

The outer leaves are removed from Chinese chard *(Bok Choy)* very much like removing the outside stalks from celery to obtain celery hearts. The leaves are tender and edible and can be reserved for another recipe. (See Chinese Chard With Oil and Salt.)

Also prepare:    **1 cup thinly sliced tender beef (about ¼ inch thick)**

In a mixing bowl place:    **½ teaspoon soy sauce**
**¼ teaspoon sugar**
**½ teaspoon cornstarch**

Mix ingredients and add:    **Sliced beef**
Marinate 5 minutes.

In a preheated *wok* or skillet, place:

**2 tablespoons vegetable oil**

Increase to high heat and add marinated beef, toss and turn until half cooked. Remove beef and place aside.

In the same utensil, place:    **2 tablespoons vegetable oil**
Add:    **Sliced chard hearts**
**½ teaspoon soy sauce**
**¼ teaspoon monosodium glutamate**
**⅓ teaspoon salt**
**¼ teaspoon sugar**

Toss and mix for 1 minute. Add:

**¼ cup chicken stock**

Cover and cook for 2 minutes, at high heat. Uncover.
Add:    **Marinated sliced beef**
Toss and mix all ingredients.
Add:    **1 teaspoon cornstarch. Make paste with 1 teaspoon water.**

Toss and mix constantly, making sure liquid ingredients are well blended with cornstarch paste. When gravy thickens sufficiently to lightly coat the chard hearts and beef (about 2 minutes), remove from fire and serve immediately with hot steamed rice. Serves 4

# SNOW PEAS WITH WATER CHESTNUTS & BAMBOO SHOOTS
*(Lon Dow Jook Soon Ma Tai)*

Have prepared:
  - ½ pound Chinese Snow Peas *(Lon Dow)* Remove tips and strings. Wash and drain.
  - 1 cup bamboo shoots sliced ¼ inch thick by 1 by 1 inch
  - ½ cup sliced water chestnuts (Use canned type if fresh are unavailable)

In a preheated *wok* or skillet, place:
  - 2 tablespoons vegetable oil
  - 4 thin slices garlic (optional)
  - ½ teaspoon salt

When garlic has browned, add:
  - Snow peas
  - Sliced bamboo shoots and water chestnuts
  - 1 teaspoon soy sauce

Toss cook at high heat for 1 minute.

Add:
  - ⅛ cup chicken stock

Cover and cook for 2 minutes. Uncover.

Gradually add:
  - 1 teaspoon cornstarch. Make paste with 1 teaspoon water.

Toss cook at high heat until sauce thickens (about 1 minute, no longer). Serve as vegetable entree. Serves 3 or 4

*Chinese Snow Peas are characteristically flat and are also called Pea Pods or Sugar Peas. To the Chinese, there is but one proper way to cook Snow Peas – quick sauté in a very hot* wok *or skillet with very little liquid to the just-tender-crisp stage to retain the delicate flavor, green color and valuable vitamins A, B and C.*


# CURED MUSTARD GREENS WITH HOT PEPPERS
*(Muey Choy Lot Jue)*

Have prepared:
  - 1 pound canned cured mustard greens *(Muey Choy)*. Soak in cold water 2 hours. Wash, drain and dice finely.
  - 4 hot green peppers, diced
  - ½ pound ground uncooked pork

In a preheated *wok* or skillet, place:

> **2 tablespoons vegetable oil**
> **½ teaspoon salt**

Bring oil to sizzling point at high heat.
Add:                    **Ground pork**
Stir and mix continuously for 8 minutes.
Add:                    **Cured mustard greens, hot peppers**
> **1 cup chicken stock**
> **½ teaspoon sugar**
> **½ teaspoon monosodium glutamate**

Stir and mix at high heat for 5 minutes. Cover and cook at low heat for 20 minutes, turning occasionally. Serve with hot steamed rice. Serves 3 or 4

## *CHINESE CABBAGE WITH FOO YEE SAUCE*

*(Siew Choy Foo Yee)*

In a preheated *wok* or skillet, place:

> **2 tablespoons vegetable oil**

Bring to high heat and add:    **2 fermented bean cakes** *(Foo Yee)* **with**
> **2 teaspoons juice from jar**
> **1½ pounds washed Chinese cabbage sliced**
> **about ½-inch wide**
> **Salt to taste**
> **½ teaspoon sugar**
> **⅓ teaspoon monosodium glutamate**
> **½ cup chicken stock**

Cover and cook at medium heat until cabbage is tender.
Add:    **1 tablespoon cornstarch. Make paste with 1 tablespoon water.**

Continue to turn and mix at high heat for another 2 or 3 minutes. Serve as a vegetable entree with hot steamed rice. Serves 4

## PICKLED MUSTARD GREENS WITH BEEF
*(Seen Choy Ngow Yuke)*

---

Have prepared:                          1½ pounds pickled Chinese mustard greens,
                                        rinsed and cut into 1-inch lengths
                                        ½ pound tender beef sliced ⅛-inch thick

In a preheated *wok* or skillet, place:
                                        1 tablespoon vegetable oil

Increase to high heat and add:          Sliced beef

Brown beef rapidly (no longer than 1 minute) and remove from pan.

In the same utensil, place:             1 tablespoon vegetable oil

Bring to high heat and add:             Prepared pickled mustard greens
                                        ½ teaspoon salt
                                        1 cup chicken stock
                                        2 tablespoons sugar

Cover and cook at high heat for 5 minutes, mixing ingredients once or twice in between times. Uncover.

Add:                                    Browned beef

Toss and mix ingredients rapidly for 1 minute.

Add gradually:                          1 tablespoon cornstarch. Make paste with 1
                                        tablespoon water.

Continue to cook at medium-high heat, turning and mixing constantly (2 to 3 minutes) until sauce is just thick enough to coat pickled greens and beef. Serve very hot as an entree with steamed rice. Serves 4

*Here is a typical "peasant style" dish which is relished by all classes in the old country. The palates of peoples all over the world often crave a stimulating pickled vegetable, served piping hot, and this Cantonese dish is refreshingly different.*

## MUSTARD GREENS WITH FOO YEE SAUCE
*(Gai Choy Chow Foo Yee)*

---

Have prepared:                          1½ pounds washed Chinese mustard greens,
                                        cut into 1½x1½-inch pieces

In a preheated *wok* or skillet, place:
                                        2 tablespoons vegetable oil
                                        ½ teaspoon salt

Bring to high heat and add:     **Chinese mustard greens**
Toss and mix for 1 minute. Add:

> **2 fermented bean cakes (*Foo Yee*) mashed
> with 2 teaspoons juice from jar**
> **1 teaspoon soy sauce**
> **½ teaspoon monosodium glutamate**
> **½ teaspoon sugar**

Toss and mix again. Add:     **½ cup chicken stock**
Cover and cook at medium heat for 3 minutes. Uncover and turn to high heat.
Add:     **1 tablespoon cornstarch. Make paste with 1
tablespoon water**

Turn and mix for 2 or 3 minutes until gravy thickens. Serve with hot steamed rice. Serves 4


# KENTUCKY WONDER STRING BEANS WITH BEEF
## (Dow Jai Chow Ngow Yuke)

Have prepared:     **1 pound Kentucky Wonder string beans,
washed and drained. Slice into 2-inch
lengths and parboil 2 minutes and drain.**
**1 cup thinly sliced beef**
**2 cloves garlic, minced very fine**

In a preheated *wok* or skillet, place:

> **2 tablespoons vegetable oil**
> **½ teaspoon salt**

Increase to high heat until oil is very hot.
Add:     **Minced garlic**
Brown garlic, then add:     **Sliced string beans**
Toss cook at high heat for 1 or 2 minutes.
Add:     **Sliced beef**
**1 teaspoon soy sauce**
**¼ teaspoon sugar**
**¼ teaspoon monosodium glutamate**
**½ teaspoon bean sauce (*Min See Jeung*)**

Toss and mix at high heat for 1 minute.
Add:     **½ cup chicken stock**
Cover and cook at medium heat for 5 minutes. Remove cover. Increase to high heat, gradually add 1 teaspoon cornstarch mixed to a paste with 1 teaspoon water. Toss and mix all ingredients for 2 minutes, or until sauce begins to thicken. Serve with hot steamed rice. Serves 3 or 4

# DICED CHINESE BROCCOLI WITH BEEF
*(Gai Lon Soong)*

Have prepared:
    **1 pound Chinese broccoli *(Gai Lon)*, washed. Slice leaves and dice stems into ¼x¼-inch pieces.**
    **½ pound chopped raw beef**

In a preheated *wok* or skillet, place:
    **2 tablespoons vegetable oil**
    **½ teaspoon salt**

Bring to high heat and add:
    **Chopped beef**
    **Diced broccoli**
    **1 teaspoon soy sauce**
    **1 teaspoon monosodium glutamate**

Toss and mix all ingredients rapidly and thoroughly for 2 minutes.
Add⁻
    **½ cup chicken stock**
    **¼ teaspoon sugar**

Cover and continue to cook at high heat for 3 minutes. Remove cover.
Add:
    **1 tablespoon cornstarch. Make paste with 1 tablespoon water.**

Toss and mix all ingredients rapidly for 2 minutes until thoroughly blended with cornstarch paste. Serve with hot steamed rice. Serves 4

# *Eggs*

## *THE FOOD OF FIVE VIRTUES*

To a people as ancient as the Chinese, the timeless mystique of life is ever cause for symbolistic application.

Thus to the Chinese, the egg is — both as a spiritual and physical truth — the beginning of life. The cycle of life itself is a continuing balance of the positive and negative forces. To the Chinese, life is symbolized by *Yin* and *Yang*. The yolk of the egg represents *Yin*, the darker, negative aspect of the earth, the female, the absorptive duad. The white of the egg is light, the positive forces of the heaven, vigor, the male and penetrative monad.

The origin of creation is the circle, which like the egg shell, surrounds the *Yin* and *Yang* — the female and male.

To the symbolistic Chinese, the joining of the *Yin* and *Yang* forces has given birth to a perfect balance of these qualities: truth, wisdom, propriety, purity and benevolence.

The egg becomes, then, the food of five virtues.

Universally, the egg is known as one of the world's oldest and most complete foods. Compared to other cuisines, the Chinese has managed to give the culinary application of the egg infinitely more variety and usage. The phrase "as American as ham and eggs" is part of the standard routine of writers and lyricists. Now to say "as Chinese as thousand-year-old eggs" may seem a little startling, but there's your comparative chronological differential!

The "thousand-year-old eggs" are a perfect example of how the Chinese have overcome the obstacles of nature in their quest for food. The lime-treating and salting of eggs are common-sense methods of food preservation in a land where refrigeration is practically non-existent for the masses. As exotic as the term "thousand-year-old" sounds, in actuality it is a 100 days' treatment of eggs, wrapped in a clay mixture of lime, salt, ashes and tea, and enmeshed in rice chaff for easy handling. The eggs then are buried in shallow ground for 100 days, during which time the heat of the lime petrifies and darkens the egg, and gives it an onyx-like glaze.

The other process, that of salting, is used in much greater volume (since the "thousand-year-old eggs" is primarily a side-dish or hors d'oeuvre) in regular cooking. Used in steamed dishes, salted eggs can be combined with fresh eggs, or pork patties. The yolk, turned an orange-red color from the saline, also is a welcome symbol of joy.

Duck's, rather than hen's eggs, are used for the liming and salting because they are stronger and tougher texturally for the preservative handling. Wonder what we do with the duck's eggs here in America?

For regular cooking, of course the Chinese use hen's eggs too. But generally the eggs are not prepared and served as a single entree, as are fried eggs or omelets. Rather, eggs are usually combined with other ingredients. Today most of you are familiar with the dish named Egg *Foo Yung*, which sounds like a first cousin to the villainous Fu Manchu. Actually, Egg *Foo Yung* is not as villainous as it sounds, if properly cooked. Many a Chinese-American restaurant fortune has been parlayed from it. Unfortunately, too often it is nothing more than a handful of bean sprouts buried in an egg omelet, which is then further buried in a mass of gravy.

All good cooks know that an omelet must be tenderly, deftly and quickly handled. Except for a difference of combination ingredients, there is no great difference between Chinese and American omelets. A gay color trick is to use a thinly spread omelet, shredding it for egg strips and making a golden garnish.

Speaking of color, when babies are born the clever Chinese send you an announcement of the occasion which you can eat! Yes, hard-boiled eggs, dyed a brilliant vermillion. An announcement basket containing an odd number of eggs — 9 or 11 — stands for a male child. An even number — 8 or 10 — symbolizes a girl.

Morrison Wood, the noted gourmet and syndicated food column writer, in his book *More Recipes With a Jug of Wine* said ". . . I don't know of any comestible that can be as varied as eggs. While there are nine basic ways to cook eggs (soft-boiled, hard-cooked, fried, broiled, baked, poached, scrambled, and in omelets and in soufflés), I'd be willing to wager that I could serve eggs three hundred and sixty-five days running, and have a different dish every day. . . ."

Mr. Wood was referring, of course, only to European and American cooking. The Chinese have a distinctly different *tenth* method which could add immeasurably to his repertoire of egg magic: STEAMING *(Jing)*.

STEAMING, indubitably, is one method of egg cooking which is so exclusively Chinese as to be almost patentable. The nearest American parallel to it would be egg soufflé, but there, the dish is baked. The steamed egg (with various ingredients) is a staple family-fare dish, a natural for the

Chinese mode of eating with rice. For this food of five virtues, one great virtue is the fact that one can mix almost any ingredient with the beaten eggs. Usually, though, it would be a salty or highly flavored ingredient chosen to give contrast to the smooth, bland, custard-like texture of the steamed concoction.

A Chinese "steamed eggs" tour de force juggles three kinds — fresh, salted and the "thousand-year-old" — into one dish, for which we have the recipe called "The Three-Toned Eggs."

Eggs, steamed method, are wondrously delicious with slivered ham, or, for a real change of pace — clams. One practice, though, which you may want to follow: In the recipes calling for water to be mixed with the beaten eggs, we have followed our mother's belief that water previously *boiled* and *cooled* is better than plain water. It is said to make for a smoother blend.

Which is the better method? Naturally we have never questioned our mother's way, so we don't know that the other *may* be better.

Anyway, here are some recipes which may egg you on to a new discovery!

## SALTED DUCK EGGS
*(Hom Don)*

Have ready:                    6 salted duck eggs *(Hom Don)*
Remove dark protective coating from eggs. Then immerse in water and rub and rinse eggs until shells are free from surplus coating.
In a small pot, place:          5 cups cold water
                                Cleaned duck eggs
Bring water to a boil and cook eggs for 10 minutes. Remove eggs, cool and remove shells. Slice eggs into quarters and serve with hot steamed rice as another entree.

# SALTED EGGS STEAMED WITH PORK
*(Hom Don Jing Gee Yuke)*

Have prepared:

1½ pounds raw pork containing some fat.
Chop very fine with two sharp cleavers
2 Salted Eggs *(Hom Don)*. Remove whites from yolks.

In a mixing bowl, place:

Chopped pork
Whites of Salted Eggs
½ teaspoon monosodium glutamate
1 teaspoon salt
1 tablespoon soy sauce
2 fresh eggs and ½ cup water

Mix thoroughly until ingredients are completely blended. Transfer to platter and press into a meat patty covering the platter. Press the firm yolks flat with side of cleaver and place over meat.

Place platter elevated on a trivet or perforated can in a large steamer which has a tight-fitting lid. Cover and steam cook at high heat for 20 to 25 minutes. Serves 3 or 4

*Whenever a Chinese housewife cannot decide what to cook for dinner, this is the old standby she can whip up, knowing it will be well received by every member of her family. Not only is* Hom Don Jing Gee Yuke *nourishing and substantial, it is highly appetizing.*

# OYSTER PURSE EGGS
*(Ho Bow Don)*

Have ready:

6 fresh eggs
6 teaspoons Oyster Sauce *(Ho Yow)*

In a preheated *wok* or skillet place:

1 teaspoon vegetable oil

Bring to medium high heat. Fry eggs sunny side up. Pour 1 teaspoon of oyster sauce over each egg yolk and fold whites over into a half moon (like "eggs over"). Ladle each egg over a bowl of hot steamed rice and serve. Serves 3

# THE THREE-TONED EGGS

*(Jin Som Wong Don)*

| | |
|---|---|
| Have prepared: | 2 large fresh eggs, whipped |
| | 1 Thousand-Year-Old Egg *(Pei Don)*. Remove clay from shell, boil 2 minutes, remove shell and dice egg. |
| | 1 Salted Egg *(Hom Don)*. Remove black protective coating from shell. Crack into dish, reserve egg white. Cut the firm yolk into small diced cubes. |
| In a mixing bowl, place: | 2 cups cold chicken broth |
| | 1 teaspoon salt |
| | 1 tablespoon vegetable oil |
| | ½ teaspoon monosodium glutamate |
| Mix thoroughly and add: | Whipped fresh eggs, diced Thousand-Year-Old Egg and white of Salted Egg and diced yolk. |

Stir entire mixture gently until all ingredients are well mixed. Pour into oiled shallow dish. Place dish elevated on a trivet or suitable substitute in a large steamer which has tight-fitting lid. Cover, steam cook over medium-high heat, removing lid frequently to drain moisture which will collect inside of cover. This will prevent excess water from dripping into eggs. Cook 15 to 20 minutes or until knife blade comes out clean when inserted. Remove dish and sprinkle steamed eggs with soy sauce. Garnish with chopped green onions. Serve hot over steamed rice. Serves 4

*This is the Cantonese method of preparing eggs, similar to a custard, only* Jim Som Wong Don, *salty instead of sweet, is a dinner entree instead of a dessert.*

## THOUSAND-YEAR-OLD EGGS WITH CHIVES
*(Pei Don Gow Choy Chow Don)*

Have prepared:

- **1½ bunches Chinese chives, cleaned and cut into 1-inch lengths**
- **\*2 Thousand-Year-Old Eggs** *(Pei Don)***, shelled and halved. Cut halves into eighths.**
- **6 fresh eggs, well beaten**

In a preheated *wok* or skillet, add:

- **2 tablespoons vegetable oil**
- **¼ teaspoon salt**

Bring oil to sizzling point and add:

- **Cut Chinese chives**

Toss cook at medium high heat for 2 minutes.

Add:

- **Beaten eggs mixed with ¼ teaspoon monosodium glutamate and Thousand-Year-Old Eggs**

Turn gently until fresh eggs are set but not overcooked. Serves 3 or 4

\*How to prepare Thousand-Year-Old Eggs *(Pei Don):* Immerse eggs in cold water and soak until the protecting coat of ''white clay'' is soft enough to be removed from the egg shell. Place eggs in hot water and boil for 5 to 7 minutes. Cool and remove shells.

## EGGS WITH GARDEN PEAS
*(Ching Dow Don)*

Have prepared:

- **1½ cups garden peas (frozen are acceptable)**
- **½ cup dried onion, diced fine**
- **6 fresh eggs, well beaten**

In a preheated *wok* or skillet, add:

- **2 tablespoons vegetable oil**
- **½ teaspoon salt**

Bring oil to sizzling point and add:

- **Diced dried onion, garden peas**

Toss and turn at high heat for 5 minutes until very hot and onion has browned.

Add:

- **Beaten eggs**

Reduce to medium-high heat, turn gently until eggs are set but not overcooked. Serve with hot steamed rice or fried rice. Serves 3 or 4

## *STEAMED EGGS WITH CLAMS*
### *(Sah Bok Jing Don)*

Have prepared:
> **4 large eggs, well beaten**
> **1 can minced clams (8 oz. size). Drain and save juices**
> **¼ cup green onions, sliced fine**

In a saucepot, place:
> **Clam juice and enough water to total 2½ cups**

Heat liquid, then cool. Reserve.

In a mixing bowl, place:
> **Beaten eggs**
> **Minced clams**
> **½ teaspoon monosodium glutamate**
> **¼ teaspoon salt**

Add and mix thoroughly:
> **Clam juice and water mixture**

Pour into an oiled shallow dish. Place dish elevated on a trivet or perforated can in a large steamer with tight-fitting lid. Cover and steam-cook 15 to 20 minutes at medium-high heat, removing cover frequently to drain moisture which will collect inside cover. Before removing dish, insert knife blade, and if it comes out clean, eggs are done. Otherwise, steam a few more minutes, but be sure not to overcook eggs.

Before serving sprinkle with 1 tablespoon soy sauce or oyster sauce and garnish with chopped green onions. Serve hot over steamed rice. Serves 4

*This is another Cantonese method of steaming eggs, for serving as an accompaniment to rice as a luncheon or dinner dish.*

# PRECIOUS FLOWER EGG
*(Gwai Fah Don)*

Have prepared:

    ½ **cup bamboo shoots, sliced fine**
    ¼ **cup snow peas, sliced fine**
    ½ **cup dried onion, sliced fine**
    ¼ **cup dried Chinese mushrooms, pre-soaked**
        **until soft, and sliced thin**
    6 **fresh eggs, well beaten**
    ¼ **cup Barbecued pork or cooked ham, sliced**
        **thin**

In a preheated *wok* or skillet, place:

    2 **tablespoons vegetable oil**
    ½ **teaspoon salt**

Bring oil to sizzling point and add:

    **All above ingredients except eggs**

Toss cook rapidly at high heat for 5 minutes or until ingredients are 70 percent done.

Add:

    **Beaten eggs mixed with ¼ teaspoon**
        **monosodium glutamate**

Reduce to medium high heat, and turn and mix gently like an omelet until eggs are done, but not overcooked. Serve with hot steamed rice or fried rice. Serves 3 or 4

*ℱ*ish

# HAPPINESS COMES IN PAIRS

A favorite subject of Chinese artists is lithe carp swimming in pairs. Their fluid movements are suited perfectly to the water-color brush technique of painting. The symbolism of fish is perfectly matched to the Chinese family pattern. Fish swimming in pairs signify connubial bliss with its attendant harmony and powers of regeneration, wealth and abundance.

Tradition alone, however, is not the only factor in the great piscatorial feeling of the Chinese. To the Chinese, fish is not just a Friday dish. Every day can be seafood day. That is, along with other dishes, it is represented daily in the menu. Chinese eat much more seafood than Americans, and in every form — dried, fresh, preserved in oil. Everything from dried inch-long fish steamed with slivered ginger to the impressive golden cartilage of the giant soup fin shark, one of the world's truly luxurious epicurean offerings, is served.

The natural environment of China played its part in making fish a staple food. It is a large country with a long coastline, many rivers and lakes and a network of canals. And every village has constructed, wherever possible, its man-made ponds. Archaeological findings have uncovered on slips of bamboo and carved animal bones pictograms, traced back to 14 B.C., showing various methods of catching fish by net, pole, line and bait. An age-old folk saying probably best expresses the position of fish in Chinese life:

"Salted fish and green vegetables (with rice) is cause for contentment." Philosophically this is sound. And dietetically, it is also sound.

The Chinese like their fish fresh. They even want them still swimming, if possible, just prior to cooking. In Old China it was a practice to obtain fish alive and to keep them alive until needed. The practice persists here in San Francisco's Chinatown, which is why in Chinese fish markets you see an uncommon number of aerated tanks where live fish cavort.

One of the dining adventures in Hong Kong today is to visit the floating restaurants in the picturesque fishing village of Aberdeen. Some small junk-restaurants had existed earlier, but it took a party of touring Frenchmen who tasted, tested, and took to heart the marvelous freshness of their seafood and cooking to spread the word, and to catapult Aberdeen to international gastronomical fame. So goes the story in Hong Kong, but it is appropriate that the discoverers were cuisine-minded Frenchmen, who rank with the Chinese in appreciation of good food for good living!

Surrounded by hundreds of junks and little sampans, several gaily decorated floating restaurants, specializing in fish and seafood, ride the waves in regal splendor. They seat 125 to 150 persons each. On deck, you can select exactly the live fish you want from an attendant who takes them thrashing from a sea pen to the kitchen. Some minutes later, the very fish you personally selected is served to you and your guests, prepared in all its succulent goodness by masters of seafood cookery.

Nowhere else in the world can you expect to get fish and shellfish or seafood any fresher than you do in this charming fishing village of Aberdeen in faraway Hong Kong.

But still, you can cook creditably at home in the fashion of the Chinese floating restaurants chefs by taking to heart these basic rules:

*Always buy the freshest fish and seafood possible. Choose fish which are clear-eyed, red gilled, firm to the touch, and have a fresh fish odor.*

*Coarse-textured fish take longer to cook than fine-textured ones.*

*Better to undercook than overcook fish, since fish should always be moist and tender. Overcooking makes a fish dry and tasteless.*

*In this respect, note that typically Chinese cooking methods, such as poaching and steaming, are naturally good ways to cook fish. Try them.*

*Chinese use "defishers" such as soy sauce, ginger, scallions and wine, as recipes will indicate.*

# FILET OF FISH WITH VEGETABLES
## (Chow Yee Peen)

Have prepared:
**1 pound fish filets sliced ¼-inch thick**
    **(Preferably rock cod, or striped bass)**
**½ cup sliced dried onion**
**½ cup sliced celery**
**½ cup sliced bamboo shoots**
**½ cup sliced water chestnuts**
**½ cup sliced button mushrooms**

In a preheated *wok* or skillet, place:
**2 tablespoons vegetable oil**

Bring oil to sizzling point at high heat, add:
**Fish filets**

Reduce to medium-high heat. Brown filets rapidly first on one side and then the other (no longer than 1 minute each side). Remove from pan and reserve.

In the same utensil, add:    **1 tablespoon vegetable oil**

Bring to high heat and add:    **Sliced dried onion, celery, bamboo shoots, water chestnuts and button mushrooms**

Toss and turn 1 minute until all vegetables are well blended.
Add:
**⅓ cup chicken stock**
**½ teaspoon salt**
**1 teaspoon soy sauce**
**1 teaspoon monosodium glutamate**

Cover and cook at high heat for about 5 minutes. Uncover.
Add:
**Fish filets**
**1 teaspoon cornstarch. Make paste with 1 teaspoon water.**

Toss and mix all ingredients gently until well mixed and sauce has thickened. Serve immediately with steamed rice. Serves 4

*A pleasant "toss-cooked" departure from the usual "fried filet" treatment.*

# SWEET AND SOUR FISH FILET
*(Teem Seen Yee Fai)*

| | |
|---|---|
| Have prepared: | **1 pound fish filets, sliced ⅜-inch thick** |
| | **Salt and pepper to taste** |
| | **½ cup finely sliced (julienne) bell pepper** |
| | **½ cup finely sliced onion** |
| | **1 medium tomato, sliced** |
| | **2 tablespoons finely sliced red ginger** |
| | **2 tablespoons finely sliced Chinese pickled scallions** |
| In a mixing bowl, combine: | **1 cup flour** |
| | **½ cup cornstarch** |
| | **1 teaspoon baking powder** |
| | **1 teaspoon salt** |
| | **¾ cup cold water** |
| | **1 beaten egg** |
| | **¼ cup vegetable oil** |

Whip batter with egg beater until smooth and free of lumps. Dip sliced fish filets in batter.

In a deep-fat fryer, place:     **4 cups vegetable oil**

Bring oil to 350°F. Gently drop battered pieces into hot oil, individually. Fry until golden brown and crisp. Do not overcook. Drain briefly on absorbent toweling. Arrange on serving platter. Keep warm.

In a preheated *wok* or skillet, place:

**½ cup vinegar**
**½ cup sugar**
**⅓ cup pineapple juice**
**¼ cup catsup**
**1 teaspoon Worcestershire sauce**
**4 drops hot sauce (Tabasco)**

Bring to boil and add:          **Sliced peppers, onion and tomato**

Stir gently and thicken this sweet and sour mixture with:

**1 tablespoon cornstarch, made into paste with**
**1 tablespoon water.**

Ladle the sweet and sour sauce over the crispy fish filet. Top with sliced ginger and scallion. Serve with pride. Serves 4

## STUFFED LOBSTER TAILS
*(Yeong Loong Hah Mei)*

Have prepared:
    **4 large lobster tails. If frozen, defrost. Remove meat and save shells. Chop meat fine.**
    **½ pound uncooked pork, ground**
    **¼ cup Black Bean Paste** *(Dow See)*
    **¼ cup dried Chinese mushrooms, pre-soaked, drained and chopped fine**
    **¼ cup water chestnuts, chopped fine**

In a preheated *wok* or skillet place:
    **1 tablespoon vegetable oil**

Bring to high heat, and add ground pork. Turn and mix until brown. Cover and cook for 5 minutes. Remove from fire and cool.

In a large mixing bowl, place:
    **Ground lobster meat, cooked pork, mushrooms and water chestnuts**

Add:
    **½ teaspoon salt**
    **½ teaspoon monosodium glutamate**

Mix all ingredients thoroughly with hands until well blended. Separate into 4 portions, form into balls. "Slap" each ball on chopping board 10 or 15 times. Stuff balls to fill lobster tail shells evenly. Arrange on shallow dish or platter.

In a hot *wok* place:
    **2 tablespoons vegetable oil**
    **1 teaspoon crushed garlic**
    **Black Bean Paste**

Toss and turn until garlic is brown.

Add:
    **½ cup water**
    **2 tablespoons soy sauce**
    **1 teaspoon cornstarch**

Stir until sauce thickens, spread over each stuffed lobster tail. Steam cook at high heat for 20 minutes. Serve hot with steamed rice. Serves 4

*A beautiful party dish which is very simple to prepare.*

# RED COOKED ROCK COD CANTONESE
*(Hoong Siew Shek Bon)*

Have prepared:
> 1 fresh rock cod, 2½ to 3 pounds, cleaned, washed and drained. Cut into 1½-inch chunks. Wipe with towels until perfectly dry.
> ⅓ cup bamboo shoots, sliced ⅛-inch thick
> ⅓ cup pre-soaked and softened dried Chinese mushrooms, sliced ¼-inch thick
> ⅓ cup water chestnuts, sliced
> ⅓ cup barbecued pork or cooked ham, sliced fine

In a mixing bowl, blend:
> 1 beaten egg
> ⅓ teaspoon salt
> 1 tablespoon soy sauce

Dip chunked rock cod in egg mixture and dust very lightly with cornstarch.
In a deep-fry utensil, bring to boil:
> 1 quart vegetable oil

Drop fish chunks into the hot oil and deep fry 4 to 6 minutes until light brown. Do not overcook. Remove fish and drain on absorbent toweling. Place on serving platter. Keep warm.
In a preheated *wok* or skillet place:
> 1 tablespoon vegetable oil

Bring oil to sizzling point and add:
> ½ teaspoon salt

Add:
> Sliced bamboo shoots, mushrooms, water chestnuts and barbecued pork or ham

Toss cook rapidly at high heat for 1 minute.
Add:
> 1 cup chicken stock
> ½ teaspoon monosodium glutamate
> 1 tablespoon soy sauce

Cover and cook at high heat until soup stock is very hot (about 4 minutes). Uncover.
Add gradually:
> 2 teaspoons cornstarch. Make paste with 2 teaspoons water.

Toss and mix at high heat until sauce thickens and all ingredients are well mixed. Pour over red cooked rock cod and serve immediately with steamed rice. Serves 4

# CRAB À LA KAN
*(Goon Yin See Jup Hai)*

Have prepared:

1 large live Dungeness crab. Scrub shells with stiff brush. Remove shell and save crab fat. Clean rest of crab. Crack legs and claws and cut at joints. Cut body portions into thirds.
1 small dried onion, sliced
1 bell pepper, sliced into 1-inch squares
1 teaspoon crushed garlic
1 beaten egg
1 teaspoon mashed *Dow See* (fermented Black Beans)

In a preheated *wok* or large skillet, place:

2 tablespoons vegetable oil
½ teaspoon salt

Bring oil to sizzling point and add:

Sliced onion, bell pepper, crushed garlic

Toss cook rapidly for 1 minute at high heat.

Add:

½ teaspoon sugar
½ teaspoon monosodium glutamate
Cracked raw crab
2 cups chicken stock
Mashed *Dow See*

Cover and cook at high heat 10 to 15 minutes, or until liquids are bubbling hot.

Add gradually:

Crab fat and beaten egg
3 teaspoons cornstarch. Make paste with 3 teaspoons water.

Turn and mix at medium high heat until sauce begins to thicken. When all ingredients are well blended and very hot, transfer to serving platter and serve at once. Serves 2 or 3

*Crab à la Kan is named after the restaurant which first introduced this delectable San Francisco Cantonese style dish to non-Chinese. To enjoy to the utmost, simply "let yourself go" and use your fingers!*

## GINGER AND ONION CRAB
*(Geong Chung Hai)*

Have prepared:

1 large live Dungeness crab, shelled and cleaned. Crack legs and claws and section at joints. Cut body portions into thirds.
8 thin slices ginger root, crushed
3 stalks green onion, cut into 1-inch sections

In a deep-fry utensil, place: 2 cups vegetable oil

Heat oil to 350°F. Cook crab pieces, stirring gently (about 2 minutes). Remove pieces and drain on absorbent toweling.

In a preheated *wok,* place: 2 tablespoons vegetable oil

Add: Ginger slices

Fry until ginger is golden brown. Add crab pieces and green onion sections. Toss cook at medium heat for 3 minutes.

Add:

½ teaspoon salt
½ teaspoon sugar
1 teaspoon soy sauce
2 tablespoons rice wine or sherry
½ teaspoon cornstarch, made into paste with
¼ cup chicken broth.

Turn all ingredients until well-mixed. Cover and cook for ½ minute or until the liquids are absorbed and slightly thickened.

Serve piping with hot steamed rice. Serves 4 to 6

## RAZOR CLAMS SAUTÉED IN GARLIC OIL
*(Seen Tow Yow Chow Dai Heen)*

Have prepared:

5 pounds fresh razor clams or cockles. Scrub the shells until free of sand. Drain.

In a preheated *wok* or large skillet, place:

3 tablespoons vegetable oil

Bring oil to sizzling heat, then add:

½ teaspoon salt
2 teaspoons garlic, chopped fine
2 teaspoon dried onion, chopped fine

Toss and mix rapidly until garlic is almost brown (about ½ minute). Immediately add washed clams or cockles, toss and mix until hot oil and garlic combination has drenched shellfish. Cover and cook at medium-high heat for 7 minutes. Uncover. Toss and turn for another minute, serve immediately. Serves 3 or 4

# STRIPED BASS À LA KAN
## (Jing Lo Yee)

Have prepared:

**4 slices of fish, ¾-inch thick, from center of a 8- or 10-pound Striper.**

Place the fish in a shallow dish.

In a mixing bowl, place:

**1 clove mashed garlic**

**2 tablespoons mashed fermented black beans (Dow See)**

**1 teaspoon sugar**

**4½ tablespoons best quality Chinese soy sauce**

**3 teaspoons vegetable oil**

Mix and mash all ingredients thoroughly until well blended. Spread evenly over fish slices.

Elevate the dish on a trivet in a large pot, containing ¾ inch of hot water, with a tight-fitting lid. Steam cook at high heat just 20 minutes. Do not overcook. Remove dish when done and garnish fish with shredded green onions and Chinese parsley. Serve immediately with hot steamed rice. Serves 4

*Since Striped bass is a salt water game fish in the West, it is not available in fish markets except on the East Coast, where Stripers are caught and sold commercially. The legal limit of Stripers is 3 fish per angler (minimum size 16 inches) in the San Francisco area. Record-size Stripers have weighed in over 68 pounds.*

## CURRIED CRAB EN SHELL
*(Gah Lay Hai)*

Have prepared:
> 1 large Dungeness crab. Scrub under cold water. Remove shell and save crab fat (custard). Clean rest of crab. Crack legs and claws and cut at joints. Cut body portions into thirds.
> 1 small dried onion, sliced
> 1 medium-sized bell pepper, sliced into ½-inch squares
> 1 large tomato, cut into eighths

In a preheated *wok*, place:
> 2 tablespoons vegetable oil
> 1 tablespoon best quality curry powder
> ½ teaspoon salt

Bring oil to sizzling point at high heat. Mix ingredients thoroughly (½ minute).

Add:
> Cracked raw crab
> Sliced onion, bell pepper and tomato
> ½ teaspoon sugar
> ½ teaspoon monosodium glutamate
> 1 cup chicken stock
> Crab custard from shell

Turn all ingredients until well mixed, cover and cook at high heat 12 to 15 minutes. Uncover.

Add gradually:
> 1 tablespoon cornstarch. Make paste with 1 tablespoon water.

Toss and turn constantly at high heat until curry sauce thickens. Crab should be thoroughly coated with sauce. Serve very hot with steamed rice, and eat the crab with your hands, first tasting the delicious sauce on the shells. Serves 2 or 3

*We are proud to say that Kan's popularized* Gah Lay Hai *and* See Jup Hai *many years ago, and these have become favorites of San Franciscans who frequent Chinatown. Since live Dungeness crabs are available only on the Pacific Coast, those of you who live on the East Coast can substitute live Maine lobster and get excellent results from the same recipe. Where neither live crabs nor lobsters are available, defrosted frozen lobster tails in the shell may be used. However, the cooking time should be increased to allow the firmer meat to become done.*

## DRY-FRIED PRAWNS EN SHELL
### (Gawn Jeen Hah Look)

Have prepared:
    **1½  pounds uncooked unshelled jumbo prawns.
Wash and drain, if fresh. Defrost if from
freezer, wash and drain.
¼  cup cleaned large green onions, cut into
½-inch lengths. Discard green portion.**

In a preheated *wok* or skillet, place:
    **2 tablespoons vegetable oil
⅓ teaspoon salt**

Bring oil to red hot sizzle at high heat. Mix salt thoroughly with hot oil.
With long chopsticks or tongs, place prawns flat in pan. Fry both sides until
shells are brown.

Add:
    **1 teaspoon soy sauce
2 tablespoons chicken stock
Cut green onions**

Toss and turn at high heat until all ingredients are very hot and well
blended. Serve immediately. Serves 4

*Once you have savored prawns cooked in this Cantonese fashion, you will
appreciate why boiled prawns lack flavor and juiciness, because all the
taste has been boiled out of them. Here again is an example of how oil and
salt, plus browning, add to the succulence which deserves to be retained in
this beneficial shellfish.*

## STEAMED SALT FISH
### (Jing Hom Yee)

Have prepared:
    **4 pieces salt fish *(Hom Yee)* cut ¾ inch wide.
Use dried flounder *(Yow Dai Day)* or
any Chinese variety. Rinse.
1 teaspoon shredded fresh ginger root**

Place salt fish in a shallow dish. Spread shredded ginger root over fish with
2 tablespoons vegetable oil. Elevate dish on a trivet, making sure water is
boiling. Steam 15 to 20 minutes. Serve as an entree with hot steamed rice.
Serves 2

*This is anothe simple, inexpensive "village-style" dish which is favored by
princes and paupers alike. Steamed* Hom Yee *is eaten in small bites,
accompanied with mouthfuls of steaming rice. However, the cost factor of
food is inconsequential when desirability is placed first.*

# DRIED ABALONE WITH OYSTER SAUCE
*(Ho Yow So Bow)*

Have prepared: **1 pound dried abalone** *(Bow Yee)*

Soak dried abalone in cold water overnight. Place in a pot and cover with boiling water and boil vigorously for 5 hours. Remove pot from fire and let stand until water is cool. Drain and clean each abalone, using the fingers and running water. When cleaned, use boiling water, but slowly this time at high simmer, for 24 hours. Drain off water and cool in colander. Sliced cooked abalone into 3/16-inch thick pieces.

In a preheated *wok* or skillet, place:

> **2 tablespoons vegetable oil**
> **⅓ teaspoon salt**

Bring oil to a sizzle at high heat, add:

> **Sliced abalone**

Turn and mix rapidly and add at once:

> **1 cup chicken stock**
> **3 tablespoons Oyster Sauce** *(Ho Yow)*
> **½ teaspoon monosodium glutamate**

Turn and mix for 1 minute, cover and cook until the stock is boiling. Uncover.

Add gradually: **1 tablespoon cornstarch. Make paste with 1 tablespoon water.**

Toss and turn until sauce thickens. Serve very hot with hot steamed rice. Serves 4 or 5

*This is a "long-cooking" recipe for which you will be well rewarded, for* Ho Yow So Bow *is strictly a fancy banquet-style entree. Here is an example of how dehydration enhances the flavor of this popular mollusk and also changes its texture. The Oyster Sauce combines with the somewhat smoky flavor of the abalone to make it a gourmet's favorite.*

# CURRIED PRAWNS
*(Gah Lay Hah Kow)*

Have prepared:    1½ pounds shelled prawns (jumbo size)
1 small dried onion, sliced
1 medium sized bell pepper, sliced into
½-inch squares

In a preheated *wok* or skillet, place:
2 tablespoons vegetable oil

Bring oil to sizzling point at high heat.

Add:    ½ teaspoon salt
1 tablespoon best quality curry powder

Mix well for ½ minute, and add:    Shelled prawns, sliced bell pepper and
onion
½ teaspoon sugar
½ teaspoon monosodium glutamate
1 cup chicken stock

Turn all ingredients until thoroughly blended, cover and cook at high heat
for 7 to 8 minutes. Uncover.

Add gradually:    1 tablespoon cornstarch. Make paste with 1
tablespoon water.

Toss and turn constantly until curry sauce thickens. Serve steaming hot
over or with hot steamed rice. Serves 4

# STEAMED SALMON WITH BLACK BEAN SAUCE
*(Dow See Jing Sah-mon Yee)*

Have prepared:    3 slices fresh salmon ¾-inch thick
In a mixing bowl, blend:    2 tablespoons fermented Black Beans *(Dow
See)*, crushed to paste
2 tablespoons vegetable oil
1 teaspoon crushed garlic
⅓ teaspoon salt
1 teaspoon fresh ginger root, shredded fine
½ teaspoon monosodium glutamate
1 teaspoon soy sauce

Place salmon neatly on platter and spread Black Bean sauce and ingredient
mixture evenly over each slice of fish. Place in steaming utensil. Steam
cook 15 to 20 minutes. Serve with steamed rice. Serves 3

## *LOBSTER SAUTÉED WITH VEGETABLES*
*(Chow Loong Hah Kow)*

Have prepared:

**Meat from 2 lobster tails, sliced into ½-inch
pieces**
**1 small can button mushrooms, drained**
**½ cup canned bamboo shoots, sliced about
¼-inch thick and into ¾-inch pieces**
**½ cup thinly sliced celery**

In a preheated *wok* or skillet, place:

**2 tablespoons vegetable oil**
**½ teaspoon salt**

Increase to high heat and bring oil to sizzling point.

Add:
**Sliced lobster meat**

Toss and turn rapidly for 2 minutes.

Add:
**Above vegetables**
**⅓ teaspoon sugar**
**1 teaspoon soy sauce**
**½ teaspoon monosodium glutamate**
**1 cup chicken stock**

Turn ingredients lightly until thoroughly mixed, cover and cook at high
heat for 7 minutes. Uncover.

Add gradually:
**1 tablespoon cornstarch. Make paste with 1
tablespoon water.**

Toss cook until sauce has thickened. Serve with hot steamed rice. Serves 4

## PRAWNS WITH BLACK BEAN SAUCE
*(See Jup Hah Kow)*

Have prepared:

**1 pound shelled prawns (jumbo size)**
**1 large dried onion, sliced ½ inch wide**
**2 bell peppers, cut into ¾-inch squares**
**2 tablespoons Black Bean Paste** *(Dow See)*
**1 teaspoon garlic**
**1 whipped egg**

In a preheated *wok* or skillet, place:

**2 tablespoons vegetable oil**

Bring oil to a sizzle, add:

**½ teaspoon salt**
**Black Bean Paste**
**Crushed garlic**

Turn and mix ingredients until garlic is brown (about 1 minute). Maintain high heat.

Add at once:

**Uncooked prawns, sliced onions and bell peppers**

Toss and turn rapidly until well blended (1 or 2 minutes).

Add:

**¾ cup chicken stock**

Cover and cook at high heat for 6 to 7 minutes. Uncover.

Add:

**½ teaspoon sugar**
**½ teaspoon monosodium glutamate**
**1 teaspoon soy sauce**

Turn and mix all ingredients again.

Add gradually:

**1 tablespoon cornstarch. Make paste with 1 tablespoon water.**
**Whipped egg**

Toss and turn at high heat very rapidly until sauce thickens. Serve with hot steamed rice. Lobster may be substituted for prawns. Serves 4

# FISH CAKES STUFFED IN BITTER MELON
*(Yeong Foo Gwa)*

Have prepared:

**1 pound fresh fish filets. Use any kind of fish that can be entirely boned.**
**1 pound shelled raw prawns**
**1 fresh egg, yolk removed**
**2 pounds Bitter Melons\*** *(Foo Gwa)*, **even-sized**
**½ teaspoon minced garlic**
**2 teaspoons fermented Black Beans†**
*(Dow See)* **crushed into paste.**

Chop fish and prawns together until minced very fine. Place in mixing bowl.

Add:

**1 teaspoon salt**
**½ teaspoon monosodium glutamate**
**White of egg**

Mix thoroughly with hands until well blended. We now have fish cake.

To stuff:

Slice Bitter Melons into 4 round segments each. Remove pulp. Stuff some fish cake in each segment, mounded on top.

In a preheated *wok* or skillet, place:

**2 tablespoons vegetable oil**

Bring oil to sizzling point and place stuffed Bitter Melon segments in utensil, flat sides down. When fish cake is brown, add garlic and black beans. When garlic is brown, add immediately:

**1½ cups chicken stock**
**½ teaspoon salt**
**½ teaspoon sugar**

Stir chicken stock, Black Bean paste, garlic, salt and sugar in the pan and blend while cooking at high heat. Cover and cook for 20 minutes. Uncover. Add gradually to liquids:

**1 tablespoon cornstarch. Make paste with 1 tablespoon water.**

Stir and mix, without disturbing stuffed Bitter Melons. When sauce thickens (3 or 4 minutes), ladle over stuffed sections several times and serve hot, with steamed rice. Serves 6

---

†See condiments
\*See Bitter Melon with Beef recipe

# SMOTHERED ROCK COD
## (Munn Shek Bon)

Have prepared:

**1 fresh rock cod (about 3 pounds) dressed**
**1 teaspoon fresh ginger root, thinly sliced**
**½ teaspoon dried Mandarin orange peel, pre-soaked and sliced**
**1 teaspoon Chinese red dates, pre-soaked and sliced**
**¼ cup dried Chinese mushrooms, pre-soaked and sliced**
**¼ cup sliced bamboo shoots**
**¼ cup sliced water chestnuts (fresh or canned)**
**1 teaspoon sliced salted vegetable root (Choong Choy), rinsed**

In a preheated *wok,* place:   **3 tablespoons vegetable oil**
Bring oil to sizzling point at high heat, then add:

**Dressed rock cod**

Brown fish rapidly (1 minute each side).
Blend and add:

**2 cups chicken stock**
**1 tablespoon soy sauce**
**1 teaspoon salt**
**½ teaspoon sugar**
**1 teaspoon monosodium glutamate**

Mix all the prepared vegetables together and place evenly over rock cod. Cover and cook at high heat for 25 minutes. Uncover.

Add gradually to the liquid:   **1 tablespoon cornstarch. Make paste with 1 tablespoon water.**

As soon as liquid thickens, ladle it carefully over fish. Transfer fish to hot serving platter, with sauce, making sure not to disturb the topping. Serve with steamed or fried rice. Serves 4 to 6

*Black rock cod, although a commercial fish, rates about second position among the favorite fishes of the Cantonese, because of the* Seen Gee Yuke *or "garlic clove characteristic" qualities, descriptive of the way the delicate meat flakes off with chopsticks. Undisputedly first in favor is the large-mouth black bass, a game fish with an even finer, flakier texture. The smother-cook method permits all the flavors of the various ingredients to infuse into the fish, resulting in a harmonious blend of taste and texture.*

## STEAMED ROCK COD
*(Jing Shek Bon)*

Have prepared:

**1 fresh black rock cod (2 to 2½ pounds) dressed**
**1 teaspoon shredded fresh ginger root**
**1 green onion shredded fine (white section)**

Place fish on a thin platter, and over it, spread evenly:

**Shredded ginger root**
**½ teaspoon salt**
**1 whole green onion**

Place platter on a trivet in a steamer, making sure water is boiling. Cover and steam about 25 minutes. Test with fork. Fish should be removed before it has a chance to become overdone.

While fish is steaming, heat: **¼ cup vegetable oil**

When fish is done drain and place on platter. Discard whole green onion, then pour over the fish: **Hot vegetable oil**
**¼ cup soy sauce**

Garnish rock cod with the shredded green onion and serve steaming hot with fried or steamed rice. Serves 2 or 3

*The secret of right timing in steam cooking rock cod can be easily discovered after a few experiments with different types of utensils. It is always important to retain the natural flavor of the fish, and this recipe, using just hot oil and soy sauce, is what the Cantonese call,* Wot, Ching-teem, *or "smooth, pure-sweet."*

*To appreciate the flaky meat of rock cod fully, spoon some of the soy sauce and oil from the platter over each morsel of fish and eat with slivers of green onions to give it "zing."*

## STEAMED FISH WITH DRIED OLIVES
*(Lom Gok Jin Yee)*

Have prepared:

**2 pounds of fish steaks ¾-inch thick. Use halibut, sea bass or striped bass.**
**¼ pound dried Chinese pitted olives**
*(Lom Gok),* **pre-soaked ½ hour, drained and chopped finely**
**1 teaspoon crushed garlic**
**½ teaspoon finely shredded fresh ginger root**

Place all ingredients except fish in a mixing bowl and blend thoroughly.
Add gradually:      ½ teaspoon salt
                    2 tablespoons vegetable oil
                    ½ teaspoon monosodium glutamate

Arrange fish steaks on a platter or shallow round dish and spread above combination over each piece so that the steaks will be evenly covered with the ingredients.

Elevate platter or dish with a trivet or perforated can in a steamer, making sure water is boiling. Steam 20 minutes. Serves 4

*This is an interesting way to spruce up any species of large, lean, salt water fish which otherwise is rather bland and coarse in texture. If you favor spicy foods, you will discover in the pleasant predominance of the* Lom Gok *and garlic an appetite-stimulating combination.*

## *SAUTÉED FRESH SCALLOPS WITH VEGETABLES*
### *(Sang Gong Yow Chee Chow Choy)*

Have prepared:      ½ pound fresh scallops cut into halves
                    ½ cup canned bamboo shoots, sliced about
                       ¼-inch thick and into ½-inch pieces
                    ½ cup celery sliced ¼-inch thick
                    ½ cup sliced dried onion
                    6-8 Chinese snow peas. Remove tips and
                       strings, wash and drain

In a preheated *wok* or skillet, place:
                    2 tablespoons vegetable oil
                    1 teaspoon salt

Bring oil to sizzling point at high heat.
Add:                Scallops and all the prepared vegetables

Toss cook at high heat for 2 minutes.
Add:                ½ teaspoon sugar
                    1 teaspoon soy sauce
                    ½ teaspoon monosodium glutamate
                    1 cup chicken stock

Turn all ingredients until well mixed. Cover and cook at high heat 5 minutes. Uncover.

Add gradually:      1 tablespoon cornstarch. Make paste with 1
                       tablespoon water.

Toss and turn until sauce thickens. Serve immediately, accompanied with hot steamed rice. Serves 4

# SWEET AND SOUR WHOLE ROCK COD
*(Teem Seen Shek Bon)*

Have prepared:                    **1 cleaned, fresh rock cod (about 2½ pounds)**

With a sharp knife, make a few incisions on both sides of fish, ¼ inch deep so sauce can penetrate. Season with salt and pepper.

In a preheated *wok* or skillet, place:

**½ cup vegetable oil**

Bring oil to boiling point and add:

**Seasoned whole rock cod**

Brown both sides (about 15 minutes) drain and transfer to hot platter.

In a preheated *wok* or skillet, place:

**½ cup sugar**
**½ cup vinegar**
**⅓ cup pineapple juice**
**¼ cup catsup**
**1 teaspoon Worcestershire sauce**
**4 drops hot sauce**

Bring to a boil and add:      **1 large bell pepper, sliced**
**2 fresh tomatoes, quartered**
**½ cup sliced dried onion (optional)**

Stir gently at high heat and again bring to a boil.

Add gradually:               **5 teaspoons cornstarch. Make paste with 5 teaspoons water.**

Continue cooking at medium-high heat, stirring mixture until sauce has thickened. Pour mixture over fish and serve immediately with steamed rice. Serves 3 or 4

# DRIED OYSTER TUMBLE WITH LETTUCE CUPS
## *(Ho See Soong)*

Have prepared:                  **½  pound dried oysters** *(Soong Ho See)*

Soak dried oysters in cold water overnight. Rinse several times to remove grit. Parboil and simmer at low heat for ½ hour. Rinse in cold water, drain and mince fine.

Also prepare:                   **1  head firm lettuce. Separate leaves.**
                                     **½  cup bamboo shoots, minced fine**
                                     **½  cup dried Chinese mushrooms, pre-soaked,**
                                          **drained and chopped fine**
                                   **½  cup water chestnuts, minced**
                                   **½  cup celery, chopped fine**
                                   **¼  pound ground pork**

In a preheated *wok* or skillet, place:
                                   **2  tablespoons vegetable oil**

Bring to high heat, add ground pork. Turn and mix until brown.

Add:                           **Minced dried oysters, bamboo shoots,**
                                   **mushrooms, water chestnuts and celery**

Turn and mix all ingredients, then add:
                                   **½  teaspoon salt**
                                   **2  tablespoons Oyster Sauce** *(Ho Yow)*
                                   **¼  teaspoon monosodium glutamate**
                                   **1  cup chicken soup stock**

Turn and mix until well blended. Cover and cook at medium-high heat for 10 minutes. Uncover.

Gradually add:               **2  teaspoons cornstarch. Make paste with 2**
                                   **teaspoons water.**

Turn and mix gently until mixture thickens. Transfer to serving dish. Each guest takes a leaf of lettuce and places a tablespoon of the oyster tumble in it, and eats it with his hands. Serves 4

## *STEAMED FISH WITH BLACK BEAN SAUCE*
*(Dow See Seen Gee Jing Yee)*

Have prepared:

In a mixing bowl, blend:

2 pounds fish steaks ¾-inch thick. Use striped
    bass, halibut or sea bass.
2 tablespoons fermented Black Beans *(Dow
    See),* crushed to paste*
1 teaspoon crushed garlic
1 green onion, finely sliced

Black Bean Paste
Crushed garlic
4 tablespoons soy sauce
1 teaspoon sugar
3 teaspoons vegetable oil
½ teaspoon monosodium glutamate

Arrange fish steaks on a platter or shallow round dish and spread the above
combination over each piece so that each steak is evenly covered with the
sauce.

Elevate the platter or dish with a trivet or suitable substitute in a steamer,
making sure water is boiling first. Steam 20 minutes. Garnish with the
sliced green onions and serve immediately with hot steamed rice. Serves 4

---

*See condiments

# SAUTÉED FRESH SQUID WITH VEGETABLES
## (Lon Dow Chow Yow Yee)

Have prepared:

**1 pound fresh squid, washed and drained. Discard tentacles, slice squid into sixths.**
**½ cup sliced dried onion**
**½ cup sliced celery**
**½ cup sliced bamboo shoots**
**¼ pound whole snow peas, blanched 2 minutes and drained**

In a preheated *wok* or skillet, place:

**2 tablespoons vegetable oil**
**½ teaspoon salt**

Bring oil to sizzling point. At high heat, add sliced squid.
Toss-cook rapidly for 2 minutes or until almost done.
Add:

**Sliced onion, celery, bamboo shoots and snow peas**
**1 teaspoon soy sauce**
**½ teaspoon sugar**
**½ teaspoon monosodium glutamate**
**⅓ cup chicken stock**

Cover and cook at high heat for 5 minutes. Uncover.
Add gradually:

**1 teaspoon cornstarch. Make paste with 1 teaspoon water.**

Turn and mix rapidly until mixture is very hot and well blended. Serve with hot steamed rice. Serves 4

# DRIED OYSTERS WITH BEAN CURD SKIM
*(Ho See Munn Foo Jook)*

Have prepared:                **½ pound dried oysters** *(Sook Ho See)*
Soak dried oysters in cold water overnight. Rinse several times to remove grit. Parboil and simmer at low heat for ½ hour. Rinse in cold water and drain.

Also have prepared:          **6 sheets Bean Curd Skim** *(Foo Jook)*
                             **pre-soaked in cold water for 2 hours.**
                             **Drain thoroughly. Cut in 2- to 3-inch**
                             **pieces.**
                             **½ cup Chinese dried mushrooms, pre-soaked**
                             **and softened in cold water 1 hour. Drain**
                             **and dice.**
                             **2 teaspoons Red Bean Cake, mashed** *(Nom Yee)*

In a preheated *wok* or skillet, place:
                             **2 tablespoons vegetable oil**
                             **½ teaspoon salt**
Bring oil to sizzling point at high heat. Reduce to medium high heat.
Add:                         **Red Bean Cake**
Toss and turn rapidly for 1 minute.
Add:                         **Bean Curd Skim and mushrooms**
                             **2 cups chicken stock**
                             **⅓ teaspoon sugar**
                             **½ teaspoon monosodium glutamate**
                             **2 tablespoons vegetable oil**
                             **Diced dried oysters**

Mix all ingredients gently until blended. Cover utensil and bring to a boil at high heat. Reduce to low heat and simmer for ¾ hour, turning mixture occasionally.

Uncover and add gradually:   **2 teaspoons cornstarch. Make paste with 2**
                             **teaspoons water.**
Turn and mix ingredients very lightly until sauce thickens. Serve hot with steamed rice. Serves 3 or 4

# CRAB LEGS SAUTÉED WITH SNOW PEAS
## (Lon Dow Chow Hai Keem)

Have prepared:
**1 pound cooked crab legs and claws. Crack shells and remove meat carefully without breaking it up.**
**½ cup dried onion, sliced**
**½ cup sliced celery**
**½ pound snow peas**

In a preheated *wok* or skillet, place:
**2 tablespoons vegetable oil**

Bring oil to sizzling point and add:
**Sliced onion, celery, snow peas**
**¼ teaspoon salt**
**½ teaspoon sugar**
**¼ teaspoon monosodium glutamate**
**1 teaspoon soy sauce**

Toss and turn rapidly at high heat for 5 minutes.
Add:
**Shelled crab legs and claws**
**½ cup chicken stock**

Cover and cook at medium high heat for 5 mintues. Uncover.
Add gradually:
**1 tablespoon cornstarch. Make paste with 1 tablespoon water.**

Toss and mix until mixture thickens. Serve immediately with steamed or fried rice. Serves 3 or 4

## STEAMED REX SOLE
*(Jing Top Sah)*

Have prepared:

    **4 dressed and washed fresh Rex sole**
    **1 teaspoon fresh ginger root, sliced thin, then shredded**

In a mixing bowl, combine:

    **¼ teaspoon salt**
    **1 teaspoon soy sauce**
    **2 teaspoons vegetable oil**
    **Shredded ginger root**
    **2 teaspoons Brown Bean Sauce** *(Min See Jeong)*

Arrange fish neatly on platter and spread on the above combination so that each fish is evenly covered with the condiments. Place the platter of fish on a trivet and into steamer, making sure that water is boiling. Cover and steam 7 to 10 minutes. Do not overcook. Serve immediately with hot steamed rice. Serves 3 or 4

*The steaming method of cooking any kind of flat fishes, especially sole and sand dabs, retains all the juices. Because it is moist cooking, the texture of the delicate meat is not destroyed. Brown Bean Sauce* (Min See Jeong) *is the accepted condiment to complement sole and sand dabs.*

## BUTTERFLY SHRIMP
*(Woo Dip Hah)*

Have prepared:    **1½ pounds prawns (medium large)**

Wash and drain prawns, remove shells but not the tails. Open prawns by splitting down the center ¾ of the way with sharp knife. Do not cut all the way through. Remove veins.

In a mixing bowl, place:

    **1 beaten egg**
    **½ teaspoon salt**
    **1 teaspoon monosodium glutamate**
    **2 teaspoons soy sauce**

Blend thoroughly for batter.

Also have prepared:

    **8-9 slices of bacon cut into 1-inch lengths**
    **¾ cup cornstarch**

Lay a piece of bacon in each prawn, fold sides together and dip in batter. Roll lightly in cornstarch. Keep in refrigerator for ½ to 1 hour. Deep fry in vegetable oil (350 degrees) until golden brown. Do not overcook. Serves 4 or 5

## FISH STUFFED IN BEAN CAKE
*(Jow Yeong Dow Foo)*

Have prepared:
> ¾ **pound fresh fish filets. Use any kind of large fish that can be entirely boned.**
> ¾ **pound raw shelled prawns**
> 1 **fresh egg, yolk removed**
> 8 **square Bean Cakes** *(Dow Foo)*

Chop fish and prawns together until minced very fine. Place in bowl.

Add:
> ½ **teaspoon salt**
> ⅓ **teaspoon monosodium glutamate**
> **White of egg**

Mix thoroughly with hands and divide into 16 balls. Drop each fish ball on a solid surface 15 or 20 times to remove air pockets.

Cut each Bean Cake straight through from corner to corner by making an X cut, which will render 4 triangular pieces from each cake. Starting from the apex of each triangle, cut a slit ¾ of the way down to form a pocket. Do not cut completely through. Stuff each triangle with a fish cake ball, smoothing it to shape of Bean Cake.

Drop triangles into a deep fat fryer with oil preheated to 350 degrees. Deep fry 3 to 5 minutes. Serves 4 or 5

## DEEP FRIED SQUID
*(Jow Yow Yee)*

Have prepared:
> 2 **pounds fresh squid. Discard tentacles, wash, clean and slice each squid into quarters**

In a mixing bowl, mix:
> 1 **cup flour**
> ½ **cup cornstarch**
> 1 **teaspoon baking powder**
> 1 **teaspoon salt**
> ⅓ **teaspoon monosodium glutamate**

Add while mixing:
> ⅔ **cup cold water**
> 1 **beaten egg**
> ¼ **cup vegetable oil**

Whip batter with egg beater until smooth and free from lumps. Dip sliced squid in batter.

In a deep fat fryer, place:    4 **cups vegetable oil**

When oil has reached 350 degrees, drop coated squid in, piece by piece, and deep-fry until golden brown. Do not overcook. Serves 4

# $\mathcal{P}$oultry

## IDYLL OF THE PEKING DUCK

---

*"The fragrance of antiquity lasts forever."* — Chinese proverb.

Beyond the hills of ten thousand yesterdays, along with the reigns of emperors and empresses from the Hsai dynasty to Hsuan T'ung and their magnificent couts in the ancient, historic city of Peking, begins the semi-legendary story of the origin of the Peking Duck.

This is one dish which is agreed upon by Chinese gourmets of all provinces — north of the Yangtze and south of the clouds — to be one of the greatest epicurean offerings ever perfected.

Though its beginning is lost in antiquity, the fame of *Kwa Law Opp* (literally meaning "hang in the oven duck" in Chinese) is well-founded and its acceptance has spread throughout the globe to wherever *haute cuisine Chinoise* is discussed, appreciated and relished. This delight of the emperors, this *pièce de résistance* of Chinese banquets, is such a symbol not only of taste enjoyment but also of culinary skill that in China, centuries ago, wealthy gourmets even went so far as to challenge each other's chefs to produce the best Peking Duck!

Little wonder then, that this most aristocratic duck still heads the poultry parade to this very day and shall forevermore, with crown unchallenged, because of the method of rearing the bird (which puts it in the luxury class) and because of the painstaking preliminary preparations. This is not to say that the true Chinese gourmet will appreciate any less a simple whole boiled chicken, Chinese style, which, patently, to the uninitiated doesn't seem to be much. (We have a recipe for it, with comments on its classic aspects). Nor will he scorn a crisp, fried young squab, which we find exquisitely tender and different — but expensive, we must warn you — as an hors d'oeuvre. Normally, it is a course of a Chinese banquet menu. Try it when you feel in the mood to be the ultra elegant hostess.

Except for the *ad astra* status of the Peking Duck, you can see that the Chinese play no favorites in the entire range of poultry and fowl. Chicken, duck, or squab; the Chinese boast hundreds of cooking interpretations for them. Indeed, the Chinese favor duck and squab more often than the American housewife does. In the soup chapter, you already have been introduced to the unusual marriage of pigeon to a fuzzy squash, and the role of a large hen as the new mother's best friend.

Beyond the Temple of Heaven in ancient Peking, in the distant hills flows a spring with water limpid and pure as precious jade. This vicinity is named "Jade Spring Hill." In the nearby waters fed by this spring lives a beautiful snow-white bird whose beak and feet are accented in deep orange. This bird is the Peking Duck.

Since the very first moment centuries ago when the nameless and unsung genius of the kitchen evolved his method of preparing the *Kwa Law Opp,* or Peking Duck, countless hundreds of thousands of these birds have ascended to the epicurean heavens. Each and every one of them had been trained, nevertheless, to the same ritualistic methods which foretell and guide the destiny of the Peking Duck. The multiple factors involved — time, skill, patience, knowledge and the irreplaceable intangibility of experience — all begin to come into play the moment a duck eggshell cracks and a fuzzy, wobbly duckling starts on its path to epicurean glory.

When the ducks reach a pound in weight, they are then selected by experts. Many are rejected for any number of reasons such as lackluster eyes, a lack of hauteur in neck poise, or even for crooked toes. The duck awarded the accolade of acceptance instantly receives pampered care. She is not allowed to feed herself anymore — for she is now force-fed. The duck is confined in a small pen where gross exertion — which is likely to coarsen the flesh texture — is impossible. (In San Francisco, White Imperial Peking Ducks have been supplied by the Otto Reichardt Duck Farm since 1901. Otto Reichardt Jr., whose father first bred and raised Imperial Pekings for Chinatown, developed his own feed formulae and nutritional program so that Peking ducklings are 5 pounds dressed in 46 days!) Distinguishing characteristics are: Head — large, broad and round; Bill — bright orange, short, round and broad; Eyes — dark, lead blue; Cheeks — bulky; Neck — long and thick; Breast — broad and full; Back and wings — the wings short and carried close to the sides and the well-spread tail carried high, the drakes having two or three curled feathers on top.

When the Peking Duck is sacrificed, it is carefully wet picked and dressed by a poultry expert and delivered immediately to the chef. At this point the genius of the chef carries on the process which makes Peking Duck the royalty of poultry. First he examines the bird to certify it is indeed a genuine descendant of the White Imperial Peking lineage. Next he marinates the cavity of the duck with his secret pungent spice mixture. Then comes the anointment, compounded partly of professional pride and partly of boiling water and diluted wheat syrup *(Muk Nga Tong)* to accomplish the base for the resultant crackling skin. The complicated skin and "beauty treatment" involving the temperament of the "south" wind through a 24-hour curing process is scientifically achieved here with room temperature control and electric fans.

The duck is then deemed eligible for the barbecue oven. It is barbecued until a sizzling brown patina, glistening with golden overtones, appears on the skin. When ready, it is removed from the oven and displayed on a silver dish. In all her majestic aplomb, the Peking Duck is beautiful to behold and even more beautiful to the taste.

First the crisp, still sizzling golden brown glazed skin is artfully separated from the bird, sliced thinly in small pieces, then replaced and arranged in its original form. This is the ambrosial offering. This is the climax which Chinese gourmets have awaited with patience. Somehow and somewhere in the metamorphosis and magic of the oven, the golden layers — so carefully nurtured — suddenly exude a heavenly blend of tastes, flavors, and textures of crispness which — of all the dishes under the Temple of Heaven — only the Peking Duck seems to embody for mere mortal man.

The true Chinese epicure, ever-mindful of his polished taste, probably would partake and relish first the thin sliced skin. Accompanied with a mere dab of a piquant bean sauce, a wisp of sliced young scallion shoots, then rolled between layers of a steamed nine-layered bun, or tortilla-like "cakes," these provide a perfect foil to the exciting Peking Duck.

With the very first morsel, one starts ascending the steps to gastronomical heaven!

Now back to the somewhat more prosaic levels of poultry, just one paragraph to inform you that there *is* a great difference between *Kwa Law Opp,* the Peking Duck, and the regular roast duck, hanging in a symmetrical row which you see in the windows of Chinatown grocery stores and poultry shops. The unpampered, literally unpedigreed roast duck (actually of a different species and requiring different preparation) has, nevertheless, merits of its own. It is eaten cold at picnics and hot at the family dinner table. Dressed up with tropical fruits such as lychee and pineapple, with a colorful sweet-and-sour sauce, it is an easily prepared party dish.

For recipes which call for a whole chicken, such as in the classical *Bok Chit Gai* (Whole Simmered Chicken) or Soy Sauce Chicken, freshly killed fowl must be used to bring out the natural flavors. Paradoxically, the Chinese also dry or salt fowl, inventing such delicacies as cured smoked duck which has a deep flavor not unlike fine Smithfield ham, and a salted fresh chicken which in a rice casserole dish is supposed to perk up the appetites of convalescents.

Chicken livers and gizzards occupy very little position in American culinary arts. But with the Chinese, they are considered delicacies, and are used as complementary ingredients and not discarded at all. They are prepared and cooked in all of the methods described. Some Chinese like giblets even better than the chicken filet, especially in toss-cooking dishes where the gizzards have the crunchy hard-yet-cooked textural quality. A Chinese spice-marinated chicken liver, deep fried in batter, is a great appetizer.

In ancient China, the cock of the walk really is a proud bird. He symbolizes the *Yang* philosophical attitude, the representation of all the warmth and optimism of universal life. So you can depend on the Chinese to invent a dish which blends philosophy and food, or the perfect union of spirit and the flesh. Served at banquets often, and especially at bridal parties is a culinary concoction, very colorful and appropriate, named *Yin Yang Gai* or "love birds looking for peach blossoms." Two colors — one the cardinal of the brilliant crest of the rooster or male, the other, the chaste white feathers of the pullet or female — are represented in this gastronomical display by the deep rich coloring of ham and slices of white chicken arranged alternately, symbolizing inseparability in a dish revering marital bliss, and surrounded by a verdant vegetable, promising the lushness of fertility.

No less poetic, the other feathered friends also have folk beliefs attributed to them. In China, the emblems of felicity are ducks. Ducks in pairs mean conjugal fidelity. The pigeon really is as gentle as its cooing. Parent pigeons macerate thoroughly the food before feeding it to their young. And the male pigeon is a wonderful husband! When weather conditions are inclement, he will direct his mate to fairer climes. He allows her to return only when the sun shines again.

The Chinese look upon the dove and pigeon as symbols of filial duty, impartiality, and faithfulness. And they prove it in the kitchen by a slow-steaming method of nesting a squab in six or eight precious herbs, whose resultant rare broth has been prescribed for centuries as a sterling rejuvenescence for new mothers.

## *ROAST CHICKEN, CANTONESE*
*(Siew Gai)*

Combine and mix together in a mixing bowl:

> **1 cup soy sauce**
> **1 tablespoon gin**
> **1 tablespoon honey**
> **1 teaspoon salt**
> **4 cloves of garlic crushed**
> **1 tablespoon fresh minced ginger root**
> **¼ cup green onions cut in ½-inch lengths**

Rub:
> **1 fryer (3½ pounds)**
> **Inside and out with mixture, then marinate for 45 minutes before roasting, in a 350° oven for 30-40 minutes on an elevated oven rack.**

Roast chicken should be cut in 2-inch segments for serving, as in Simmered Whole Chicken recipe. Serves 4

*The difference between this and ordinary roast chicken is the secret blend of the marinade!*

## *CHICKEN À LA KAN*
*(Goon Yin – Yin Yang Gai)*

Have prepared:
> **½ of a cooked chicken (Use Simmered Whole Chicken Recipe, page 147)**

Separate leg portion and filet the meat evenly. With a sharp cleaver, split chicken into 4 parts, and filet meat carefully from bones. Match filet of chicken on chopping block so it will retain the natural form of half a chicken. Slice filets into 2 x 1-inch pieces. Carefully scoop up sections and slide onto serving platter.

Also prepare:                    25 slices cooked Virginia ham, ⅛-inch thick
                                 and sliced into 2 x 1-inch pieces
                                 1 pound washed Chinese broccoli cut into
                                 2-inch lengths

Insert a piece of Virginia ham evenly between each piece of chicken so that alternate slices of ham and chicken are arranged on serving platter.

In a preheated *wok* or skillet, place:
                                 1 tablespoon vegetable oil
                                 ½ teaspoon salt

Turn to high heat until oil is very hot.

Add:                             Sliced Chinese broccoli
                                 1 teaspoon soy sauce
                                 Dash of sugar
                                 Dash of monosodium glutamate

Toss and mix for about 1 minute.

Add:                             ¼ cup chicken stock

Cover and cook for 2 minutes. Uncover.

Add gradually:                   1 tablespoon cornstarch. Make paste with 1
                                 tablespoon water.

Continue to toss cook at high heat until gravy thickens and is well blended with broccoli. Remove from skillet and place around chicken and ham slices on serving platter.

In a saucepot, place:           ½ cup chicken stock
Bring to a boil and add:        ¼ teaspoon salt
                                 ¼ teaspoon soy sauce
                                 ¼ teaspoon monosodium glutamate

Mix thoroughly and add gradually:
                                 ½ teaspoon cornstarch. Make paste with ½
                                 teaspoon water.

Stir constantly and when gravy thickens, pour entire mixture over chicken and ham, but not on the broccoli. Serve at once. Serves 4 or 5

This is a formal dish, usually served at wedding banquets, which is as beautiful to behold as it is delicious to the taste. Preserved Chinese Duck may be substituted for Virginia ham, which represents the *Yin* or male and chicken, *Yang* or female. Slices of each are placed alternately, representing inseparability in a dish revering marital bliss.

# CHICKEN SMOTHERED IN ROCK SALT
*(Yim Gai)*

Have ready:
**1 5-pound dressed roaster sized chicken (Must be fresh, wet picked)**

Hang chicken in cool place to drain and wipe dry with absorbent toweling.

Combine:
**½ teaspoon Chinese Rose Liqueur or any brand of gin**
**1 cup water**
**1 teaspoon minced ginger root**
**2 teaspoons Kantonese Salt (see condiments)**
**½ teaspoon chopped Chinese parsley, optional**
**1 green onion, flattened**
**¼ teaspoon monosodium glutamate**

Tie neck of chicken with string and fill cavity with the above marinade. Sew up tightly all openings of the bird so that no liquid will leak out.

In a huge pot, place:
**10 pounds rock salt**

At high heat, stir occasionally and mix rock salt until red hot. Thirty or more minutes will suffice. Make a deep impression in the center, place chicken in it, making sure there is at least 2 inches of salt "bedding" underneath. Cover pot tightly, cook over low heat 30 minutes.

Remove chicken from pot, cut the strings and drain the cavity marinade into a pot. Keep it hot over a low fire until ready to place in a gravy boat. Cut and serve as in Simmered Whole Chicken *(Bot Chit Gai)* recipe. Serves 4

*When we were children, it was an adventure to cook stolen potatoes smothered in coals, and we still find the same spirit of adventure in cooking a chicken, Chinese style, smothered in this manner. Though literally "baked" in salt, the chicken is moist and flavorful.*

## PINEAPPLE CHICKEN
*(Bo Law Gai Kow)*

Have prepared:

**2 cups uncooked chicken filets (1 x 1-inch pieces)**
**½ teaspoon salt**
**1 fresh egg**
**½ teaspoon soy sauce**

Mix all ingredients with chicken, then dust chicken lightly and evenly with cornstarch.

In a preheated *wok* or skillet, place:

**2 inches vegetable oil**

Bring oil to sizzling point at high heat.

Add chicken and deep fry until brown. Drain on absorbent toweling.

Drain oil from *wok*. In same *wok* or skillet, place:

**½ cup vinegar**
**½ cup sugar**
**⅓ cup pineapple juice**
**¼ cup catsup**
**4 drops hot sauce (Tabasco)**
**1 teaspoon Worcestershire sauce**

Cook at medium heat to boiling point, then thicken with cornstarch paste until medium thick.

Add:

**1 cup pineapple chunks**
**½ cup green pepper, sliced into 1 x 1-inch pieces**
**Browned chicken**

Toss and mix thoroughly until chicken is heated through. Serves 4

## *BUTTON MUSHROOM CHICKEN WITH BAMBOO SHOOTS*
*(Mo Goo Jook Gai Kow)*

Have prepared:

**Boned uncooked meat from a medium sized fryer chicken, sliced ¼-inch thick and cut into 1½ x 1½-inch squares**

**2 cups washed whole Chinese Snow Peas**

**1 tall can of small button mushrooms, drained. Save liquid.**

**1 cup canned bamboo shoots, sliced ¼-inch thick. Cut into about ¾-inch pieces.**

**½ cup sliced celery**

In a preheated *wok* or skillet, place:

**2 tablespoons vegetable oil**

Bring to high heat and add:

**½ teaspoon minced garlic**

**1 teaspoon salt**

Stir and mix, then add:

**Boned chicken**

Toss and mix for about 1 minute, then add all the above ingredients. Continue mixing.

Add:

**1 teaspoon soy sauce**

**¾ cup chicken stock**

**¼ teaspoon monosodium glutamate**

Mix all ingredients thoroughly, then cover and cook for 5 minutes. Remove cover.

Add:

**2 tablespoons cornstarch. Make paste with 2 tablespoons water**

Toss and mix at high heat until gravy thickens. Serve with hot steamed rice. Serves 5 or 6

*An extremely palatable dish that the Chinese love for its pleasant constrasting texture. Equally acceptable for both simple family meals or for company.*

## *ASPARAGUS CHICKEN*
*(Lee Soon Wot Gai)*

Have prepared:

**1 young hen, 3½ to 4 pounds, fresh dressed. With a sharp cleaver, make a slash from neck to tail, turn bird and make a slash from breast to tail. Do not cut through bone.**

Have prepared for flavoring:

12 star anise *(Bot Gok)* washed
1 teaspoon finely minced ginger root
1 teaspoon dried Mandarin orange peel
 *(Gaw Pay)* pre-soaked, minced finely
1 teaspoon minced garlic
1 bunch Chinese parsley, washed
1 teaspoon salt
½ teaspoon monosodium glutamate
½ teaspoon sugar

Mix all ingredients thoroughly in a bowl. Ladle mixture into cavity of bird and spread evenly over surfaces. Sew openings.

Place chicken in a deep thin pan and elevate in a steaming utensil. Cover and steam cook for 40 minutes. Remove chicken but save juices for gravy.

With a very sharp cleaver, make deep incisions 1½ inches apart the entire length of bird. Carefully filet strips of skin attached to meat from carcass. Match strips on cutting board as they are removed and cut into 1½ x 1½-inch squares. Hold.

In a large shallow bowl, place evenly:

Drained white asparagus tips from 16 oz.
can

Next, carefully scoop up sliced chicken squares with cleaver or spatula and turn them over so that skin sides are resting on asparagus. Place entire bowl, elevated, in a steaming utensil, cover and steam cook until very hot (about 20 minutes). Meanwhile make gravy.

In a saucepot, place:

Reserved chicken juices
½ cup mashed white asparagus tips (canned)
½ cup half & half cream
¼ teaspoon salt
¼ teaspoon monosodium glutamate

Bring to high heat, stir and mix until sauce comes to a boil.

Add gradually:

Paste made with 2 tablespoons cornstarch
and 2 tablespoons water

Reduce to medium high heat and continue stirring until gravy thickens. Keep hot.

Remove bowl containing chicken and asparagus from steamer. Place a large round serving platter over bowl and flip it over so that asparagus will be on top when bowl is removed. Pour the hot gravy over asparagus chicken and serve immediately with hot steamed rice. Serves 4 or 5

*This is a sumptuous semi-banquet dish everyone will favor. The combination of smooth textured chicken infused with the bouquet of Chinese spices and the harmonious blending of it with asparagus makes this entrée singularly Chinese in character.*

# ALMOND CHICKEN
*(Hung Ngon Gai Kow)*

In a preheated *wok* or skillet, place:

**3 tablespoons vegetable oil**
**½ teaspoon salt**

Bring oil to a sizzling point.
Add:

**1 cup uncooked chicken filets cut into 1 x**
**1-inch pieces**

At high heat, toss and turn chicken until almost done (about 5 minutes).
Reduce to medium heat and add:

**½ cup diced water chestnuts**
**½ cup diced bamboo shoots**
**½ cup diced celery**
**¼ cup diced button mushrooms**
**½ teaspoon monosodium glutamate**

Increase to high heat, toss and turn until all ingredients are blended (about 3 minutes).
Add:

**½ cup chicken stock**
**1 teaspoon soy sauce**

Cover and cook at medium high heat for 5 minutes. Uncover.
Add gradually:

**Paste made with 2 tablespoons cornstarch, 2 tablespoons water**

Continue to cook at medium high heat turning rapidly until liquids thicken and mixture is very hot (about 3 minutes). With spatula, scoop mixture into a large ladle or bowl and turn over in a mound on a compote. Garnish generously with whole French-fried almonds. Serve with hot steamed or fried rice. Serves 3

# CHICKEN WINGS WITH BLACK BEAN SAUCE
## (See Jup Gai Yik)

Have prepared:

> **2 pounds large chicken wings (fresh or frozen)**
> **Clean and wash thoroughly and chop each**
> **wing into 5 segments.**
> **¼ cup fermented black beans** *(Dow See)*.
> **Rinse, drain and crush.**
> **2 teaspoons crushed garlic**
> **½ cup green peppers cut into 1 x 1-inch pieces**
> **½ cup dried onion cut into 1 x 1-inch pieces**

In a preheated *wok* or skillet, place:

> **4 tablespoons vegetable oil**
> **1 teaspoon salt**

Bring to high heat. When oil is hot, add chicken wings and crushed black beans mixed with crushed garlic. Brown lightly on both sides.

Add:

> **1 cup chicken stock**
> **½ teaspoon monosodium glutamate**

Turn and mix all ingredients thoroughly. Cover and cook at high heat for 10 minutes. Uncover.

Add:

> **Sliced green peppers, onion**

Again cover and cook at medium heat for 10 minutes. Uncover.

Add:

> **1 teaspoon soy sauce**
> **Dash of pepper**
> **1 tablespoon cornstarch. Make paste with 1**
> **tablespoon water.**

Turn and mix at medium heat until sauce thickens, making sure chicken wings do not burn. Serve over or with hot steamed rice. Serves 4 or 5

*Here is a way to prepare chicken wings which will pleasantly surprise your family and guests alike, and yet is comparatively economical. Again, the use of Chinese black bean sauce works wonders and transforms a rather plebeian food into something to rave about. Another advantage in preparing this dish is that you can double the recipe and reserve half of it for use from the refrigerator for days afterwards, since it tastes even better when aged. It makes a great heat-and-serve entrée for busy people who have to prepare their meals a day in advance. This is one of our favorites to take along on a weekend boating and fishing trip. On one burner of the galley stove we heat the pre-cooked chicken wings, while the rice is being cooked on the other burner, and within half an hour a delicious substantial hot lunch is ready for all hands.*

## PINEAPPLE CHICKEN WINGS SWEET AND SOUR
*(Bo Law Teem Seen Gai Yik)*

Clean and dry:              **12 large chicken wings**

Dip in:                   **2 beaten eggs**

In a large heavy paper bag, place:

         **½ cup cornstarch**
         **¼ teaspoon salt**
         **Dash of pepper**

Drop egg-coated chicken wings into bag, shake until completely coated.

In a large deep skillet, place:    **2 inches vegetable oil heated to boiling point**

Deep fry chicken wings until golden brown. Drain on absorbent toweling. Pour off oil from skillet except 1 tablespoon. Keep skillet hot.

Mix well and pour into skillet:    **½ cup vinegar**
                              **¼ cup catsup**
                              **⅓ cup pineapple juice**
                              **½ cup sugar**
                              **1 teaspoon Worcestershire sauce**
                              **4 drops hot sauce**

Cook at high heat to boiling point, then thicken with cornstarch paste until medium thick.

Add:                         **1 cup pineapple chunks**
                            **Chicken wings**

Turn and mix thoroughly for 5 minutes at high heat until blended. Serves 4

*Chicken wings are to many Caucasians, "something to throw away." To the Chinese, "meat closest to the bone" is the sweetest and most delectable, so to those who turn their noses up at the mention of chicken wings, this recipe will come as a revelation in dining delight. Relish the sauce and eat like fried chicken – with your fingers, and pour the remaining sweet and sour sauce over steamed rice!*

## HONG KONG LEMON CHICKEN
*(Nom Moong Gai)*

Have prepared:            **1 young hen, 3½ to 4 pounds, fresh dressed**

Also have prepared for flavoring:

12 star anise, washed
½ teaspoon ground cinnamon
1 teaspoon finely minced ginger root
1 teaspoon dried Mandarin orange peel,
    pre-soaked and minced finely
1 teaspoon minced garlic
½ bunch Chinese parsley, washed
1 teaspoon salt
½ teaspoon monosodium glutamate
1 teaspoon sugar
1 lemon, sliced thinly

Mix flavoring ingredients thoroughly in a bowl. Place chicken in a deep thin pan and spread ingredients evenly over chicken. Lower pan into steaming utensil with trivet. Cover and steam cook for 15 minutes. Uncover. Roll chicken over, cover utensil, and steam cook another 15 to 20 minutes. Remove chicken. Reserve juices for gravy.

Rub steamed chicken with natural uncolored soy sauce *(Sin Cho)*. Dust bird lightly but evenly with cornstarch.

Return chicken to a clean pan and again steam cook for 10 minutes. Remove and cool.

In a deep-fry utensil, place:          Enough vegetable oil to cover chicken

Bring to a boil. Carefully lower chicken into the hot oil and deep fry until all sides are golden brown. Remove chicken and drain on absorbent toweling.

Cut bird into segments this way: First, separate wings and legs. With sharp cleaver, split chicken lengthwise down the spine into 4 quarters, then with fast decisive strokes, chop quarters into 1-inch wide pieces. Carefully scoop up the cut quartered pieces with cleaver and slide onto platter. Legs and wings can be cut in halves and scooped up in the same manner; then all can be arranged in a natural whole chicken shape on the serving platter.

For gravy, place in a saucepot:      Reserved chicken juices
                                     1 teaspoon lemon juice
                                     1 teaspoon finely grated lemon rind

Bring to a boil and gradually add:

                              2 teaspoons cornstarch, made into paste with
                              2 teaspoons water

Stir continuously until gravy thickens.

Pour the hot gravy over chicken, garnish platter with lemon wedges and serve at once, as an entrée. Serves 4 or 5

*Lemon Chicken is a great favorite in Hong Kong restaurants. There are several other ways of preparing Lemon Chicken, among them, the steamed variations. However, this deep fry method is our favorite and we think will be yours also. The flavoring ingredients are identical to those in Asparagus Chicken, with the exception that the lemon flavor predominates, as it should.*

## *CORIANDER CHICKEN SALAD*
*(So See Gai)*

Deep fry in vegetable oil:    **1 whole 4½- to 5-pound roasting chicken**

Place on clean absorbent towel, let drain and cool. Strip off all meat from carcass. Then with hands strip the meat into fine shreds.

Prepare:
- **1 bunch green onion tops, shredded finely lengthwise**
- **1 bunch washed Chinese parsley (coriander) stems removed**
- **1 tablespoon sesame seeds, lightly fried in pan (no oil)**
- **1 tablespoon mixed hot mustard**
- **½ head shredded lettuce**
- **½ teaspoon monosodium glutamate**
- **½ teaspoon salt and sugar**

First, mix shredded chicken with the hot mustard, followed with sesame seeds. Add monosodium glutamate, salt, sugar, coriander and green onions and toss in salad bowl until thoroughly mixed. Line platter with shredded lettuce, place the chicken salad over it. Garnish with more coriander before serving. Serves 4

*This is not a true salad in the American menu sense, since it is served as one of the continuing array of dishes at big dinners and banquets. For home parties, the coriander chicken salad can be one of the several main entrées.*

# PINEAPPLE CHICKEN SALAD**
## (Baw Law Gai See Sai Lud)

Soak in warm water for ½ hour:

> **2 oz. white agar agar strips, cut into 3-inch lengths**

Drain and squeeze out excess water. Set aside.

Pan fry into thin sheets:    **½ cup whole beaten eggs**

When done, shred cut into ⅛-inch wide pieces. Set aside.

Prepare:

> **1 cup fresh cucumber slices, cored and cut into 2-inch lengths, medium thin slices**
> **¾ cup shredded carrots**
> **1 cup crushed pineapple, drained**
> **½ cup chicken meat, cooked and shredded**

On a large serving platter, begin assembling the salad by lining the platter with the softened agar agar strips. For the next layer distribute the fried shredded egg, making sure to leave a margin so that the bottom layer shows. In the same fashion, in a smaller circle, arrange the cucumber slices over the egg layer. Then the chicken pieces, followed by the crushed pineapple, each layer smaller than the first, so that you end up with a cone shape. Last, sprinkle over evenly with the shredded carrots. Keep refrigerated until ready to serve.

Salad Dressing:

Lightly toast in skillet or *wok:*

> **4 tablespoons sesame seeds**

Blend together in medium mixing bowl until smooth:

> **1 cup soy sauce**
> **1 cup vinegar**
> **½ cup granulated sugar**
> **1 cup sesame oil**
> **2 tablespoons dry mustard, mixed with water**
> **4 tablespoons water**
> **3 tablespoons smooth peanut butter**

To serve, sprinkle sesame seeds over the center of the salad and spoon dressing over individual servings. Serves 4

Variation: As a substitute to agar agar strips, shredded deep-fried wonton noodle can be used as the salad base (¼ pound to yield 4 servings of the same salad).

*\*\*This recipe won Executive Chef Sun Pui Wong first prize in the salad competition category in the 1978 Pineapple Growers' Association Cooking Contest in Hawaii.*

## WALNUT CHICKEN
*(Hop To Gai Kow)*

Have prepared:
> **1 cup boned uncooked chicken cut into ¾ x ¾-inch pieces**
> **¼ cup canned bamboo shoots sliced ⅛-inch thick and into ¾-inch squares**
> **1 cup blanched and deep fried walnut halves**

In a preheated *wok* or skillet, place:
> **2 tablespoons vegetable oil**
> **¼ teaspoon salt**

Bring oil to sizzling point and add:
> **Sliced chicken**

Toss and turn at high heat for 1 minute and add:
> **1 teaspoon soy sauce**
> **¼ teaspoon monosodium glutamate**
> **Sliced bamboo shoots**

Toss cook at high heat for 1 minute and add:
> **¾ cup chicken stock**

Cover and cook at high heat for 2 to 3 minutes. Uncover.

Add:     **Walnut halves**

Turn and mix thoroughly with other ingredients.

Add gradually:     **2 tablespoons cornstarch. Make paste with 2 tablespoons water.**

Turn all ingredients until sauce thickens, about 2 minutes. Serve with steamed or fried rice. Serves 3 or 4


## CASHEW CHICKEN
*(Yew Dow Gai Kow)*

Use same recipe as above, but substitute deep fried cashews for walnut halves.

# SIMMERED WHOLE CHICKEN
## (Bok Chit Gai)

Into a large heavy pot with tight-fitting lid, place

**Enough hot water to cover chicken**

Bring to a boil and add:        **1½ teaspoons salt**

Decrease to medium heat and add:

**1 whole dressed 4- or 5-pound pullet**

Cover pot with lid and simmer chicken for 30 to 35 minutes. Drain chicken and cool with cold running water. Cut bird in segments this way: First, separate wings and legs. With sharp cleaver, split chicken lengthwise down the spine, into 4 quarters, then with fast decisive strokes, chop quarters into 1-inch-wide pieces. Carefully scoop up cut quartered sections, slide onto platter. Legs and wings can be cut in halves and scooped up in the same manner, then arranged in a natural whole chicken shape on the serving platter.

Cut into vertical slivers, first flattening with side of cleaver:

**2 bunches large green onions (using only the heads)**

Prepare and mix thoroughly:     **2 tablespoons salt**

**3 tablespoons boiled and cooled vegetable oil**

Place salt and oil sauce on half of the compote dish and green onions on the other. Dip each piece of chicken in sauce and eat with green onions. Serves 4

With some experimentation, you will eventually hit the texture of perfection. But since the timing may vary, the chicken may be overcooked. Yet, you may succeed the very first try. And if not, the recipe is worth chancing again, because this dish represents an essence of purity and naturalness of flavor retained through the simple cooking method of just simmering. To the Chinese gourmet, undercooking in this case is more desirable than overcooking, since they believe chicken should be *wot* or smooth, instead of *cho* or coarse. You may also wonder about the "why" of cooling with running water, as noted in the recipe. This process keeps the skin from becoming soggy, to retain its *al dente* quality, similar to what Italian epicures say about the precise bite texture of their *pasta*. This is another example of the small, but important, attention which the Chinese pay to the texture in foods. When accompanied with the oil and salt sauce with green onions, this is indeed a classical Chinese dish, royal in its very simplicity.

# STEAMED CHICKEN WITH GRASS MUSHROOMS
## (Cho Goo Jing Gai)

Have prepared:

**1 dressed fryer-size chicken, cut into 1½-inch segments**

**Cleaned giblets, cut into ½-inch pieces**

Place chicken and giblets evenly on a large platter. Drain off all excess fluid.

Also have prepared:

**4 Chinese dried dates** *(Hoong Jo)*, **(previously soaked for 15 minutes in water). Drain dates, remove pits. Slice into thin strips.**

**10 dried Chinese grass mushrooms** *(Cho Goo)*, **previously soaked in water for 15 minutes, then sliced very thin**

**½ cup bamboo shoots** *(Jook Soon)*, **sliced very thin**

**1 piece dried Mandarin orange peel** *(Gaw Pay)* **about the size of a 25¢ piece, previously softened in warm water and sliced very thin.**

**5 slices ginger root sliced paper thin and shredded into strips**

Into a large mixing bowl, place all the above ingredients and add:

**1½ teaspoons salt**

**½ teaspoon sugar**

**2 teaspoons soy sauce**

**1 teaspoon monosodium glutamate**

**1 tablespoon cornstarch**

Mix all ingredients thoroughly until completely blended. Spread evenly over chicken in the platter.

In a *wok* or deep pot, place 3 inches of hot water and trivet. Place platter of chicken on trivet. Cover and increase to high heat until steam begins to generate. Steam cook chicken 30 to 40 minutes. Serve with hot steamed rice. Serves 4

*This is a long-time favorite of the Chinese housewife, because it is relatively simple to prepare and is so satisfying as* Soong *(accompaniment) with hot steamed rice. The contrasting flavors of the fragrant grass mushrooms and many other ingredients are steamed right through the chicken, resulting in a heavenly combination. Poured over steamed rice with some of the juices, it is most appetizing.*

## STEAMED CHICKEN WITH LILY FLOWERS
### (Gum Jum Jing Gai)

Use same recipe as Steamed Chicken with Grass Mushrooms *(Cho Goo Jing Gai)*, except with the substitution of 2 ounces of Lily Flowers for grass mushrooms.


## CHICKEN WITH SNOW PEAS, BAMBOO SHOOTS
### (Lon Dow Jook Soon Gai Kow)

Have prepared:
**1 cup uncooked, boneless breast of chicken, cut in 1 x 1-inch pieces**
**½ pound Chinese Snow Peas, strings removed, washed and drained**
**½ cup canned bamboo shoots, sliced ¼-inch thick and in 1 x 1-inch squares**
**½ cup sliced celery**

In a preheated *wok* or skillet, place:
**2 tablespoons vegetable oil**

Bring oil to sizzling point and add:
**Sliced chicken**

Toss and turn rapidly at high heat 1 minute.

Add:
**Snow Peas**
**Sliced bamboo shoots, celery**
**½ teaspoon salt**
**1 teaspoon soy sauce**
**½ teaspoon monosodium glutamate**

Toss cook 1 minute and add: **1 cup chicken stock**

Cover and cook at high heat for 2 to 3 minutes. Uncover.

Add gradually: **2 tablespoons cornstarch. Make paste with 2 tablespoons water**

Turn all ingredients until sauce thickens. Toss cook for another minute. Serve with steamed or fried rice. Serves 3 or 4

# GLUTINOUS RICE CHICKEN
*(Naw Mai Gai)*

---

Have prepared:

**1 young hen, 3½ to 4 pounds, fresh dressed. Bone completely, making sure the chicken is kept in its natural form and skin is intact.***

*The practical solution for a home cook is to leave the task of deboning to the poultry shop. Most Chinatown poultrymen are familiar with requests of this nature and are experts in this field.

Have prepared for stuffing:

**3 cups glutinous rice *(Naw Mai)* washed like ordinary rice. Pour off final wash water and cover with clear water. Soak overnight and drain.**

Also prepare:

**½ cup lotus seeds *(Leen Gee)* washed and drained**

**¼ cup diced raw or cooked ham (Virginia type if available)**

**¼ cup diced Chinese sausage *(Lop Cheong)***

**¼ cup presoaked Chinese dried mushrooms, diced**

**1 teaspoon salt**

**1 teaspoon monosodium glutamate**

Combine soaked rice with other ingredients in mixing bowl. When thoroughly blended, stuff into cavity of the boned chicken and sew all openings. Place stuffed chicken in deep pan, pour enough boiling chicken stock over the chicken to cover it. Elevate in a steaming utensil. Cover and steam cook for 3 hours. Carefully remove chicken and place in a flat pan. With a spatula or hotcake turner, gently press stuffed bird into a flat shape but be careful not to let it burst. Dust lightly with cornstarch on both sides.

Transfer chicken back to deep pan and into steaming utensil. Steam cook another 15 minutes and remove bird to cool.

Meanwhile, bring vegetable oil in deep-fry utensil to a boil. Lower chicken into hot oil and deep fry until brown on all sides. (About 20 minutes.) Drain on absorbent toweling. Transfer chicken to serving platter. Without disturbing form of bird, slice chicken straight through the stuffing, into 2½-inch squares. Surround chicken with lemon wedges for garnish. Serves 4 or 5

*This is a super banquet-style chicken. Each bite is an epicure's gem of boneless meat with a pleasingly textural contrast of tacky rice stuffing combined with bits of ham, mushrooms and Chinese sausage, surrounded by crispy skin.*

# CHICKEN IN PARCHMENT
## (Gee Bow Gai)

Combine in a large mixing bowl:

½ teaspoon vegetable oil
½ tablespoon soy sauce
1 teaspoon Chinese parsley, minced
1 teaspoon green onions, minced
½ teaspoon red seasoning sauce *(Hoy Sein Jeong)*
1 pinch salt
1 pinch monosodium glutamate

Add: 1 cup uncooked chicken filets cut into 1-inch square thin slices

Mix thoroughly and marinate for 1 hour.

Wrap each piece of chicken in 2½-inch square pieces of parchment paper securely with all loose corners tucked in.

Fry: Parchment chicken in deep, hot vegetable oil as for French fries, for 5 minutes

Drain on absorbent paper toweling and serve immediately. Serves 3

*Somehow, every nationality has a food specialty wrapped and cooked in paper to retain the natural juices. This is the accepted Chinese treatment of chicken in parchment. Its tenderness, flavor and succulence preserved in the parchment envelope is a gastronomical delight.*

## *SESAME CHICKEN*
*(Gee Mah Gai)*

Bone and filet in about ¼-inch thick slices:

**1 5-pound uncooked roasting chicken**

Mix together:

**1 beaten egg**
**4 drops gin**
**Dash of salt and pepper**

Marinate chicken slices in above mixture for about 10 minutes, then coat lightly with: **Water chestnut flour or cornstarch**

In a large skillet, place: **1 inch vegetable oil heated to boiling point**

Deep fry chicken for 5 minutes. Drain on absorbent paper toweling. Place on warm platter.

Make a white sauce by combining:

**2 cups water**
**½ cup half & half cream**
**½ cup diced button mushrooms**
**2 tablespoons cornstarch**
**½ teaspoon monosodium glutamate**
**1 teaspoon salt**

Cook and stir constantly at low heat until mixture begins to thicken and is smooth and free from lumps.

Pour white sauce over: **Deep fried chicken filets**

Sprinkle with: **1 tablespoon toasted sesame seeds**

Serves 6-8

# CURRIED CHICKEN CANTONESE
## (Gah Lay Gai)

In a preheated *wok* or skillet, place:

> 3 tablespoons vegetable oil
> ½ teaspoon salt

Bring oil to sizzling point.
Add:                                    1 four-pound fryer, cut into 2-inch segments
Brown chicken, but do not overcook. Transfer to large pot.
Add:

> ½ cup sliced dried onions
> 1 clove crushed garlic
> 2 stalks diced celery
> 1 teaspoon monosodium glutamate
> ½ cup bell pepper cut into 1-inch squares
> 3 tablespoons curry powder
> 2 cups chicken stock
> 2 teaspoons soy sauce

Bring to high heat, stir and mix, then cover. Cook at medium high heat for 30 minutes or until chicken is tender. If a thicker sauce is desired, add 2 tablespoons cornstarch mixed with 2 tablespoons water. Add paste gradually. Stir and mix until gravy thickens.

Serve chicken curry with or over hot steamed rice. Serves 4 or 5

*The pungent condiment known as curry, both in powder and paste forms, is said to have trickled into Chinese cuisine centuries ago through the borders of Yunnan province from its neighbor India. Chinese use curry in many dishes, including seafoods and meats.*

# SOY SAUCE CHICKEN
*(See Yow Gai)*

If possible, purchase from Chinese apothecary:

> **2 ounces Licorice Root** *(Gum Cho)*
> **20 Star Anise** *(Bot Gok)*
> **1 ounce Anise Seed** *(Sew Wai)*
> **1 ounce Kaemferia Galanga** *(Sahn Lai)*

In a small pot place:  **10 cups water**
> **Above herbs**

Boil violently for half an hour, strain through cheesecloth, save all of liquid. Tie cheesecloth like a bag around herbs with a long string. If herbs are unavailable use Star Anise *(Bot Gok)* only, which is always available at Chinese grocery stores.

Combine and mix thoroughly in a large soup pot:

> **Liquid from herbs or Star Anise**
> **10 cups soy sauce**
> **8 cups sugar**
> **1 1-inch-square piece dried Mandarin orange peel, washed**
> **1 stick cinnamon**
> **1 1-inch piece peeled ginger root**
> **2 teaspoons monosodium glutamate**

Suspend bag of herbs or Star Anise below liquid level and secure string so bag will simply hang in that position. Cover pot and bring to a rolling boil.

Add:  **1 whole 4- or 5-pound dressed pullet and giblets**

Simmer the chicken at medium heat for 30 minutes for medium, 40 minutes for well done. Turn frequently to equalize cooking the sauce through the bird. Remove chicken from pot, drain and cool.

Cut into segments the same way as in Boiled Whole Chicken recipe and serve with plain slivered green onions. Serves 4

*As in the boiled chicken, at first glance the cooking method in this recipe appears deceptively simple. But for smoothness in texture, it requires much patience. Pointers for the thrifty housewife: One, you can use the same sauce to cook several chickens. The sauce will keep in the refrigerator for several days. Or, for occasions when you require many servings – such as for a buffet – you can cook as many as 4 chickens again in the same prepared sauce. Two, do what the Chinese children love, mix the chicken-flavored sauce with steamed white rice.*

# RED BEAN CURD CHICKEN
## (Nom Yee Gai)

In a preheated *wok* or skillet, place:

> 3 tablespoons vegetable oil
> ½ teaspoon salt

Bring oil to sizzling point, add:    1 four-pound fryer, cut into 2-inch segments
Brown chicken, but do not overcook.
In a mixing bowl, place:

> 2 tablespoons spiced red bean curd *(Nom Yee)*
> 1 teaspoon sugar
> 3 tablespoons soy sauce
> ½ teaspoon five fragrant spice *(Ng Lew Fun)*
> 2½ cups water
> 1 teaspoon monosodium glutamate
> ¼ teaspoon salt

Blend ingredients into a smooth mixture and pour into large pot with chicken.

Add:    2 large potatoes cut into 1-inch cubes

Bring to high heat until mixture reaches boiling point, stirring constantly. Simmer at medium high heat for approximately 20 minutes or until potatoes are done. Serve with or over hot steamed rice. Serves 4 or 5

*Here is an example of a poultry dish in which the predominant flavor of the condiment – Nom Yee – provides the setting to blend chicken and potatoes into a culinary achievement.*

## DEEP FRIED SQUAB
*(Sang Jow Bok Opp)*

In a large mixing bowl, place:  **2 young dressed, uncooked squabs, cut into**
**1½ x 1½-inch pieces**

Add:  **¼ teaspoon monosodium glutamate**
**2 teaspoons soy sauce**
**1 teaspoon salt**
**¼ teaspoon ground pepper**
**½ teaspoon minced garlic**
**1 beaten egg**
**½ cup water chestnut flour or cornstarch**
**1 teaspoon minced onion**

Stir and mix squab with mixture thoroughly.

In a deep-fry utensil, place:  **1 quart vegetable oil**

Bring oil to a violent boil and add:

**Coated squab segments**

Deep fry at high heat (350°) for 4 minutes. Remove squab with strainer, drain on absorbent toweling, then transfer to serving platter. Serves 4

*The Chinese are masters in the preparation of squab, especially in crisp, deep-fried dishes such as this. The secret of the light crispness is in the water chestnut flour batter.*

# CHUNG KWONG SQUAB
## (Chung Kwong Bok Opp)

In a large mixing bowl place:    **2 young, dressed uncooked squabs**
Mince very fine:    **1 1-inch piece ginger root**
    **1 teaspoon cinnamon**
    **1 1-inch piece Mandarin orange peel**
      **(previously washed and softened in**
      **water)**
    **1 teaspoon monosodium glutamate**
    **1½ teaspoons salt**
    **2 cloves star anise**
    **1 bud fresh garlic**

Spread minced ingredients over squabs with one whole green onion over each. Steam cook for ¾ hour. Remove squabs, gently rinse off ingredients. Dry squabs with clean towel and brush squabs lightly with soy sauce. Roll the whole squabs until they are coated with cornstarch. Place squabs in pan and steam cook 10 minutes. Remove and cool, then place squabs in refrigerator overnight.

In a deep-fry utensil, place:    **Enough vegetable oil to cover squabs**
    **(about 6 inches)**

Bring oil to a violent boil at high heat.

Add:    **Cured whole squabs**

Deep fry at high heat 5 minutes or until golden brown.

Cut and serve as in Soy Squab recipe, with the exception that lemon quarters are used in place of Kantonese salt for garnishing flavor. Serves 4

*One of the aristocrats of squab dishes. The subtlety of harmonious flavor steamed into the tender meat, at the same time giving it a smooth texture, is reason enough for a true epicure's appreciation.*

# SOY SQUAB RED FRIED
*(Hoong Siew Bok Opp)*

Combine and mix thoroughly in a large soup pot:

**8 cups cold water**
**2 quarts soy sauce**
**9 cups sugar or 3 pounds Chinese rock sugar**
  ***(Bing Tong)***
**3 ounces star anise**
**1 1 x 1-inch piece dried Mandarin orange peel, washed**
**2 sticks cinnamon**
**1 1-inch piece peeled ginger root**
**2 teaspoons monosodium glutamate**

Cover pot and bring to a boil.
Add: **3 large dressed squabs**

Simmer squab at medium heat for 30 minutes, turn frequently to equalize cooking the sauce through the birds. Remove squabs from pot, drain and cool.

In a deep-fry utensil, place: **Enough vegetable oil to cover squabs (about 6 inches)**

Bring oil to violent boil at high heat.
Add: **Soy-cooked squabs**

Deep fry for 5 minutes or until dark brown. Remove squabs, drain on absorbent toweling. With a sharp Chinese cleaver, remove legs and wings. Cut squabs straight down the spine into halves, then into quarters or eighths as desired.

Carefully scoop up cut segments with cleaver and slide onto platter. Legs and wings can be scooped up in same manner then arranged in a natural whole squab shape on the serving platter. Serve with Kantonese salt. Serves 4 or 5

*Probably one of the best ways to really savor the difference between the Chinese style of flavoring fowl and other limited methods is to try this recipe. We cannot emphasize strongly enough the necessity of using only the best grade of naturally fermented Chinese soy sauce. It is the prerequisite for a genuine soy sauce flavor and the secret of a good marinade, when combined with the ingredients in this recipe.*

# DICED SQUAB TUMBLE IN LETTUCE CUPS
## (Bok Opp Soong)

Completely bone:        **2 large dressed, uncooked squabs**
With a Chinese chopping cleaver, mince squab meat very fine.
Finely dice:        **1 pound peeled water chestnuts (canned type is suitable if fresh is not available)**

        **6 dried Chinese black mushrooms (previously softened in water)**

        **½ cup celery**

        **2 tablespoons lean raw pork**

        **2 teaspoons smoked Chinese duck liver** *(Opp Geok Bow)*. **(Optional)**

        **½ cup bamboo shoots**

In a preheated skillet, place:        **4 tablespoons vegetable oil**

        **1 pinch salt**

Add:        **Meat of squab**

        **Minced pork**

At high heat, stir and mix for 2 minutes.
Add:        **Diced ingredients**
Stir and mix at medium heat for 2 minutes.
Add:        **1 cup chicken stock**

        **1 teaspoon soy sauce**

        **Dash of ground pepper**

        **½ teaspoon monosodium glutamate**

Stir and mix, then cover skillet and cook at medium heat for 10 minutes. Remove cover.
Add:        **1 tablespoon cornstarch. Make paste with 1 tablespoon water**

Cook at medium heat, tossing and mixing constantly until very hot. Transfer to serving compote or platter.
Have prepared:        **Crisped leaves of 1 head lettuce on platter**
Method of serving: Each guest takes a lettuce leaf, and places two tablespoons of the *Soong* in it and eats it with his hands. Serves 4

# SQUAB STUFFED WITH BIRD'S NEST
*(Yeen Wo Bok Opp)*

Have prepared:

**2 whole squabs, dressed and boned, as in Glutinous Rice Chicken**
**1 ounce genuine bird's nest** *(Yeen Wo)*
**½ teaspoon baking soda**

Cover bird's nest with hot water and boil for 10 minutes. Transfer to colander and rinse with running cold water. Remove foreign materials, if any, from bird's nest. Drain.

Stuff squab with the bird's nest and sew up all openings. In a bowl about 8 inches in diameter, place:

**Stuffed squab**
**4 cups water**
**½ teaspoon salt**
**½ teaspoon monosodium glutamate**

In a pot large enough to accommodate the bowl, place:

**2 to 3 inches boiling water**
**Trivet to elevate bowl**

Bring to high heat and steam the stuffed squab in the bowl for 3 hours, replacing boiling water in bottom of pot as it steams off. Lift bowl from steaming pot and place on serving table. The liquid in which the squab was steamed has now become a rich broth, which should be served with the squab and bird's nest stuffing and eaten as a soup.

## *PEKING DUCK*
### *(Kwa Law Opp)*

Prepare:

**1 4-5 pound duckling, eviscerate and remove excess fatty tissue, clean entire carcass.**

In a small mixing bowl, mix:

**1 small amount chopped fresh ginger root**
**2 cloves chopped garlic**
**1 tablespoon spiced salt (q.v.)**
**1 small amount Chinese parsley (coriander)**
**Dried Mandarin orange peel**

Rub the cavity of the duck with this mixture. Seal opening of duck with thread as with a turkey.

In a saucepan, mix:

**2 quarts lukewarm water**
**2 tablespoons honey**
**½ cup white vinegar**

Bring water and honey to quick boil, then add the vinegar. Keep warm.

Blend together:

**¾ cup cornstarch**
**1 cup cold water**

Bring honey water to boil, then slowly add cornstarch mixture, stirring constantly.

While the entire mixture is at slow boil, ladle mixture over hanging duck repeatedly.

Hang duck in cool place, preferably in a windy area, for two days.

To barbecue, the duck must be hung by the neck. Roast the duck for 15 minutes at 400°F, then for 30 to 40 minutes at 350°F. Remove feet and carve.

Serve with 1,000 layered buns or Chinese Pancakes, *Hoy Sien* Sauce and slivered Chinese green scallions.

*This gourmet specialty is prized for its delicately crispy skin and is a finger dish, widely imitated but rarely duplicated.*

# CHINESE PANCAKES
*(Bock Beang)*

These delicate pancakes are always cooked in pairs because, when rolled out, the pancakes are too thin and fragile to cook individually.

Have prepared:

 1½ cups all-purpose flour
 ¼ teaspoon salt
 ½ cup boiling water
 3 tablespoons cold water
 2 tablespoons all-purpose flour
 Shortening, cooking oil, or sesame oil

Stir together the 1½ cups flour and the salt. Pour boiling water slowly into flour, stirring constantly with a fork or chopsticks till well blended. Stir in cold water. When dough is cool enough to handle, knead in the 2 tablespoons flour for 8 to 10 minutes, or until smooth and elastic. Shape dough into a ball. Place the dough back in bowl; cover with damp towel. Let stand for 15 to 20 minutes.

Turn dough out onto a lightly floured surface. Form into a 12-inch-long roll. Cut roll into 1-inch pieces. Flatten each piece of dough with the palm of the hand. To make pancake, roll each piece of dough into a 6-inch circle. Brush the entire surface of top of each pancake lightly with shortening, cooking or sesame oil.

Stack two pancakes together, greased sides together. In a heavy ungreased skillet or griddle, cook the pancake stacks over medium heat 20 to 30 seconds on each side or till bubbles appear on surface of pancakes (a few golden spots will appear). Quickly remove from pan and gently separate the paired pancakes.

# LYCHEE PINEAPPLE ROAST DUCK
### (Leong Bon Faw Opp Peen)

Purchase from Chinatown poultry shop:

**1 Roast Duck, fileted, with juice in separate container**

To serve: Cut filets into 2 x ¾-inch pieces. The leg portions are also boned and cut to the same size. Carefully scoop up cut sections from chopping block with cleaver, and slide onto serving platter evenly. Place platter in warm oven for a few minutes until warm.

Have prepared:

**1 small can pineapple cubes (reserve juice)**
**1 medium sized bell pepper, cut into ½-inch pieces**
**1 can Lychees, drained**
**1 cup maraschino cherries**

In a preheated *wok* or skillet, place:

**3 tablespoons vegetable oil**

Bring oil to sizzling point and add all the above ingredients.

Also add:

**⅓ cup duck juice**
**¼ cup brown sugar**
**½ cup pineapple juice**

Turn and mix all ingredients. Cover and cook at medium high heat 5 minutes. Uncover.

Add gradually:

**2 teaspoons cornstarch. Make paste with 2 teaspoons water**

Increase to high heat, toss and turn for 2 to 3 minutes until sauce thickens and mixture is very hot. Pour over warmed roast duck filets and serve at once with steamed rice. Serves 4 or 5

*As we mentioned in the commentary under the Roast Duck recipe,* Faw Opp *is the forte of Chinatown poultry shopkeepers. One poultry-delicatessen enjoys such a great reputation, that Chinese visitors from Honolulu purchase his succulent* Faw Opp *by the dozen, to be flown back to the Islands with them on the same jetliner. Packed individually in special cartons, San Francisco's Roast Duck is the most welcome of all gifts to Islanders. For this recipe, request your Chinatown poultryman to filet the Roast Duck for you. Like magic, you will emerge from the kitchen with a quickly prepared culinary masterpiece, containing exotic fruits of the Orient. Recognized as a banquet dish,* Leong Bon Faw Opp *will impress the most distinguished company.*

# LOTUS STUFFED DUCK
*(Leen Gee Opp)*

Have prepared:

1 large fresh dressed duckling (do not use wild duck). Have Chinatown poultryman bone the duck, making sure the bird is kept in its natural form. Hang and drain.

For stuffing, prepare:

1 cup barley, softened in water. Drain.

1 cup lotus nut meats *(Leen Gee)*. Wash well.

1 cup Chinese dried mushrooms *(Heong Soon)*. Soften in water, drain and dice into ¼-inch squares.

1 cup Gingko nut meats *(Bok Gaw)*, if fresh unavailable, use canned.

½ teaspoon monosodium glutamate

¼ cup diced ham

Place ingredients for stuffing in large mixing bowl and mix thoroughly.

Add:

1½ teaspoons salt

½ teaspoon sugar

Continue to mix all ingredients until well blended. Place stuffing into cavity of the boned duck. Sew all openings. Rub entire bird lightly with soy sauce. In a large pot, place: 2 cups vegetable oil. Bring to boiling point.

Carefully lower into pot: Stuffed duckling

Brown all sides, turning frequently in the hot oil, then remove and drain bird on absorbent toweling. Place browned duck in a deep dish.

In a pot large enough to accommodate the large dish, place duckling and cover with:

½ bunch Chinese parsley

2 whole green onions

10 star anise

1 1-inch piece Mandarin orange peel, softened in water

Place on trivet to elevate the dish over 3 inches boiling water.

Bring to high heat, cover and steam the stuffed duckling for 3 hours, replacing boiling water in bottom of pot as it steams off. Remove duck, discard topping.

In a sauce pot, for gravy, place: 2 cups chicken stock

Bring to a boil and add:

¼ teaspoon salt

¼ teaspoon soy sauce

Dash of ground pepper

Mix ingredients constantly at high heat and gradually add:

2 teaspoons cornstarch. Make paste with 2 teaspoons water.

Stir vigorously and continuously until gravy thickens. Maintain at boiling point. Pour hot gravy over duckling, then garnish with Chinese parsley (coriander). Slice duck straight through into convenient portions and serve from the platter with stuffing.

*The browned rich skin of the duck to the Chinese gourmet is considered the delicacy and is relished more than the meaty part. As you notice in the recipe, great pains in the cooking process are taken to brown and steam the skin so that it will result in the desired texture and at the same time not be "broken" so that the duckling will appear appetizingly on the table as a whole bird.*

# *PRESSED MANDARIN DUCK*
## *(Wo Siew Opp)*

| In a large deep pan, place: | **1 medium-sized dressed duckling** |
|---|---|
| Make a marinade with: | **1 teaspoon salt** |
| | **½ cup soy sauce** |
| | **1 teaspoon sugar** |

First, rub the marinade all over the bird, then pour the remainder into the cavity, swishing it around until cavity is drenched. Drain. Place duck on a dish and place three whole green onions and 2 stalks of celery over it. Steam in a large utensil for 2½ hours. Remove and when cool enough to handle, carefully remove all the bones making sure that the original shape of the duck is disturbed as little as possible. Place the boned duck on a large platter and press down to ¾-inch thickness with hands. Sprinkle cornstarch generously over both sides until completely coated. Steam for ½ hour. Remove and cool. Cut steamed duck into four quarters. (While duck is steaming, prepare Sweet and Sour Sauce.)

In a deep-fry utensil bring to a boil:

**2 quarts vegetable oil**

Add: **Quartered duck**

Deep-fry until golden brown, remove with strainer and drain on absorbent toweling. With a sharp cleaver, slice duck into 1½ x 1½-inch pieces. Line the serving platter with sliced lettuce. Scoop up duck squares evenly with cleaver and slide them off over lettuce. Top with hot Sweet and Sour Sauce and garnish with finely chopped toasted almonds. Serve with hot steamed rice. Serves 4 or 5

## SWEET AND SOUR SAUCE

Mix well and pour into skillet:

½ **cup vinegar**
½ **cup sugar**
⅓ **cup pineapple juice**
¼ **cup catsup**
1 **teaspoon Worcestershire sauce**
4 **drops hot sauce**

Cook at high heat to boiling point, then thicken with cornstarch paste until medium thick.

*The title of this familiar duck dish is a misnomer, for want of a better description. Even the Chinese term for Pressed Mandarin Duck,* Wo Siew Opp *(Wo alludes to crispness,* Siew *means braised,* Opp *is duck, adding up to Crisp Braised Duck) does not completely describe it, but comes closer than the popular American term. It is sometimes called Peanut Duck, Almond Duck, etc.* Wo Siew Opp *really should be renamed Pressed Braised Duck.*

*The Chinese do not use a duck press. As you will notice in our recipe, the bird is steamed and boned, then pressed flat with the hands onto a platter and deep fried later, giving the skin a wonderfully crisp texture. A subtlety of flavors – as you can detect in the blend of many ingredients used in the recipe – marks this duck dish as a strong favorite at banquets. All children love the sweet and sour sauce and nut topping plus the fact that the duck is boneless.*

# *ROAST DUCK*
## *(Faw Opp)*

Purchase from Chinatown poultry shop:

**1 Roast duck, with juices in separate container**
**Plum Sauce** *(Seen Mooey Jeong)* **is**
**furnished with duck**

To serve:
First, separate wings and legs. With sharp cleaver, split duck lengthwise down the spine in 4 quarters, then with fast decisive strokes, chop quarters into 1 x 1½-inch pieces. Carefully scoop up quartered, cut sections with cleaver and slide onto platter. Legs and wings can be cut in halves and scooped up in the same manner, then arranged in a natural whole duck shape on the serving dish. Heat the duck juices and pour over roast duck. Place Plum Sauce in small condiment dishes. Dip each piece of roast duck in Plum Sauce and eat with steamed rice. Serves 4 or 5

*This is an answer to the oft-asked question "How do you serve the roast duck that we see hanging in the Chinatown poultry shop windows?" This above method is the simplest and fastest. In another recipe, page 163, we explain how to serve* Leong Bon Faw Opp, *a sauce containing whole lychees and pineapple.*

*Although roast duck is primarily a ready-to-eat delicatessen item, it requires a preparation that would stump an expert amateur chef. A bellows or bicycle pump to blow the duck up like a balloon is merely the beginning of a lengthy complicated pre-preparation. Unlike Peking Duck* (Kwa Law Opp) *which is prepared successfully only by master chefs in restaurants, Roast Duck is the forte of the Chinese poultry-delicatessen shopkeepers; so even restaurant chefs order* Faw Opp *from them, for convenience.*

# SAI WO DUCK
*(Sai Wo Opp)*

In a large deep-fry utensil, place:

**Enough vegetable oil to cover medium-sized duckling**

Bring oil to boiling point and add:

**1 whole dressed duckling, rubbed with soy sauce**

Deep fry until entire bird is well browned. Remove and drain on absorbent toweling.

Slash the duck starting from the breast down to the lower belly with a sharp cleaver. Do not cut through bone.

Place browned duck in a pan, then place evenly inside cavity:

**2 stalks celery**
**1 whole green onion**
**4 thin slices ginger root**
**5 pre-soaked Chinese black mushrooms**
**2 pre-soaked pieces of dried Mandarin orange peel (size of half-dollar)**
**5 thinly sliced pieces bamboo shoots**
**10 star anise**
**1 teaspoon salt**
**¼ teaspoon sugar**
**Dash of pepper**
**1 teaspoon monosodium glutamate**

Place duck on platter, elevate in a steamer, cover and steam cook for 2½ hours, making sure water is replenished as it steams off. Remove platter and let duck cool.

Discard all ingredients except bamboo shoots and mushrooms. Save all the juices for later use in gravy.

Carefully remove wings and legs. Starting from the slash, gently separate the flesh from carcass with hands, while keeping the skin intact. Be sure not to make any more holes in the skin and to keep the bird in its natural shape. (Carcass will make good soup.)

Spread duck, meat side up, evenly in deep platter. Debone legs and place with wings, spreading evenly mushrooms and bamboo shoots over duck meat. Replace in steaming utensil and steam cook again for 20 minutes. Remove.

Line a large serving platter with loose lettuce leaves.

Take the platter with the duck and turn it upside down so that the duck will rest on the nest of lettuce, skin up.

In a saucepot, place: **Juices from duck (about 2 cups)**

Turn to high heat until it boils.

Add:
1 tablespoon cornstarch
1 tablespoon soy sauce
¼ teaspoon salt

Stir continuously until gravy thickens. Pour evenly over the whole duck. Garnish with Chinese Parsley (Coriander) and serve immediately with hot steamed rice. Serves 4 to 5

*For all of you who have the instincts of a gourmet and relish the delicious aromatic browned skin of a tender duckling, laced with aromatic flavors,* Sai Wo Opp *will become one of your favorites. The presentation of this banquet dish is most impressive in appearance and your guests will exclaim over your culinary prowess at the very first taste.*

# CURRIED DUCK
## (Gah Lay Opp)

In a preheated pot, place:
2 tablespoons vegetable oil
1 teaspoon salt

Add:
1 medium sized duckling, cut into 2-inch segments

Brown duck slightly and pour off excess fat.

Add:
4 thin slices ginger root
Browned duck and giblets
3 tablespoons curry powder
1 teaspoon soy sauce
3 tablespoons catsup
1 teaspoon monosodium glutamate

Stir and mix thoroughly for 5 minutes.

Add:
3 cups hot water

Cover pot and cook at medium heat for ¾ hour, stirring occasionally.

Add:
1 cup sliced dried onion
1 cup green pepper, sliced into 1-inch squares

Continue cooking for another 10 minutes. Add cornstarch paste to thicken to desired consistency. Serve Curried Duck with or over hot steamed rice. Serves 5 or 6

*With what are listed here as easily obtainable ingredients, this Cantonese method transforms duck into an exotic and mouth-watering dish. The ginger root dissipates the oftentimes "gamy" flavor of duck and adds zip.*

## *TARO ROOT DUCK WITH NOM YEE SAUCE*
*(Nom Yee Woo Tow Opp)*

Have prepared:
> 1 whole 5 pound duckling, dressed. Rinse and dry with toweling. Rub cavity with soy sauce

In a deep pot or *wok,* place:  ½ cup vegetable oil

Bring oil to boiling point at high heat. Lower whole duck carefully into utensil and brown evenly on all sides. Remove bird, drain and cool.

In a mixing bowl, place:
> 1 square red bean cake *(Nom Yee),* mashed
> ½ teaspoon salt
> ½ teaspoon sugar
> 2 thin slices ginger root, crushed
> 1 teaspoon monosodium glutamate
> 1 cup chicken stock
> 10 whole star anise *(Bot Gok)*

Mix all ingredients thoroughly. Pour mixture into cavity of duck.

Add:
> ½ bundle Chinese parsley (fresh coriander)
> 2 whole green onions

Sew openings to keep juices from escaping.

Have prepared:
> 1½ pounds taro root, peeled and sliced 1 inch thick

Place duck in deep dish. Surround with sliced taro root. Place in steaming utensil, cover and steam cook at medium high heat for 1½ hours. Carefully remove taro root and place on serving platter. Remove duck, open cavity and save juices.

Cut in same manner as Simmered Whole Chicken *(Bot Chit Gai)* recipe, but place on top of taro root instead.

In a saucepot, place:  Juices from duck cavity

Bring to a boil. Add:
> 2 teaspoons cornstarch. Make paste with 2 teaspoons water.

Stir continuously and when gravy thickens, pour over duck. Serve immediately with steamed rice. Serves 4 to 5

# Meats

# ANOTHER "DISSERTATION UPON ROAST PIG"

Thanks to Charles Lamb and his charming essay classic "A Dissertation Upon Roast Pig," many Americans probably have a tantalizing picture of the Chinese people toothsomely enjoying roast pig. They are not too wrong.

Daily in the heart of the native section of San Francisco's Chinatown, grocery stores in every block offer the rather spectacular sight of whole glazed roast pigs which always awe the tourists. Festive occasions such as weddings and receptions also give reason for the colorful procession of a crackling roast pig — beribboned and serenely enthroned on a gilded wooden tray — wending its proud way to highlight some happy party.

Even country towns in California with any sizable colony of Chinese try to manage a regular culinary weekend treat for their people. It's chicken on Sunday for Americans. For the Chinese, it's roast pig. And Chinese from all around the countryside would come on Sunday to buy it. This weekly roast pig session combines all the gaiety and social aspects of an American country store gathering.

So you see, there really is a lot of truth to Charles Lamb's fictional parable about the roast pig. And the pig is the most common source of meat in China. This whole picture brings out a point:

In Chinese grocery and delicatessen displays you will see whole glazed roast pigs, racks of barbecued spareribs and strips of barbecued pork *(Cha Siew)*. These are commercially prepared in large quantities for selling in small quantities, because it is most unusual in a Chinese home to see meats served in the form of roasts, steaks or chops.

One of the fundamental differences between the Chinese and American styles of meat preparation is the fact that Chinese meat dishes are cut into slices or small chunks — bite size — or finely chopped as meat patties.

171

Also, even the "pure" meat items are served as one of several dishes on the table, to be enjoyed by all — and not as a single entree for just one person as a steak would be. As you recall in the *Vegetable* chapter, another characteristic of meat usage in Chinese cooking is the infinite combinations of meat with vegetables.

One more purely Chinese technique of meat usage is the practice of STEAMING *(Jing)* of pork patties or sliced beef, laced with native condiments and ingredients ranging from a tangy shrimp paste to pickled bamboo membranes. Chinese steaming, of course, retains all the natural juices right in the serving vessel.

The greater use of flavoring agents or marinades in the preparation of all meats is another characteristic of the Chinese handling of meats. Most of the sliced meats in the vegetable combinations, for instance, call for the use of a basic soy sauce marinade.

## PORK

When Mrs. Wong tells her husband they will have, among other things, a *Yuke Beong,* or literally a *meat patty,* on the dinner menu, Mr. Wong knows that it will be a pork patty. Through the centuries pigs have proven to be the easiest domestic animal to raise under the conditions of an agricultural country teeming with small farmers and checkered with small foraging areas, rather than the vast grazing land needed for cattle.

Mr. Porky also leads the Chinese meat parade because his meat has a more delicate flavor than beef, a less coarse grain, and consequently is more adaptable for the infinite varieties of dishes of the Celestial cuisine. For all-purpose use (patties and toss-cooking shreds) what is the best piece of pork to buy?

Get a piece of Boston Butt and put it in the refrigerator for convenience of future use. Boston Butt runs about 4 pounds. Of course, all gristle and some of the fat should be trimmed. For patties, a small amount of fat should be chopped and minced in the mixture for smoothness of texture and to help "hold" it together. For barbecued pork *(Cha Siew)* pork tenderloin is best.

## BEEF

Beef, as we have discussed previously and in the *Vegetable* chapter, is not eaten in China as much as pork. Cattle per se are not raised in China expressly for food. However, in the United States good beef is plentiful and the Chinese-Americans have availed themselves of a greater use of it.

For the predominantly toss-cooked dishes, flank steak is the beef to buy. Its flat slab-like structure, with the grain running long, makes for easy handling in the cross-grain cutting. Flank steak strips turn out tender morsels in the fast toss-cooking process, and it is not an extremely expensive cut of meat.

Novitiates of the Chinese knife *(Choy Doh)* may find a strip of flank steak just a little difficult to handle. Freeze it just enough, but not too hard, for easy cutting. Since it is a staple like Boston Butt, flank steak also can be bought in quantity and stored in the freezer.

## LAMB AND MUTTON

To the Chinese, both lamb and mutton are the same. Although texturally both are very tender, the Chinese are not too fond of them, perhaps because of the pronounced "muttony" taste, except in North China where there are many persons of the Moslem faith who naturally prefer them to pork. The Cantonese, whose school of cooking we are featuring, do not use it much.

## ON VARIETY MEATS

The Chinese, like the Europeans, are much more exposed than Americans to the enjoyment of variety items like kidney and liver. Kidney toss-cooked, for instance, is enjoyed immensely for texture. The Chinese skillfully manage to utilize almost every bit of a butchered animal to the very end — including a pig's tail.

# BELL PEPPER BEEF
*(Ching Jiew Ngow Yuke)*

Have prepared:

**1 pound tender beef, sliced ¼-inch thick, in 2 x 1-inch pieces**
**2 medium bell peppers, cored, cut into ¾ x ¾-inch pieces**
**1 small onion, cut in ¾-inch pieces**

In a mixing bowl, marinate beef with:

**1 tablespoon light soy sauce**
**1 teaspoon granulated sugar**
**1½ tablespoons cornstarch**
**Dash white pepper**
**1 teaspoon rice wine or sherry**
**3 tablespoons water**
**2 tablespoons vegetable oil**

In a preheated *wok* or skillet, place:

**2 tablespoons vegetable oil**

Bring oil to sizzling point at high heat. Add marinated beef, toss and turn until half-cooked, remove beef and set aside.

In the same *wok* or skillet, place:

**1 tablespoon vegetable oil**
**1 tablespoon brown bean sauce**
**Pepper and onion pieces**

Toss and mix for one minute. Add:

**1 cup chicken stock**

Cover and cook for 2 minutes at high heat. Remove cover. Return the partially-cooked beef to the pan. Toss and mix all ingredients thoroughly.

Thicken mixture with:          **1 tablespoon cornstarch. Make paste with 1 tablespoon water.**

Serve immediately with hot rice. Serves 4

# CHOPPED BEEF WITH GREEN PEAS
### (Ngow Yuke Beong Chow Ching Dow)

Have prepared: **2 pounds green peas, frozen or fresh**
**8 ounces ground beef**

In a preheated *wok* or skillet, place:
**2 tablespoons vegetable oil**

Bring oil to sizzling point and add:
**Chopped beef**
**Green peas**
**¾ teaspoon salt**
**½ teaspoon monosodium glutamate**
**¼ teaspoon sugar**

Toss and mix rapidly at high heat for two minutes.
Add: **½ cup chicken stock**
Cover and cook at medium-high heat for 3 or 4 minutes. Uncover.
Add gradually: **2 tablespoons cornstarch. Make paste with 2 tablespoons water**

Turn ingredients 2 or 3 minutes until sauce thickens. Serve with steamed or fried rice. Serves 4-5

# PIG TROTTERS VINAIGRETTE
### (Seen Gee Geok)

Have prepared: **4 large pig's feet, well-cleaned, and cut into eighths**

In a large pot, place: **Cut pig's feet**
**Enough boiling water to cover**

Bring to high heat and boil for 15 minutes. Drain off boiling water in colander and rinse pig's feet in cold running water until excess fat is washed off.

In the same utensil, place: **10 slices fresh ginger, ¼-inch thick**
**2 cups strong cider vinegar**
**1½ cups cold water**
**2 cups brown sugar**
**½ teaspoon salt**

Bring vinegar sauce to a boil, add:
**Pig's feet**

Continue boiling for 10 minutes, then simmer for 1 hour or until meat is tender. Serve with hot steamed rice. Serves 4

## STEAMED BEEF WITH PICKLED BAMBOO SHOOT MEMBRANES
*(Soon Yee Jing Ngow Yuke)*

| | |
|---|---|
| Have prepared: | 1½  pounds tender raw beef, sliced into 1 x 1½-inch pieces, ¼-inch thick |
| | 1  cup Bamboo Shoot Membranes *(Soon Yee)*, washed and drained |
| In a mixing bowl, blend: | Sliced beef |
| | 2  tablespoons soy sauce |
| | 1  teaspoon sugar |
| | 1  tablespoon cornstarch |
| | ½  teaspoon monosodium glutamate |

After thoroughly mixed, spread beef out on platter or round dish. Spread Bamboo Shoot Membranes evenly over beef.

Place platter elevated on a trivet or perforated can in a large steamer which has a tight fitting lid. Cover and steam at high heat 7 to 10 minutes. Serve with steamed rice. Serves 4

*A tangy dish in which the crispy texture of the* Soon Ye *contrasts with slices of beef.*

# LYCHEE PINEAPPLE PORK SWEET AND SOUR
## *(Lychee Baw Law Goo Lo Yuke)*

Have prepared: 
**1 pound lean pork, cut into ¾-inch squares**
**1 egg, well beaten**

Coat pork by dipping in beaten egg.

In a pan, place: 
**1 cup flour**
**½ teaspoon monosodium glutamate**
**½ teaspoon salt**
**Egg coated pork**

Mix well until pork is thoroughly coated with flour and remove from pan.

In a deep-fry utensil, place:     **4-5 cups vegetable oil**

Bring oil to a boil (360° F), drop in coated pork and deep fry 6 to 8 minutes until browned and done. Remove pork and drain on absorbent paper toweling. Keep warm.

Also have prepared: 
**15 (canned) lychees, drained**
**1 cup pineapple chunks, drained (reserve pineapple juice)**
**1 medium green pepper cut in ½-inch pieces**

In a *wok* or deep skillet, place: 
**½ cup vinegar**
**½ cup sugar**
**⅓ cup pineapple juice**
**¼ cup catsup**
**1 teaspoon Worcestershire sauce**
**4 drops hot sauce**

Blend all the ingredients well and bring to a boil.

Add gradually: 
**2 tablespoons cornstarch. Make paste with 2 tablespoons water.**

Continue to boil at high heat, stirring continuously until sauce thickens.

Add: 
**Pre-cooked pork**
**Lychees**
**Pineapple chunks**
**Sliced green pepper**

Turn and mix rapidly for about 5 minutes or until all ingredients are very hot. Serve with hot steamed rice. Serves 3 or 4

## *PINEAPPLE PORK SWEET AND SOUR*
*(Baw Law Goo Lo Yuke)*

Have prepared:
    **1 pound raw lean pork, cut into ¾-inch squares**
    **1 egg, well beaten**

Coat pork by dipping in beaten egg.

In a pan, place:
    **1 cup flour**
    **½ teaspoon monosodium glutamate**
    **½ teaspoon salt**
    **Egg coated pork**

Mix well until pork is thoroughly coated with flour and remove from pan.

In a deep fry utensil, place:    **4-5 cups vegetable oil**

Bring oil to a boil (360° F), drop in coated pork and deep fry 6 to 8 minutes or until browned and done. Remove pork and drain on absorbent paper toweling. Keep warm.

Also have prepared:
    **1 cup pineapple chunks, drained (Reserve pineapple juice)**
    **1 medium green pepper, cut in ½-inch pieces**

In a *wok* or deep skillet, place:
    **1 teaspoon soy sauce**
    **½ cup sugar**
    **⅓ cup pineapple juice**
    **¼ cup catsup**
    **½ cup vinegar**

Blend all the ingredients well and bring to a boil.

Add gradually:
    **2 tablespoons cornstarch. Make paste with 2 tablespoons water.**

Continue to boil at high heat, stirring continously until sauce thickens.

Add:
    **Pre-cooked pork**
    **Pineapple chunks**
    **Sliced green pepper**

Turn and mix rapidly for about 5 minutes or until all ingredients are very hot. Serve with hot steamed rice. Serves 3 or 4

# SAUTÉED KIDNEYS WITH VEGETABLES
### (Gee Yew Chow Gwa Choy)

Have prepared:

**4 fresh pork kidneys, halved and deveined. Slice ¼-inch thick. Parboil 10 minutes. Rinse 15 minutes with running water. Drain.**

**½ cup celery, sliced 3/16-inch thick**

**½ cup dried onion, sliced in ½-inch squares**

**2 cups Chinese snow peas, strings removed, washed and drained**

**1 teaspoon fresh ginger root, peeled and shredded thread-fine**

In a preheated *wok* or skillet, place:

**2 tablespoons vegetable oil**

Bring oil to sizzling point at high heat.

Add:

**Parboiled sliced kidneys**

**Shredded ginger root, celery and onion**

**1 teaspoon salt**

Toss cook rapidly for 2 minutes.

Add:

**2 tablespoons soy sauce**

**1 tablespoon bourbon or gin**

**¼ teaspoon monosodium glutamate**

**¼ teaspoon sugar**

Continue to toss cook for 1 minute.

Add:                                   **¼ cup chicken stock**

Cover and cook at medium heat 2 minutes. Uncover.

Add:                                   **Snow peas**

Cover and cook 1 minute. Uncover.

Add gradually:                 **⅓ cup cornstarch. Make paste with ⅓ cup water.**

Toss and turn all ingredients until sauce thickens and mixture is very hot. Serve with steamed or fried rice. Serves 4

## *SPARERIBS WITH BLACK BEAN SAUCE*
*(See Jup Pai Gwut)*

Have prepared:

2 pounds fresh spareribs, cut into 1½-inch lengths. Parboil 15 minutes, rinse in cold water.
2 teaspoons minced garlic
2 teaspoons fermented Black Beans *(Dow See)*, crushed into paste
¼ teaspoon minced fresh ginger root
1 cup bell pepper, sliced 1 x 1-inch square
¼ cup scallion tops, halved and in 1-inch lengths

In a mixing bowl place:

Black Bean Paste
Minced ginger root and garlic
1 teaspoon soy sauce (Combination is now Black Bean Sauce)

In a preheated *wok* or skillet, place:

2 tablespoons vegetable oil

Bring oil to sizzling point and add:

Sparerib sections

Brown rapidly and add:

Black Bean Sauce
½ teaspoon monosodium glutamate
½ teaspoon salt

Toss and mix for 1 minute and add:

1½ cups chicken stock
Pepper to taste

Cover and cook 25 minutes at high heat. Uncover occasionally, turn and add more chicken stock if liquid evaporates too fast. When spareribs are thoroughly cooked through, uncover.

Add gradually:

2 tablespoons cornstarch. Make paste with 2 tablespoons water.

Turn and mix at high heat until sauce thickens. Add onion. Serve with steamed rice. Serves 3 or 4

*This is an ideal dish to take on an outdoor trip as overnight aging actually improves the flavor. While the spareribs are being reheated, you can be cooking a pot of steamed rice. In less than half an hour, you have a meal fit for a king.*

# SPARERIBS WITH RED BEAN CAKE SAUCE
## (Nom Yee Pai Gwut)

Have prepared:

> **2 pounds fresh spareribs, cut into 1½-inch lengths. Parboil 15 minutes, rinse with cold water.**
> **½ teaspoon minced garlic**
> **2 tablespoons Red Bean Cake** *(Nom Yee)*
> **½ teaspoon minced fresh ginger root**
> **¼ cup scallion tops, cut ½-inch long**

In a preheated *wok* or skillet, place:

> **2 tablespoons vegetable oil**

Bring oil to sizzling point at high heat.

Add:   **Minced garlic and ginger root**

Brown garlic rapidly and add:
> **Sparerib sections**
> **½ teaspoon salt**
> **1 teaspoon soy sauce**
> **Red Bean Cake**
> **½ teaspoon sugar**
> **½ teaspoon monosodium glutamate**

Stir and mix 1 minute and add:   **1 cup chicken stock**

Cover and bring to a boil, then lower heat and cook 25 minutes. Uncover occasionally and turn ingredients. Add more chicken stock if liquid evaporates too fast. When spareribs are thoroughly cooked through, uncover.

Add:   **Scallions**

Turn and mix.

Add gradually:
> **2 tablespoons cornstarch. Make paste with 2 tablespoons water.**

Turn and mix at high heat until sauce thickens. Serve with steamed rice. Serves 3 or 4

*By using Red Bean Cake instead of Black Bean paste, this identical recipe offers spareribs with an entirely different flavor.*

## *STEWED PORK SPARERIBS*
*(Wut Pai Gwut)*

Have prepared:

**2** pounds pork spareribs, cut into 2-inch
    lengths. Parboil 15 minutes and rinse in
    cold water.
**9** dried Chinese mushrooms *(Heong Soon)*
    softened in water. Slice into ¼-inch strips
**4** star anise, rinsed

In a large pot, place:

Parboiled spareribs
Cold water to cover
**1** teaspoon salt
**3** tablespoons soy sauce
**½** teaspoon monosodium glutamate
Chinese mushrooms
Star anise

Cover pot, bring water to boil. Reduce to simmer, and cook spareribs until tender (about 1 hour). Uncover.

Gradually add:

**4** tablespoons cornstarch. Make paste with 4
    tablespoons water.

Stir continuously until gravy thickens. Serve over or with steamed rice. Serves 4

*We highly recommend this favorite recipe of ours as an ideal "cooked in advance" meat dish for sportsmen because it actually improves in flavor when kept cool overnight. Reheat the spareribs on a galley burner or camp stove while cooking up a pot of steamed rice, and serve together as a "one-dish" lunch or dinner. This delicious meat and rice combination is not only nutritious, it "sticks to the ribs" and supplies satisfying body warmth all day in nippy weather.*

# *FUKIEN PORK*
## *(Fook Geen Lot Ding)*

Have prepared:
- **12 ounces lean pork, cut into ½-inch squares**
- **½ cup diced lotus root**
- **½ cup canned Gingko nuts**
- **¼ cup diced water chestnuts**
- **¼ cup green peas**

In a mixing bowl, marinate the pork with:
- **1 tablespoon soy sauce**
- **½ teaspoon sugar**
- **1 tablespoon rice wine or sherry**
- **2 tablespoons cornstarch**

Set aside.

In a preheated *wok* or skillet, place:
- **2 tablespoons vegetable oil**

Bring oil to sizzling point at medium heat. Add marinated pork. Toss cook gradually until browned (about 2 minutes).

Add:
- **Vegetables: lotus root, Gingko nuts, water chestnuts and peas.**
- **2 cups chicken broth**
- **2 tablespoons chili bean sauce**
- **½ teaspoon salt**
- **1 tablespoon dark soy sauce**
- **1 teaspoon sugar**

Cover and continue to cook until little liquid remains. Remove cover. Thicken with:
- **1 teaspoon cornstarch, made into paste with**
- **¼ cup water.**

Toss and mix well.

If desired, garnish with roasted lotus seed. Serves 3 or 4

## STEAMED PORK PATTY WITH CURED DUCK LIVERS

*(Opp Geoke Bow Jing Gee Yuke Beong)*

Have prepared:

1½ pounds fresh raw pork containing some fat
3 cured duck livers *(Opp Geoke Bow)*.
   Presoak ½ hour, rinse and drain.
   Remove livers.
½ cup canned or fresh water chestnuts, diced

Chop pork very fine with two sharp cleavers. Add cured livers and chop into pork. Turn and chop several times.

Into a mixing bowl, place:

Chopped pork and livers
Diced water chestnuts
½ teaspoon salt
1 teaspoon soy sauce
   Sprinkle of monosodium glutamate
1 tablespoon cornstarch

Mix all ingredients until thoroughly blended. Transfer to platter and press into patty about ½ inch thick.

Place platter elevated on trivet or substitute in a large steamer with tight-fitting lid. Cover and steam cook at high heat 20 to 25 minutes, until pork is well done. Serve immediately with hot steamed rice. Serves 3 or 4

*For those who do not care for Salted Eggs or Salt Fish, this style of pork patty should appeal to you. Cured Duck Livers are a delicacy. At times, they will be scarce at the Chinatown grocer's due to import restrictions. Make sure they are fresh stock. When in doubt, don't accept them – substitute ½ cup diced ham for the livers.*

# STEAMED PORK PATTY WITH SALT FISH
## (Hom Yee Jing Gee Yuke Beong)

| Have prepared: | 1½ | pounds raw pork containing some fat. Chop very fine with two sharp cleavers. |
|---|---|---|
| | 4 | pieces Salt fish *(Hom Yee),* cut ¾ x 2 inches. Soak and wash in cold water 10 minutes. Drain. |
| | 1 | teaspoon sliced ginger |
| In a mixing bowl, place: | | Chopped pork |
| | ½ | teaspoon salt |
| | 1 | teaspoon soy sauce |
| | | Sprinkle of ground pepper |
| | | Sprinkle of monosodium glutamate |
| | 1 | tablespoon cornstarch |

Mix pork with other ingredients until well blended. Transfer to platter and press into a meat patty, covering the platter. Place salt fish and ginger over patty evenly.

Place platter elevated on a trivet or perforated can in a large steamer with tight-fitting lid. Cover and steam cook at high heat 20 to 25 minutes, or until pork is well done. Serve at once with hot steamed rice. Serves 3 or 4

*This recipe is similar to Salted Eggs Steamed with Pork. There are countless varieties of* Hom Yee *in Chinese grocery stores, but we suggest that you try the domestic dried Flounder* (Yow Dai Day) *to begin with, before sampling the stronger and saltier imported varieties.*

## *STEAMED PORK PATTY WITH VEGETABLE ROOT*
*(Choong Choy Jing Gee Yuke Beong)*

Have prepared:

**1½ pounds raw pork containing some fat**
**½ cup Salted Vegetable Root** *(Choong Choy)*, **pre-soaked ½ hour and rinsed until free of possible grit. Drain and chop very fine.**

Chop pork very fine with two sharp cleavers. Turn frequently.

In a mixing bowl, place:

**Chopped pork**
**½ teaspoon salt**
**1 teaspoon soy sauce**
**Sprinkle of ground pepper**
**Sprinkle of monosodium glutamate**
**1½ teaspoons cornstarch**
**Chopped Salted Vegetable Root**

Mix thoroughly until all ingredients are completely blended. Transfer to platter and press into meat patty about ½ inch thick.

Place patty elevated on a trivet or perforated can in a large steamer with tight-fitting lid. Cover and steam cook at high heat 25 minutes or until pork is done. Serve immediately with hot steamed rice. Serves 3 or 4

## *STEAMED PORK PATTY WITH TEA SQUASH*
*(Cha Gwa Jing Gee Yuke Beong)*

Use same recipe as above, substituting Tea Squash *(Cha Gwa)* in place of Salted Vegetable Root *(Choong Choy)*. Since Tea Squash comes packed in tins, you only need to rinse them and slice 3/16-inch thick, before adding to pork patty.

# STEAMED PORK PATTY WITH CHINESE SAUSAGE
## (Lop Cheong Jing Gee Yuke Beong)

The same recipe applies again, substituting 4 Chinese Dried Sausages *(Lop Cheong)* for *Choong Choy* or *Cha Gwa*. Slice sausages diagonally ½-inch thick, then place over pork patty.

# ROAST PORK WITH SHRIMP PASTE
## (Hom Hah Jing Diew Yuke)

Purchase from Chinatown grocery:

**1 pound roast pork from roast pig. Have shopkeeper chop into 1½x1½-inch pieces by ¾-inch thick. The crackling skin is the best part, do not remove.**

Prepare and mix:

**3 tablespoons Shrimp Paste** *(Hom Hah)*
**½ teaspoon minced fresh ginger root**
**½ teaspoon monosodium glutamate**
**¼ teaspoon sugar**

Arrange roast pork evenly on a platter or round shallow dish. Over it, spread the Shrimp Paste, diluted with a few drops of bourbon.

Place the platter or dish elevated on a trivet or perforated can in a steamer, cover and cook at high heat for 20 minutes. Uncover. Serve at once with steamed rice. Serves 2 or 3

*Once one develops a taste for* Hom Hah, *he is considered a gourmet of the first order and his pantry is never without a handy supply. It has an aroma of its own, seemingly strong at first, but what the Chinese call* Heong *or pungent-fragrant. Canned imported anchovies are similar in degree of saltiness and few learn to enjoy them with their first experience.*

## OYSTER SAUCE BEEF
*(Ho Yow Ngow Yuke)*

Have prepared:

**1 pound tender beef, sliced ¼-inch thick (2 x 1-inch pieces)**
**½ cup scallions. Use white sections cut into 1-inch lengths.**

In a mixing bowl, place:

**¼ teaspoon salt**
**½ teaspoon soy sauce**
**1 teaspoon cornstarch**
**Dash of sugar**

Mix ingredients thoroughly, add:

**Sliced beef**

Marinate for 5 minutes.
In a preheated *wok* or skillet, place:

**2 tablespoons vegetable oil**
**Sliced beef and scallions**
**2 tablespoons oyster sauce** *(Ho Yow)*

Toss cook at high heat for 3 minutes.
Add:

**¼ cup chicken stock**
**½ teaspoon monosodium glutamate**
**1 tablespoon cornstarch. Make paste with 1 tablespoon water.**

Toss and mix until gravy thickens and has coated the beef and scallions. Serve while very hot with steamed rice. Serves 3

*This recipe, like Ginger Beef, is a quickly prepared toss-cooked meat dish, which is perfect for those who have unexpected company.*

# GINGER BEEF
## (Sang Geong Ngow Yuke)

Have prepared:
> 1 pound tender beef, sliced ¼-inch thick (2 x 1-inch pieces)
> ¼ cup peeled ginger root, sliced vertically as thin as possible
> ¼ cup scallions. Use white sections cut into 1-inch lengths

In a preheated *wok* or skillet, place:
> 2 tablespoons vegetable oil
> ¼ teaspoon salt

Turn to high heat until oil is very hot.

Add:
> Sliced beef, ginger root and scallions
> 2 teaspoons soy sauce
> Dash of sugar
> ½ teaspoon monosodium glutamate

Toss cook rapidly at high heat for 3 minutes.

Add:
> ¼ cup chicken stock
> 1 tablespoon cornstarch. Make paste with 1 tablespoon water.

Continue to stir and mix until gravy thickens. Serve with hot steamed rice.
Serves 3 or 4

## *PEKING BEEF*
*(Buck Ging Ngow Yuke)*

Have prepared:

> 1 pound flank steak, cut into 1-inch cubes. Pound each cube once with tenderizing mallet.
> 1 medium onion, shredded

In a mixing bowl, marinate beef with:

> 1 tablespoon dark soy sauce
> 1 tablespoon *Hoy Sien* Sauce
> 1 tablespoon tomato catsup
> 1 teaspoon Worcestershire sauce
> 1 tablespoon rice wine or sherry
> 1 tablespoon *Tientsin* Preserved Vegetables
> 2 tablespoons cornstarch, with
> 2 tablespoons water
> 1 tablespoon sesame oil
> 2 tablespoons vegetable oil
> 1 clove finely crushed garlic

Let stand for 2 hours.

In a preheated *wok* or skillet, place:

> 2 tablespoons vegetable oil

Bring oil to sizzling point at high heat. Add marinated beef. Toss cook gradually to brown beef until just half-cooked. Add the shredded onion and continue to toss-cook for one minute.

Add:

> 1 tablespoon dark soy sauce
> 1 teaspoon granulated sugar

Blend well. Serve hot. Serves 4.

*This recipe has been a closely guarded secret of Kan's executive Chef Sun Pui Wong for many years. Many diners at the restaurant have tried to duplicate this dish in their own homes. The Chef is now proud to present it to the many who have coveted this recipe.*

# KAN'S LAMB
## (How Yeong Yuke)

Have prepared:
                              1 pound fresh lamb (preferably leg of lamb),
                                cut into 1½-inch squares, ⅛-inch thick.

In a mixing bowl, marinate lamb with:

                              1 tablespoon soy sauce
                              2 tablespoons *Hoy Sien Sauce*
                              1 tablespoon granulated sugar
                              1 teaspoon sesame oil
                              1 teaspoon rice wine or sherry
                                Dash of white pepper
                              1 small clove garlic, finely minced
                              1 tablespoon cornstarch
                              1 tablespoon vegetable oil

In a preheated *wok* or skillet, place:

                              2 tablespoons vegetable oil
                                Sliced lamb

Toss cook to brown both sides of the lamb slices at high heat.

Add:
                              1 tablespoon dark soy sauce
                              1 teaspoon sugar

Toss and mix for an additional ½ minute. Garnish with:

                              1½ cups rice sticks *(Mai Fun)*, puffed in deep
                                 fryer at 350°.

Serve piping. Serves 4

# Desserts

## THE "EIGHT PRECIOUS" PUDDING

Maybe we *are* clever, we Chinese.

Consider even the average American family dinner, when for a triumphant finale, the lady of the house proudly brings out a deep cream-laden pie, or a massive cake — the dessert.

Beautiful four-color magazine ads and TV commercials tout desserts as the glorious end of a meal. Lovely to look at, so easy to eat, but so hard to shed — to paraphrase a perennially popular song. That is, the calories are so hard to shed.

Have you ever observed the clinging *cheong-sham* native gowns which Chinese women wear? Seductively figure-revealing, but hardly the most flattering garments for obese individuals. Maybe one reason Chinese women can wear them is because in the serving of Chinese meals they *do not* indulge in the daily gastronomical ritual of desserts. Maybe it is cleverness, or maybe common sense.

However, it doesn't mean that the Chinese do not indulge in sweet things to eat. We just don't make it a habit.

At sumptuous banquets, a dessert or "sweet thing" is served shortly after half the courses have been savored. This plan makes for a welcome contrast and pace change to the perhaps repeated salty and highly spiced dishes. Also, in the Chinese mode of dining, there is a succession of dishes and ofttimes a sweet-and-sour sauce concoction, such as in chicken wings or a rock cod which will satisfy readily the craving for something sweet.

At Chinese teahouses, where the *Deem Sum* type of luncheon — steaming hot tiny meat and seafood tidbits wrapped in dough — is served, there is also a choice of the dessert kind of pastry, such as a sweet rice flour steamed pudding. Here again, choosing a dessert-type pastry is an optional matter rather than a practice.

In the indulgence of "sweet things" the Chinese sometimes even sip Hot Almond Paste *(Hung Ngon Woo)*, usually a banquet item but sometimes enjoyed as a sweet-tooth appeaser. This *Hung Ngon Woo*, called by some Almond Tea, really is a creamy sauce served in small soup bowls. Several San Francisco Chinatown native-type restaurants feature nightly a dried green bean gruel, with the bean ground coarsely, blended with sugar and minced dried Mandarin orange peel *(Gaw Pay)* simmered for hours to a thick, smooth soupiness. This indigenous dish, called *Look Dow Sah,* though served boiling hot, gives a coolish, soothing sensation which is due partly to the orange peel undertone. It is very good to the throat when you've been smoking too much.

In step with their partial American as well as Chinese cooking, many Chinese-American housewives now defer to practice and do serve dessert, or "something sweet" at the end of a Chinese dinner on a party or company occasion. Something like, for instance, our recipe *Lychee Delight.*

Suppose all the Chinese restaurants suddenly went strictly native and traditional? Why, there would be no moments of joyful suspense and fun at the end of a Chinese dinner — because there would be no dessert fortune cookies to break! Fortune cookies, purely an invention of Chinese-Yankees, were unknown in Old Cathay.

To soothe your disillusionment over the cracked fortune cookies, we now offer you some truly traditional Chinese sweets, one harmonizing with our octaval taste theme, called the Eight Precious Pudding.

## HOT LOTUS TEA
*(Teem Choy)*

Have prepared:     **1 pound dried lotus nuts** *(Leen Gee)*
**½ teaspoon baking soda**

Cover lotus nuts with boiling water, add baking soda and stir. When cool enough, clean lotus nuts in soda and water with fingers. Rinse and drain.

In a sauce pot, place:     **5 cups boiling water**
**1 cup cane sugar**
**Lotus nuts**

Boil at medium heat for 1 hour.
Stir and add:     **2 beaten eggs**
Serve hot in small bowls. Serves 4

## HOT ALMOND PASTE
*(Hung Ngon Woo)*

---

In a saucepan place:      **3 cups boiling water**
Keep water boiling and add:    **¾ cup sugar**
In a bowl, mix into a smooth paste:

        **¼ cup cornstarch**
        **¼ cup cold water**

Bring sugar and water to a boil and gradually add cornstarch paste while stirring constantly. Turn off fire.
Add:      **½ cup canned milk**
        **1 teaspoon pure almond extract**

Continue to stir until well blended. Serve very hot. Serves 4

Hung Ngon Woo *is usually served in small bowls as a dessert after a Chinese banquet, and is very sweet. Try it with reduced amounts of sugar to suit your taste.*

## CHINESE GELATIN
*(Tai Choy Go)*

---

Have ready:      **1½ sticks agar agar** *(Tai Choy Go)*
        **½ cup cane sugar**
        **1 small can evaporated milk**
        **1 teaspoon banana extract**
In a sauce pot place:    **4 cups boiling water**
Keep water at boiling point and add:

        **Agar agar and sugar**

Boil for 15 minutes or until agar agar has dissolved.
Add:      **Canned milk, and extract**
        **Red, yellow or orange vegetable coloring to suit**

Remove from fire and cool, then pour mixture into a shallow pan and refrigerate for 2 hours. When dessert is jelled, slice into 1-inch squares. Transfer gelatin squares to dessert dishes. Serve plain or garnish with preserved Chinese fruits in syrup. Serves 4

# EIGHT PRECIOUS PUDDING
## (Bot Bo Go)

In a heavy pot, place:          **4 cups glutinous rice** *(Naw Mai)*, **washed and drained**
                                **2½ cups cold water**

Cover and cook at high heat until water boils (about 20 minutes). Turn to very low heat and continue cooking another 30 minutes.

Thoroughly mix and add:         **1 cup sugar**
                                **3 tablespoons oil**

Blend with rice until sugar dissolves.

On bottom of large deep bowl, which has been oiled, arrange in a decorative design:

**Raisins**
**Canned gingko nuts**
**Chestnuts**
**Walnuts**
**Candied red and green cherries**
**Candied melon**
**Candied ginger**
**Candied kumquats**

Add layers of rice and Sweet Black Bean Paste* *(Dow Sah)* alternately in bowl on top of eight ingredients above.

Rest bowl on trivet in steaming utensil. Steam for one hour. Take bowl out of pot, place large round plate over top of bowl. Quickly invert bowl on plate and remove bowl. Pudding should be intact with fruit design on top. Serve warm or cold. Serves 6 to 8

### *SWEET BLACK BEAN PASTE *(Dow Sah)*

*Prepare:*                      **1 pound Chinese small red beans** *(Hoong Dow)*

Wash until clean and boil in sufficient water to cover beans. Boil for one hour, or until beans are separated from their skins. Strain in a piece of cheesecloth. The bean mixture will be of a thick paste consistency to which add:

**1 cup sugar**
**4 tablespoons oil**

Mix thoroughly and place in an oiled skillet at low heat. Stir constantly and rapidly for five minutes to prevent scorching.

*Through many centuries of Chinese history the Eight Treasures have served as charms to ward off evil and induce goodness. Abstractions of the Eight Treasures are used in clothing, and as motifs in porcelain and embroidery as well as for this traditional holiday dessert.*

## *LYCHEE DELIGHT*
*(Lychee Tai Choy Go)*

Have ready:

> **3 pints water**
> **4 sticks agar agar** *(Tai Choy Go)* **(1½ ounces)**
> **1½ cups sugar**
> **2 cups pineapple syrup**
> **½ teaspoon yellow vegetable coloring**
> **1 small can lychee nuts**

Put all ingredients into pot. Boil briskly until agar agar melts. Cool enough for handling. Pour into individual jello molds, allowing space to place one lychee nut. (A pineapple chunk or a canned kumquat may be substituted). Put in refrigerator to chill. Makes 24 jello molds.

## *PEKING CANDIED APPLES*
*(Chuey Tong Ping Gaw)*

Peel, core and cut into 12 sections:

> **2 medium size crisp apples**

Coat apples in:  **1 beaten egg**

Dust very lightly with  **Flour**

Deep fry apples in hot oil until golden brown. Drain.

Make a thick mixture of:  **1½ cups sugar**

Add sufficient oil to moisten sugar. Heat over low flame, stirring constantly, until sugar dissolves and becomes a syrup consistency. Pour over apple sections, covering all apple completely. Have a large bowl of ice cold water at table in which to immerse apple sections individually with chopsticks to crystallize the coating. Eat immediately. Serves 6

## ALMOND COOKIES
### (Hung Ngon Beang)

Have prepared:

3 cups sifted flour
1 teaspoon soda
½ teaspoon salt
1 cup sugar
1½ cups vegetable shortening
1 teaspoon almond extract
1 fresh egg, beaten
1 cup blanched almonds

Sift flour, salt, and soda together.

In a mixing bowl cream shortening, add egg and almond extract and thoroughly mix. Gradually add dry ingredients, mix well with hands. Roll into 1-inch balls, place on greased cooky pan. Make indentation in center of each ball in which place 1 blanched almond. Bake at 350° F for 20 minutes. Recipe makes approximately 50 cookies.

# Chinese Tidbits

## MORNING, NOON AND NIGHT

This chapter will deal with party-type dishes (some of them the 25 percent portion of our recipes which are more difficult to do) and with the delightful between meals and midnight snacks which are part of the informal eating custom of the Chinese.

To quote an ancient philosopher, "Sameness in food and habits depresses; variety stimulates." Chinese are great lovers of food. Any excuse to eat evokes laughter and gaiety no matter what the occasion. So little wonder then, that through the centuries the Chinese have refined so many dishes to serve for morning, noon and night!

We will try to describe briefly some of the special aspects of Chinese snacks — all of which are available in various restaurants in San Francisco's Chinatown as precise in their specialties as your take-out *pizza* places or favorite hamburger and chili spots — so that you will see the comparison and understand the transition of these dishes to the home.

In old China, a familiar sound was the wooden clack-clack of the *Won Ton* and noodles vendor as he shuffled through the streets with a charcoal brazier and served these hot foods to you right at your door.

The traditional noonday meeting place for those who liked to sip tea, chat and enjoy a wonderful array of delicate, steaming hot tidbits was the teahouse. Here business was transacted, politics discussed and congenial friends met to enjoy such delicacies as deep-fried taro root paste turnovers stuffed with chopped meat, or ivory-white steamed buns filled with marinated diced meats and mushrooms. Perhaps the choice would be the crackling, glazed skin from a just-out-of-the-oven suckling pig, or merely simple noodles or rice rolls topped with sesame oil and soy sauce.

Probably the best testimonial to the importance of this venerable institution is the fact that today in San Francisco's Chinatown, the Chinese capital of America, there are more teahouses flourishing than ever before.

When you are invited to *Yum Cha* or "to sip tea" it really means "having lunch at a teahouse."

A dozen places, from plush restaurants to holes-in-the-wall serve *Deem Sum* which means literally "a touch of the heart" and is truly the heart of the elaborate specialties of the Chinese teahouse.

This same *Deem Sum* is the world's original hot hors d'oeuvres!

Another San Francisco Chinatown institution is the eating place which specializes in *Jook,* the Chinese rice gruel. One such place is dubbed "the house that *Jook* built" because of its tremendous and lucrative popularity. This springs not only from regular, repeat local customers but from the patronage of Chinese visitors from all over the world. There is a tranquilizing satisfaction in a bowl of hot *Jook* with congenial friends as dawn breaks after a night of celebration.

In the large Chinese centers of America some of the morning, noon and night snacks we describe can be bought from the specialty food places and taken home. But the average Chinese-American housewife who lives outside the orbit of these epicurean centers can and does prepare many of the dishes we are including in this chapter. For the San Franciscan, dishes such as *Jook* and *Mien* can be prepared at home. But not the *Deem Sum.* The former two are relatively simple to make at home; the last item can always be bought cooked in any variety requiring only reheating before serving.

One of the most traditional dishes, the Winter Chafing Dish, can be adapted beautifully to the latest modern appliance, the electrical skillet. This *Dah Bin Lo* on a cold night — dunking a dozen varieties of sliced foods in a "community" soup pot — is the Chinese version of togetherness in the warmth of good fellowship, witty conversation and the fun of an indoor picnic.

The shouting, good-natured ribbing and toasting to each other which goes on during a Ceremony of the Fish Party is a colorful manner of enjoying the day's fresh catch of striped bass. This can be a big, gay, hospitable party.

So, here you will see that aside from regular meals, the perfect Chinese host or hostess can be kept busy in the kitchen MORNING, NOON AND NIGHT with a tremendous range of dishes designed for around the clock enjoyment.

## *EGG ROLL*
*(Choon Geen)*

Sift into mixing bowl:      **3 cups flour**
**2 teaspoons salt**

Add:      **2 eggs**
**4 tablespoons cold water**

Mix together, place on floured board. Knead until smooth. Place dough in refrigerator for half an hour. Roll out paper thin. Cut in 6½-inch squares.

Prepare for filling:    **½ cup shredded barbecued pork or ham**
**½ cup shredded cooked chicken**
**½ cup finely sliced dried mushrooms (which have previously soaked)**
**½ cup finely sliced bamboo shoots**
**1 cup finely sliced young celery**

Toss and mix above ingredients in oiled hot skillet until soft.

Add:    **½ teaspoon monosodium glutamate**
**½ teaspoon salt**
**½ teaspoon sugar**
**1 teaspoon soy sauce**
**2 teaspoons cornstarch**

Toss and mix constantly for 5 minutes.

Add:    **4 drops sesame seed oil**

Cool mixture.

Place:    **¼ cup filling on each 6½-inch square of dough**

Roll and fold in ends of egg rolls. Put in container and steam 10 minutes. Cool. Have ready pan containing:

**2 beaten eggs**

Have ready another pan with:    **Cornstarch**

Dip each roll first in egg, then lightly in cornstarch. Dust off excess cornstarch. Deep fry in hot vegetable oil until brown. Drain on absorbent paper toweling. Slice 1½ inches long before serving. Makes 6 egg rolls.

# STEAMED EGG SPONGE CAKE

## (Gai Don Go)

Have prepared:

**6 large fresh eggs, separated**
**1 cup cane sugar**
**1½ cups flour**
**½ teaspoon baking powder**
**1 teaspoon pure vanilla extract**

Beat egg whites in electric mixer until stiff. Add sugar gradually and beat 2 minutes. Add egg yolks and vanilla and beat another 2 minutes.

Sift flour and baking powder together. Mix with above ingredients until batter is smooth and well blended.

Line a 9 x 9-inch pan at least 3 inches deep, with paper coated with vegetable oil. Pour batter into pan and elevate in steaming utensil containing 3 or 4 inches of hot water. Cover pot with cloth under lid to absorb water created by steaming. Turn to high heat and steam cake for 20 to 25 minutes. Remove lid and cloth, test for doneness with toothpick. If toothpick comes out clean with no trace of stickiness, remove from steamer. Turn cake upside down on a rack and cool. Cut into 2½x2½-inch squares for serving. Delicious with Oolong or Jasmine tea. Serves 5 or 6

# CHINESE BARBECUED PORK

## (Cha Siew)

In a mixing bowl, combine:

**½ teaspoon monosodium glutamate**
**½ cup soy sauce**
**¼ cup granulated sugar**
**½ teaspoon garlic powder**
**2 tablespoons catsup**
**¼ teaspoon salt**

Slice into two strips:      **1 pound pork tenderloin**

Marinate pork for at least 3 hours in sauce, turning frequently. Drain pork and place on oven rack; roast at 350° F. for 40 minutes, turning every 10 minutes to assure even brownness. Slice into ¼-inch thickness, sprinkle with toasted sesame seeds. Hot mustard and soy sauce dip optional.

*Chinese-style barbecued pork is not only great for a snack, it is as versatile as cooked ham, but with better flavor.* Cha Siew *can be used for sandwiches, for garnishing* Won Ton, *and can be cooked with rice, among many other uses. So whenever you make* Cha Siew, *triple the above recipe, and keep it in reserve in your refrigerator. It will keep nicely for many days.*

# SHRIMP BALLS
*(Hah Yin)*

Chop finely:
- ½ pound fresh cleaned prawns
- ¼ cup bamboo shoots
- ¼ cup canned button mushrooms
- 1 whole green onion

Add:
- Dash pepper
- ½ teaspoon salt
- Few drops sesame seed oil

Place in mixing bowl and add:  White of one egg

Mix together thoroughly until fluffy. Form into small balls the size of marbles.

Dip balls in batter of:
- 1 beaten egg
- 1 cup flour
- 1 teaspoon baking powder
- 3 teaspoons oil
- Sufficient water to make smooth batter of pancake consistency

Fry until golden brown; serve on toothpicks.

*This festive dish, a combination of both white and golden-brown balls perched on toothpicks, stuck on a bright orange (with one end cut off to prevent rolling), creates a gay, jewel-like edible table ornament. Oranges are Chinese good luck symbols and they are artfully displayed during the native holidays.*

# WINTER CHAFING DISH
*(Dah Bin Lo)*

Into a large ten-quart soup pot, place:
- 5 quarts boiling water
- 6 Chinese dried scallops, washed well
- 1 whole chicken carcass (bone chicken and retain meat)
- 1 medium size ham bone
- 1 can abalone (cut in small pieces) with liquid
- 1 pound Chinese lean roast pork*
- 1 tablespoon monosodium glutamate
- Salt to taste

*Chinese roast pork *(Siew Gee Yuke)* Roast Pig. To be distinguished from barbecued pork *(Cha Siew)*

Boil at high heat for 1½ hours. Remove chicken carcass, ham and chicken bone particles.

While soup is cooking — prepare and put in individual serving dishes (Slice in ⅛-inch thin pieces approximately in 1½-inch widths):

**1 pound calf's liver**
**2 pounds flank steak**
**Chicken filet**
**4 pork kidneys, cleaned and blanched**

Following fish may be used, cut in 2 x 2-inch pieces:

**2 whole filets of 4-pound rock cod**
**— or —**
**2 whole filets of 10-pound striped bass**
**— or —**
**2 whole filets of 5-pound black bass**
**— or —**
**6 whole filets of 3-pound hardhead**

Drain liquid of following into soup and transfer to serving dishes:

**1 pint fresh or frozen clams**
**1 pint fresh or frozen oysters**

Wash and clean following vegetables — place in individual large serving bowls:

**4 bunches spinach**
**1 pound young Chinese mustard greens**
**2 heads lettuce, separated leaves**
**1 bunch dandelion greens**
**1 head Chinese celery cabbage (cut in 5-inch pieces)**
**2 bunches Chinese parsley**
**2 bunches green onions (slice in small pieces)**

Condiments to be used on table (serve in small condiment or sauce dishes):

**Oyster Sauce** *(Ho Yow)*
**Pure soy sauce** *(Sin Cho)* **devoid of caramel coloring (soy sauce,** *See Yow,* **contains caramel coloring)**
**Mixed hot red seasoning sauce†**

---

†Red seasoning sauce *(Hoy Sein Jeong)*

*Table setting:*

Each setting should have a dinner plate, small soup bowl and two pairs of chopsticks — one pair being bamboo to be used for cooking.

Fill the chafing dish (or large electric skillet) with the boiling hot soup (set degree of heat on high, then keep at boiling point for first 10 minutes. Reduce heat to medium). The chafing dish should be placed in the center of the table, to be accessible to everyone, and the dishes of various ingredients surrounding it. Use two chafing dishes if you have more guests.

To the hot soup, add:                **2 squares of bean cake cut in cubes**

*Procedure of self-serving:*

Each guest will select whatever morsel of food he wishes with his bamboo chopsticks — meat, fowl and fish generally precede the vegetables — dunk his tidbit in the hot broth, transfer it after cooking to his eating bowl. The cooked food may be eaten with whatever condiment he chooses or the green onions or parsley for added flavor. Soup may also be spooned from chafing dish to another bowl for consumption. As needed, the soup is replenished in chafing dish from main soup pot. Serves 10 to 12

*Like the Ceremony of the Fish, this, too, is an epicurean excuse for togetherness, possibly in a more quiet mood. This Chinese Winter Chafing Dish may be the indoor answer to finding a substitute for outdoor barbecuing, especially in parts of the country where snow and other inclement weather conditions make outdoor entertaining impossible.*

*A glance at the recipe will show the extensive range of ingredients and choices – with meats, seafoods and vegetables – to appeal to all tastes. Each guest blends the combinations to suit himself while cooking his own morsels of food.*

# *TURKEY RICE GRUEL*
## *(Foh Gai Jook)*

Place in a 10-quart heavy soup pot with a tight-fitting lid:

> **Carcass of roast turkey which has been cut into six large pieces**
> **Cold water to cover, at least 5 quarts**
> **1 level tablespoon salt**
> **1 teaspoon monosodium glutamate**

Boil at high heat for 2 hours. Remove bones and skim excess fat from turkey broth.

Have prepared while broth is cooking:

> **1 full cup washed rice**
> **½ teaspoon vegetable oil**
> **½ tablespoon salt, mixed thoroughly with rice. Let stand one hour.**

Add rice to broth and cook at medium heat until rice disintegrates completely into broth (about 2 hours). Stir occasionally to prevent sticking and burning in bottom of pot.

Add:

> **½ canned shelled Gingko nuts, stirred thoroughly into turkey gruel (optional)**

Ladle *jook* into large bowls.

Garnish each serving with finely sliced green onions, cooked ham and shredded roast turkey. Serves 8

*In their native land, for breakfast the Chinese eat plain gruel as the Americans would eat cereal. Here in America, the Chinese enjoy* jook *mostly as a late nighttime snack. In San Francisco's Chinatown, a native* jook *specialty house, serving a dozen varieties of the rice gruel all night through dawn, attracts patrons from all over the world. At last, here's a fresh new answer for the housewife to her eternal question of how to fully use what's left of the festive bird.*

# CHOUY-CHOUY CHICKEN LIVER
*(Gai Gon)*

Boil for 15 minutes:
       **6 cleaned chicken livers**
       **3 cups water**
       **1 teaspoon salt**
       **4 star anise**
       **½ teaspoon monosodium glutamate**

Drain and cool.
Cut:
       **Each liver into 5 pieces**
       **15 water chestnuts in half**
       **15 slices bacon cut in half**

Wrap:
       **Liver and water chestnut which have been placed together into the half-slice of bacon.**

Deep fry until bacon is crisp. Drain on absorbent toweling, then serve immediately.

*In Chinese* chouy-chouy *means crunchy, and this cocktail appetizer gives you a tidbit endowed with three contrasting taste textures.*

# ABALONE CUBES
### (Say Fong Bow Yee)

Drain and cube into ¾-inch squares:

**1 can abalone. Save liquid.**

Place in mixing bowl:
- **½ teaspoon soy sauce**
- **¼ cup abalone liquid**
- **¼ teaspoon salad oil**

Add abalone to marinade until it is drenched uniformly. Let stand for 15 minutes.

Spear each piece of abalone with a toothpick and arrange on a platter, sprinkle ground white or black pepper over abalone before serving. Marinade may be used optionally as a dip.

*There are several kinds of canned abalone. The above recipe calls for the type which is canned in Mexico, a special variety which possesses wonderful flavor, and is tender yet meaty.*

# CEREMONY OF THE FISH
*(Yee Sang)*

Want to change your luck for the better? Then arrange a Ceremony of the Fish party. Besides its function in seeking the gleaming road to good fortune, it is also a sort of Chinese expression of "togetherness" among friends. But it's only fair to warn you that to perform this Ceremony of the Fish correctly, traditionally, and with flair, you certainly will need a lot of friends with the togetherness spirit. This party is one time when you can gather sincere friends together — and do a lot of cutting up. It's worth it, though.

Prepare 1 hour prior to party:

Clean, peel and shred:  **8 pounds fresh long Chinese turnips**

(Use fine blade of vegetable shredder)

As turnips are shredded, place and soak in pan of cold water. Drain turnips in colander. Transfer turnips to clean absorbent cloth, large enough to roll turnips around in several layers, as a jelly roll. Grasp each end of the roll firmly with each hand and wring out as much liquid as possible from the turnips. Remove turnips from cloth to large surface pan which has been lined with absorbent paper toweling. Spread turnips out as evenly as possible to permit them to dry and retain their crispness. Turn turnips occasionally for drainage. Turnips will have the appearance of fresh grated coconut.

Shred:  **3 medium size young carrots**
**Put shredded carrots in dish**

Clean and filet:  **1 10-pound striped bass**

Slice filets paper-thin with sharp Chinese cleaver into 1 x 1-inch pieces. Place on serving platter and refrigerate.

Prepare:
- **½ pound rice sticks, deep fried**
- **1 pound noodles, deep fried**
- **¼ pound toasted sesame seeds**
- **½ pound salted peanuts chopped fine**
- **½ cup thinly sliced pickled scallions**
- **½ cup thinly sliced red ginger**
- **6 halves of lemon**
- **½ cup thinly sliced white ginger**
- **¼ cup sweet baby squash**
- **6 bunches Chinese parsley, stems removed**
- **6 bunches green onions, using the heads only, cut in small slices**

Place on table:
**Sugar**
**Cinnamon**
**Salt**

**Mixed hot mustard**
**Salad oil in decanter**
**Sesame oil in decanter**

Every ingredient should be placed separately in an individual dish and arranged around the platter of fish on a table to accommodate eight or more persons. Each place setting should consist of one dinner plate, bowl and two pairs of chopsticks, one pair being bamboo for mixing.

At the command of the host, the guests arise from their seats at the table, assemble near the food with bamboo chopsticks in hand ready to participate in mixing the ingredients when the signal, LO! Mix! is given!

Procedure of mixing:
(As directed by host)

1. Pour the oil on the fish (everybody mix)
2. Add sweet baby squash and scallions
3. Add more oil, continue mixing with chopsticks
4. Add red and white ginger, squeeze lemon halves for juice
5. Add mustard, sugar, salt and cinnamon to taste. Host says *"Lo hay sai gai!"* (Stir up the good fortune!)
6. Do not mix any further
7. Spread turnips over fish, followed with layer of:
   Peanuts
   Green onions
   Parsley
   Carrots
   Sesame seeds
   Rice sticks

Serve immediately without disturbing mixture to retain texture of each ingredient and crispness.

Each guest then helps himself, picking up the ingredients in a "bunch" with his chopsticks.

Serve *jook* afterwards. (See Turkey Rice Gruel recipe.) Serves 8 to 10

The traditional serving of this visually colorful and subtly taste-blended dish occurs during the Chinese Moon Festival, which falls in autumn when the populace gives thanks for bountiful crops and honors the Moon Goddess. However, any other time is permissible. The real proof of it as a respected and perennial symbol of propitiousness is the fact that a busy Chinese may turn down many dinner invitations, but he *never* turns down an invitation to a Ceremony of the Fish (or *Yee Sang*) party unless there is a grave emergency which prevents his attendance.

In itself, purely as a gay affair in glamorizing a fish, it's unadulterated fun. But follow the directions carefully. Properly done, the display is colorful enough to be a candidate for a food magazine cover. At the last Ceremony party which we attended, the arrangement reminded us of a decorated Christmas tree, with its green parsley, red ginger, white turnips, orange carrots and golden sesame colorings.

This is one dish whose perfect symphony of taste completely disguises the fact that in reality you are eating uncooked fileted fish.

The fun begins when (as you will note in the recipe) the oil is poured on the fish and everyone mixes. Frankly, those assigned to the cutting of the various ingredients are by this time pretty much in need of oil, too. The host never fails to reward these faithful volunteer workers with spirits.

Even for guests who are strangers to each other, the ice is broken when the oil is poured. Everyone has to start mixing the shredded fish and condiments with chopsticks at the spirited commands of the Chief of Ceremonies, so designated not because he is the host, but because the assigned one is best versed in the preparation and protocol of the ceremony.

Happy shouts of *"Lo"* – *"Lo hay sai gai!"* fill the air.

After the various layers of ingredients are spread over the basic foundation of fish, the guests can enjoy the fruits of their labors. Though lots of mixing precedes all this, the Chinese epicure now will carefully refrain from *mixing* the assortment further as he dips his chopsticks in for a portion. The reason? The crisp shreds are placed on top, and to keep the taste contrast of crispness, and the softness on the bottom, the chopsticks must lift only from the bottom up.

By this time, toasting to each other becomes a necessary part of the ceremony. The Chinese literary allusions, and phonetic play on words add to the intensity of the toasting. The words *Yee Sang,* with *Yee* meaning fish, and *Sang* meaning Life, are the name of the dish. Thus one is partaking of more Life with each bite, and each drink.

In the mixing process, the term *Lo* means "to mix." Also, the popular reference to "seeking good fortune" is *Lo Hay Sai Gai*. Again, one thus woos the Goddess of Fortune. It's little wonder then that an invitation to a Ceremony of the Fish party is seldom turned down.

But in spite of top-heavy tradition and beliefs, it's always a lot of fun, although not without much preliminary cutting up on the host's part, too. When will we be invited to your Ceremony of the Fish party?

# CHINESE BARBECUED SPARERIBS
## (Siew Pai Gwut)

In a large baking pan, place:    **1 2½-pound slab pork spareribs, which has been cracked down the center**

In a mixing bowl, blend together:

    **¼ teaspoon saltpeter**
    **1 tablespoon red bean cake**
    **½ teaspoon salt**
    **2 tablespoons sugar**
    **½ teaspoon monosodium glutamate**
    **½ cup catsup**
    **¼ cup red seasoning sauce**

Spread mixture over both sides of spareribs. Let stand in cool place overnight.

Place ribs on racks in shallow baking pan. Place in oven and roast at 350 degrees for 1 hour.

Turn ribs frequently to assure even browning.

*Spareribs properly barbecued always are a spectacular success, and this secret recipe should be even more so because of the distinctive flavor which comes from the Chinese condiments in the marinade. A good standby, this same oven recipe can be used for outdoor charcoal barbecuing also. Here's a hint, however, on open barbecues: Mix more marinade for basting to keep the ribs from drying out too quickly.*

## *RICE ROLL*
*(Geen Fun)*

Mix together in large mixing bowl:

**1 cup unsifted Swansdown\*cake flour**
**1 tablespoon cornstarch**
**1 teaspoon salt**
**2 tablespoons vegetable oil**
**1¼ cups cold water**

Mix well, eliminating as many lumps as possible. Pour through a strainer into another bowl to make a smooth batter.

Have available two 8-inch well-oiled cake pans and large steamer filled with hot water, 2 inches deep.

Pour a scant ¼ cup of batter into each pan, place pan into steamer, rolling batter around until bottom of pan is coated and batter is partially cooked. This will be when batter becomes translucent. Cover steamer and cook additional 5 to 7 minutes. When large air bubbles appear under the batter, remove from steamer. Cool 10 minutes before lifting cooked batter *(fun)* from pans.

### FILLING FOR GEEN FUN

*Shredded egg:* Beat together well:

**2 eggs**
**4 tablespoons water**
**1 pinch salt**

Preheat skillet which has been slightly but thoroughly oiled.

Pour sufficient egg mixture into skillet to coat bottom of pan, rolling skillet constantly until mixture is set. Cook under very low heat until top of mixture is dry, remove from pan and cool. Repeat process until all egg is cooked. Cut in quarters and stack for shredding.

Cut into extremely thin vertical slices:

**½ pound barbecued Chinese pork**
**1 bunch green onions**
**Chinese parsley (optional)**

---

\*Our extensive experiments have proven that of many American cake flours, Swansdown seems to approximate the desirable qualities of true rice paste. That is why it is specifically called for by name. True rice paste gives a translucent, firm texture. As made by the native method, it is stone-ground in tedious fashion and takes hours. So, for the busy American housewife, we definitely recommend Swansdown.

Spread individual pieces of *fun* on a smooth flat surface.

Sprinkle evenly small amount of each ingredient on each round *fun* and roll over filling (as a jelly roll) until it is completed in one long roll. Cut and serve in pieces of one to two inches in length. *Fun* may be garnished with sesame seeds.

Dip in Chinese mustard and soy sauce.

*Rice Roll is a versatile morning, noon and night dish for the Chinese. A recipe which can be prepared in advance, this makes a good luncheon or buffet dish. Geen* fun *is great to pack for picnics as a novel change from sandwiches.*

## WRAPPED MEAT BALLS
### (Siew Mai)

In a small pot of boiling water, place:

**1 piece of fat pork (3 ounces)**

Cook for 5 minutes, drain off water and cool. Dice pork fat into very small pieces.

Mince finely:     **4 ounces raw pork**
**4 ounces raw prawns**

Add:     **Diced pork fat**
**A dash of salt, pepper and monosodium glutamate**

Mix all ingredients thoroughly with hands.

Divide the mixture into 20 portions, rolling each portion into a ball. Place ball between palms, and roll into cylindrical shape. Place each portion in the center of a *won ton* skin\*, wrap, and crimp edges. Leave the top of each *Siew Mai* exposed.

Steam for 20 minutes.

The teahouses of Old China served many variations of this wrapped meat ball. This recipe advantageously allows you to use either fresh or cooked meat to test your ingenuity in varying the filling. The addition of finely chopped Chinese parsley, leeks, or water chestnuts, will add a lightness to the filling.

---

\*May be purchased in Chinatown.

# SOFT FRIED NOODLES
*(Gon Lo Mein)*

In salted boiling water, cook until soft:

**1 pound noodles. Drain.**

Have prepared:

**1 cup sliced Chinese barbecued pork**
**2 cups bean sprouts**
**1 cup Chinese chard cut in 1-inch pieces**

In a preheated *wok* or skillet place:

**⅓ cup vegetable oil**
**1 teaspoon salt**

At high heat, bring oil to a sizzle, add:

**All ingredients except noodles**

Toss and mix for five minutes, reduce to medium heat and add:

**Noodles**

Continue to turn and mix all ingredients and noodles for five minutes.
Add:

**⅓ cup soy sauce**
**1 teaspoon monosodium glutamate**

At medium heat, gently turn and mix noodles until sauce is thoroughly mixed in and noodles are very hot. Serve with mixed Chinese mustard and soy sauce. Serves 4


# YEE FOO NOODLES
*(Yee Foo Mein)*

In boiling water, cook until soft:

**1 pound noodles. Drain.**

In a deep fryer, place enough vegetable oil to cover noodles. Bring oil to a boil, then add noodles and fry until golden brown. Drain.

In a soup pot, place:

**6 cups chicken stock**
**½ teaspoon salt**
**¼ teaspoon monosodium glutamate**

Bring to a boil.
Add:

**1 cup diced bamboo shoots**
**½ cup frozen green peas**
**½ cup diced button mushrooms**
**½ pound diced uncooked chicken filet**

Cook at high heat for 5 minutes. Thicken soup with cornstarch to a thin gravy consistency. Add the fried noodles and divide into four portions, add some of the hot thickened soup to each bowl. Serves 4

# THOUSAND-YEAR-OLD EGGS
*(Pei Don)*

Immerse in cold water:          **4 whole thousand-year-old eggs**

Soak until the protecting coat of white "clay" is soft enough to be removed from the egg shell. Place eggs in hot water and boil for 7 minutes. Cool and remove shells.

With a very sharp knife, slice the dark eggs about ¼-inch thick. Arrange slices on platter alternately with sliced pickled scallions and red ginger. A geologist-gourmet must have christened Chinese preserved eggs with the fancy and awe-inspiring name "Thousand-Year-Old Eggs" — known to the Chinese simply as *Pei Don,* or "egg with skin." Once its rough layer is removed and it is shelled, however, the ancient egg (which really is cured only for 100 days) glistens like an aged, petrified rock polished to a deep amber tone. Hence our suspicion that a geologist, or a lapidary, named it. When cut, the outer egg white, now darkened too, is crystalline in appearance.

The Chinese serve it as a banquet starter, because the mouth-watering *gum* or "gold flavor" makes it a true appetizer.

# ABALONE YEE TON
*(So Bow Yee Ton)*

Have prepared:          **2 cans of No. 1 size abalone, Mexican or Japanese, water packed. Drain off liquid and slice ¼-inch thick**

In a preheated *wok* or skillet place:

                             **2 tablespoons vegetable oil**
                             **½ teaspoon salt**

Add:          **Sliced abalone**
                             **1 tablespoon imported Chinese Oyster Sauce**
                                *(Ho Yow)*
                             **1 teaspoon soy sauce**
                             **½ teaspoon monosodium glutamate**
                             **1 cup chicken stock**

Cover and cook at high heat for 5 minutes. Uncover. Turn and mix ingredients until liquids begin to bubble.

Add gradually:          **2 teaspoons cornstarch. Make paste with 2 teaspoons water.**

Turn and mix until sauce thickens. Pour over hot fried *won ton* and serve at once. Serves 4

# BASIC WON TON RECIPE

*Dough\*:*
Sift into a mixing bowl:        1½  cups flour
                                1  teaspoon salt

Add:                            1  beaten egg
                                2  tablespoons cold water

Knead until smooth, place dough in refrigerator for 1 hour, then place on floured board and roll until paper thin with rolling pin. Dust dough with flour, cut into 3-inch squares and stack.

*Filling:*
Combine and mix well:           ¼  pound finely chopped pork
                                ¼  pound chopped raw shrimps or prawns
                                ½  teaspoon monosodium glutamate
                                2  teaspoons finely chopped green onions
                                2  tablespoons finely chopped button
                                    mushrooms
                                2  tablespoons soy sauce
                                ½  teaspoon salt

*To wrap Won Ton:*
Hold square of dough on palm of left hand. Place about ½ teaspoon filling ½-inch from corner of square nearest you. Fold this corner over the dough, then roll it once more toward the center of the square. Your *Won Ton* is now shaped.

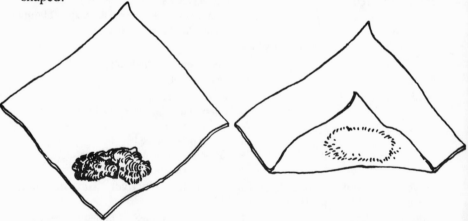

\*May be purchased by the dozen at your Chinatown grocery.

Spread a tiny bit of the filling on the right-hand corner, compress the left-hand corner to it. This leaves the corner opposite the one you have rolled to ramble freely. It sounds harder to do than it really is. With practice, a beautiful billowy shape, termed by the Chinese "the butterfly," will be the result.

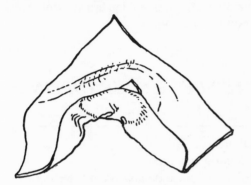 

## OYSTER SAUCE BEEF WON TON
### (How Yow Ngow Yuke Yee Ton)

In a preheated *wok* or skillet, place:

> **2 tablespoons vegetable oil**
> **½ teaspoon salt**

Bring oil to sizzling point and add:

> **1½ pounds tender beef, sliced ¼-inch thick**

Turn and mix for 1 minute at high heat or until both sides of sliced beef are light brown. Center should be rare.

Add:

> **1 tablespoon imported Chinese Oyster Sauce**
> **1 teaspoon soy sauce**
> **1 cup chicken stock**
> **½ teaspoon monosodium glutamate**

Continue to cook at medium high heat until liquids begin to bubble.

Add gradually:

> **2 teaspoons cornstarch. Make paste with 2 teaspoons water.**

Turn and mix all ingredients until sauce thickens. Pour over hot fried *won ton* and serve at once.

# CRUNCHY MIDGET WON TON

The dough and filling are made exactly like regular *Won Ton,* but the dough is cut in 2-inch squares, the filling reduced to ¼ of a teaspoon. Fold each square diagonally ¾ of the way down, press edges with fork to secure filling. Deep fry in preheated (350° F) hot oil until golden brown. Remove with slotted spoon and drain on absorbent toweling.

# FRIED WON TON WITH SWEET & SOUR TOPPING
*(Jow Won Ton)*

Deep fry in hot vegetable oil until brown:

**3 dozen** *won ton*

Remove with ladle strainer carefully and place on absorbent toweling.

*SWEET AND SOUR SAUCE:*
In a mixing bowl, place:

**½ cup vinegar**
**½ cup sugar**
**⅓ cup pineapple juice**
**¼ cup catsup**
**1 teaspoon Worcestershire sauce**
**4 drops hot sauce**

Stir and mix thoroughly and have ready.

*TOPPING:*
In a preheated skillet, place:  **1 teaspoon vegetable oil**
Add:  **½ cup bell peppers, sliced into one-inch squares**
**½ cup sliced dried onions**
**1 cup fresh tomatoes, cut into eighths**
**½ cup sliced Chinese barbecued pork**

At medium heat, toss cook for three minutes.
Add:  **Sweet and sour**
**1 tablespoon cornstarch. Make paste with 1 tablespoon water**

Continue cooking at medium heat, tossing and mixing continously until sauce and topping is thick and very hot.

Place the fried *won ton* on a large platter, pour cooked topping over them and serve at once. Serves 4

# WON TON IN SOUP
## (Wo Won Ton)

In salted boiling water, cook until soft:
    **60 wrapped** *won ton*. **Drain.**

Have ready:
    **2 chicken gizzards, sliced**
    **2 chicken livers, quartered**
    **5 shelled prawns, sliced in half**

Parboil in very little water for three minutes and drain.

In a soup pot, place:    **6 cups chicken stock**

Bring to a boil. Reduce to medium heat.

Add:
    **Chicken gizzards, livers and prawns**
    **5 sliced button mushrooms**
    **5 sliced water chestnuts**
    **½ cup sliced bamboo shoots**
    **2 cups Chinese chard, cut into 1-inch lengths**

Cook at medium heat for 5 minutes.

Divide *won ton* into four portions and place in separate bowls. Pour the hot soup over *won ton,* saving the ingredients for garnishing on top of each bowl. Decorate with slices of Chinese barbecued pork and chopped green onions. Serve with soy sauce and mixed hot Chinese mustard. Serves 4

# WON TON IN THICK SOUP
## (Mun Yee Won Ton)

Use same recipe above but thicken the soup with cornstarch to a thin gravy consistency.

# WON TON YEE FOO
## (Yee Foo Won Ton)

Use same recipe as *Yee Foo* Noodles, using fried *won ton* instead of noodles.

# *J*eas and Wines

## A CUP OF JOY

---

Tea is one of the world's most popular beverages and everyone knows that it is the national beverage of the Chinese. Since time immemorial, tea has been enjoyed by every Chinese person — from prince to pauper.

Tea is always offered to the caller as a gesture of hospitality. An oft-quoted legend about Emperor Sheng Nung, circa 2737 B.C., a most intelligent ruler noted for his interest in agriculture and welfare, observed that persons who drank boiled water were less prone to disease than those who did not. Therefore, he decreed that all his subjects drink boiled water. While in a forest one day, a royal servant was adding wood to a fire for boiling water, and some withered leaves from a bush dropped into the pot. The fragrance from the steaming water attracted the emperor. He sipped and enjoyed it.

Another story describes a Buddhist saint named Bodhidharma who journeyed from India to China in 519 A.D. to convert the Chinese to Buddhism. In his fervor he swore to teach the virtues of Buddha for nine years without sleep or rest. For six long years he preached, but one night, weary beyond endurance, Bodhidharma dropped to sleep. Upon awakening, he was filled with shame. He cut off his eyelids in repentance and cast them to the ground. Lo and behold, the next day, on the very spot, an evergreen tree sprang up — becoming the first tea tree on earth — from which Bodhidharma nibbled leaves which renewed his strength and faith.

Legends notwithstanding, it is a recorded fact that in China tea was cultivated extensively from the fifth century A.D. The tea plant, a cousin of the camellia, has the virtue of existing where other crops cannot be grown — in small areas around houses, hillsides, and high-up mountain crags. Some of the world's finest connoisseurs' teas are said to be harvested by trained monkeys, because these tea trees grow so high on steep cliffs they are too difficult for man to reach. These are premium teas grown by

Buddhist priests, and sold under many Buddhist names such as Iron Kwan Yin, Iron Lo Hun or Iron Buddha. The green type Cloud Mist tea, grown on a mountain top of Kiangsi, also is said to be plucked by trained monkeys.

Besides the exotica described, what then are the main general types of Chinese tea? They are the green, black (called "red tea" in Chinese) and *oolong*. The leaves of all three can come from the same plant. It is basically the curing process which differentiates them. For green tea, the leaves are plucked before withering and given a quick drying. Smaller and more tender leaves are selected for the green, with less handling, so the color remains verdant-grey. A famous type of green tea is *Lung-Cheong* or Dragon Well.

For black tea, the leaves are withered, rolled and fermented. This forms an oxidation which turns them dark. *Oolong* tea is a semi-fermented tea. The fermentation is curbed at a certain state in order to create that distinctive *oolong* bouquet. The infusions appear partly red and partly green. Infused with jasmine, it becomes the familiar jasmine tea. Chinese tea blends also incorporate the charming idea of packing and mixing various dried flowers or leaves to emphasize a certain flavor and fragrance — or simply as a lyrical expression of one's feelings. So individual touches may be expressed through the use of roses, camellias, chrysanthemums, jasmine or orange blossoms.

September is the month when the farmer plants the tea seed, which takes three years to mature to first harvest. The tree plant is trimmed to a height of five feet or less, and has partial crops through its sixth year, then gradually builds to a complete full crop by the tenth year. It will bear good leaves for another ten years. April is the month for the "flush" or period of best active growth, when the leaves are most tender and delicate in flavor. May and August are the other harvest months. The leaves are picked by women, who are more dexterous than men. Sixty pounds per person is the average picking, and four pounds of freshly plucked leaves process into one pound of tea. Curled by hand to release their flavor, the leaves then are sorted to sizes and classifications. The intriguing grading names — such as *Young Hysen, Twankey, Fannings* and *Pekoe Souchong* — resemble a word painting from a Somerset Maugham story. There are more kinds of Chinese teas than California wines, so we leave the detailed classification to those more qualified in the scholarly pursuit of them.

Rather, you will want to know: How is tea properly made — and served?

Tea leaves are delicate, they absorb other flavors and moisture and lose their own fragrance if exposed too long.

To fully enjoy this satisfying beverage:

Buy the finest tea leaves within your budget. Use a porcelain ware teapot for metal ones alter the delicate flavor. The water should be brought to a rolling boil, and poured immediately over the tea leaves.

One heaping teaspoon of tea leaves to six cups of boiling water is a good average. Steep Chinese teas ten to fifteen minutes. (Non-Chinese teas such as Orange Pekoe steep immediately.)

After the first potful is empty, add a few leaves and pour in more boiling water. The second infusion improves the taste even more.

Tea is unchallenged as the beverage for people in all walks of Chinese life and has developed social mores to accompany it. Tea is a symbol of fidelity, and any attempt to move or transplant a mature tea plant would destroy it.

A gift of tea means friendship. Thus tea is necessary among the gifts sent to a girl's family by the fiancé when an engagement is announced. A delicate reference to a broken engagement is "The tea has been spilled."

After the engagement, the ceremonial aspect of tea is pursued to the climax of marriage, when the bride must personally pour and serve tea to all her relatives, her husband's relatives and the assembled guests in order of protocol.

The potful of tea is a daily functional routine. It is the first order of the day in a Chinese household, as the breakfast cup of coffee is in an American one. In China, stores and offices keep a supply of hot tea all the time just as American places have water coolers. Every caller is offered a cup of tea as a gesture of welcome and hospitality.

For formal occasions, however, a more ceremonial tea ritual is observed, consisting of a *Cha Joong,* a saucer, bowl and lid for each person. The tea leaves are placed directly in the cup, boiled water is poured over it, and the lid used as in a teapot. When pouring, each individual uses the lid as a "strainer" to hold back the tea leaves.

When a person is asked obliquely to do a favor, he is delicately offered "tea money." But when one is invited to a midday tidbits luncheon at a teahouse, he goes to "drink tea" or *"yum cha."*

Teahouses in China are the great public social centers where people have a snack, exchange conversations and make transactions — all amid a lively, congenial atmosphere. Legends abound attesting to the choice teahouses as places of intrigue where revolutions, kingdoms, fortunes as well as romances have been plotted and conceived. In San Francisco's Chinatown today, because of an increased population, more teahouses than ever are flourishing. Here's a tea tip: the teahouse, aside from being a place where you can indulge in tidbits, also is a spot where you can sample rare, premium teas you may not buy in quantity for home usage, and the waiter may ask you: "What is your pleasure in choice of tea?" (See Morning, Noon and Night.)

# – OR WINE –

Popular usage has termed the alcoholic beverages of China "wines" although they originate from rice and grain rather than grapes. But to avoid confusion we will use the same word.

Thousands of years before Christ, "wine" was imbibed in China. Its origin can be traced in a passage from an ancient Chinese classic, "The Country's Policy," which credited a man named Yi Dick with the discovery of wine. The Emperor Yu sampled it and was delighted by its after-effects.

However, this astute ruler who had tamed the unruly Yellow River feared that one day the unwise use of wine would have the power to destroy the empire. He banished wine-discoverer Yi Dick.

Wine seems to be a part of the flow of life, and Emperor Yu's edict was a mere stop-gap. A later Chinese classic records how a host invited his guests to libation with these literary lines:

"Emperor Yao drank one thousand measures,
Confucius a hundred goblets.
And Tse-Loo, a Confucius disciple, drank
A hundred wooden cups of wine
All sages, in fact, partake of the cup,
So how can you not honor us with a drink?"

The two main types of Chinese wine are yellow and white. The common yellow wine is *Shooching,* a rice wine used also for cooking. It usually is warmed when served in porcelain wine pots and tiny thin cups.

*Kaoling,* distilled from the grain of that name in Northern China, is white wine and similar to vodka, except that it is much smoother.

Indigenous to Canton is *Ng Gah Pei,* a dark yellow wine laced with herbs, and somewhat reminiscent of a 100-proof bourbon, but with a strong medicinal flavor. *Ng Gah Pei* comes in a flared neck jug.

Wine has a great literary tradition in China, and a capacity for alcohol has been a source of pride among Chinese poets and writers for many centuries. One writer, Wang Chi, was known as the "Five-Bottle Scholar"!

Li Po, one of China's greatest poets wrote: "No man who is sober deserves the rapture of drinking and wine's dizzy spell."

A legend in his time, Li Po truly lived — or died, depending on how one looks at it — believing in the virtues of drinking. He died a celebrated death, by having fallen out of a boat while inebriated trying to embrace the reflection of the moon. And drowned.

Such are the excesses of drinking, but nevertheless, the Chinese also have many proverbs of warning against over-indulgence. One of the most practical safeguards is the general Chinese habit of drinking only at the dinner table with food.

The older-generation Chinese do not favor the dubious institution known as the "cocktail party." When they drink, they "drink it straight," but they eat also.

\* \* \*

Chinese liqueurs also are distilled from grains, and embellished with various natural fragrances. One of the more popular enjoyed in America is *Mui Kwei Lu,* a potent liqueur with a rose petal flavor.

Wine, like tea, also plays a ceremonial role in marriage. At the end of the old-fashioned traditional ceremony, wine is poured into two cups from pots which are tied together. The bride and groom each sips the wine. Then some of the wine of each cup is poured into the other. The bride and groom exchange cups and drink the mingled wine symbolizing the intermingling of their two bodies and spirits.

Thusly do the Chinese express life's cup of joy.

# ⓜenus

## REALM OF THE KITCHEN GOD

By now, we hope the invisible guidance of *Tsao Shen*, the Kitchen God, has given you more than a nodding acquaintance with the Eight Immortal Flavors. You can recognize a gingko nut when you see one. You may even have been initiated into the Ceremony of the Fish. In any case, you have made some explorations into the myriad mysteries of the Chinese cuisine, and you are ready to map out some menu expeditions yourself.

Because Chinese food is *prepared* and *served* differently from American fare — with many dishes to complement a meal rather than just a single unit entrée served each person — the possibilities for infinite variety in a menu are unlimited. This is the prime principle of Chinese cuisine to remember.

It is one which the hostess or menu planner should use to the best advantage to enhance both appetite appeal and nutritional balance.

The American phrase "from soup to nuts" has its keynote in the word *soup* in the determination of a Chinese dinner. Did you know that when you invite a Chinese guest to a dinner, the *soup course* you serve will tell the guest immediately which type of dinner he will be enjoying?

Even though as a matter of traditional Chinese courtesy the host or hostess would emphasize with apologies that the meal "really is only *bien fon*," literally meaning "a casual bit of rice," one may guess the repast to be anything from a really simple dinner to an elegant banquet. That is, until the "tip-off" comes in the serving of the soup, although the guest may not be able to peek in the kitchen.

When the Chinese host invites guests, he is most careful about his choice of soup. Certain soups are appropriate to certain styles of dining. For example, if your host is a man of moderate means, you will probably be served the simple Village Style food, starting with something like a hearty

Mustard Green Soup *(Gai Choy Tong)*, followed by Bean Cake with Meat *(Dow Foo Yuke)* and a steamed Pork Patty with Salted Fish *(Hom Yee Jing Gee Yuke Beong)*, plus a vegetable dish like Chard Hearts with Prawns *(Choy Sum Hah Kow)*. And, of course, heaping bowls of steamed rice.

On the other hand, if your host is a well-to-do intimate friend who is tired of elaborate Banquet Style dishes, and knows you will relish the more down-to-earth, simple, nourishing Village Style dishes with him, he, too, will serve you the more humble yet delicious foods. Hence the Chinese expression when you are extended an invitation to dine at someone's home, "Please come — it is only to eat *'bien fon'* or *'hom yee choy'* '' (convenient rice or salt fish-vegetable fare). This polite gesture is to assure you of the host's humility — and is not a true indication of the possibly elaborate dinner that may be served you!

Between Village Style cooking and the elaborate Banquet Style are the Dinner Style dishes, which may begin with Abalone Soup *(Bow Yee Tong)* followed by Coriander Chicken Salad *(So See Gai)*, Prawns with Black Bean Sauce *(See Jup Loong Hah Kow)*, Roast Duck *(Faw Opp)*, and perhaps a sweet and sour dish like Pineapple Pork *(Goo Lo Yuke)* — accompanied with properly cooked steamed rice *(Bok Fon)*, etc.

Last comes the *Choy* (Banquet Style) type of cooking. (There is still another category called *Dai Choy* (Super Banquet Style), where two or three kinds of soups are served. These complicated dishes which require special equipment and several days of pre-preparation, are the forte of top-notch restaurant chefs — so we will not include them here.)

*Choy* (Banquet Style) — for entertaining six to ten guests elaborately at home — a host can make a good impression by starting off the dinner with Bird's Nest Soup, followed by Stuffed Lobster Tails *(Yeong Loong Hah Mei)*, Hong Kong Lemon Chicken *(Nom Moong Gai)*, Diced Squab in Lettuce Cups *(Bok Opp Soong)*, Pressed Duck *(Wo Siew Opp)* and Black and White Mushrooms with Oyster Sauce *(Ho Yow Song Goo)*, etc. In a formal dinner like this, rice should be available and optional to a company dinner only after the guests have partaken of the dishes. Again this is custom, since a good host expects his guests to feast on the "pure" entrees he provides not as *Soong* (accompaniment for rice) as distinguished from the informal Village or Dinner Style called *Fon Soong* (rice and accompaniments).

Summarized the three types of dining are:
1. Village Style
2. Dinner Style
3. Banquet Style

In serving (1) Village Style or (2) Dinner Style — a good rule for the number of entrées to serve for a given number of persons is:

For a party of two people, a soup and 2 or 3 other dishes plus rice are sufficient.

For larger groups, serve a soup and other dishes in the same number as there are people, plus "one for the table." (Example: for a group of five, serve a soup, 6 dishes, and rice.)

For a party of eight or ten, dishes must be enlarged to double the given recipe, which is twice the ordinary quantity. In this case reduce the variety in accordance to your desire.

What to include for five or more persons dining in Banquet Style:
A soup
A vegetable and a vegetable combination dish
A seafood dish
A meat dish
One or two poultry dishes
A sweet and sour dish (meat or poultry)
Rice, steamed or fried

Here are some more suggested combination menus:

### VILLAGE STYLE

Watercress Soup *(Ching Sai Yong Choy Tong)*
Steamed Fish with Black Bean Sauce *(Seen Tow Dow See Jing Yee)*
Sautéed Kidneys with Vegetables *(Gee Yew Chow Gwa Choy)*
Chinese Chard with Oil and Salt *(Yow Yim Bok Choy)*
Steamed Rice *(Bok Fon)*

### DINNER STYLE

Diced Winter Melon Soup *(Doong Gwa Nupp Tong)*
Lobster Sauté with Vegetables *(Chow Loong Hah Kow)*
Cashew Chicken *(Yew Dow Gai Kow)*
Pineapple Pork Sweet and Sour *(Goo Lo Yuke)*
Snow Peas with Water Chestnuts and Bamboo Shoots *(Lon Dow Jook Soon Ma Tai)*
Oyster Beef *(Ho Yow Ngow Yuke)*
Fried Rice or Steamed Rice *(Chow Fon, Bok Fon)*

### BANQUET STYLE

Melon Cup Soup *(Doong Gwa Joong)*
*Chung Kwong* Squab *(Chung Kwong Bok Opp)*
Lotus Stuffed Duck *(Leen Gee Opp)*
Soy Squab Red Fried *(Hoong Siew Bok Opp)*
Lychee Pineapple Pork Sweet and Sour *(Lychee Baw Law Goo Lo Yuke)*
Chicken à La Kan *(Goon Yin – Yin Yang Gai)*
Water Chestnut Tumble in Lettuce Cups *(Mai Tai Soong)*
Dessert

This is, of course, only an infinitesimal sample of the endless range of Chinese food combinations which could satisfy the reach and taste of either peasant or prince. By adhering to the principles, you yourself can blend various combinations. There will be occasions when perhaps only one Chinese dish will give variety and interest to an American dinner.

One of the great pleasures of life for the Chinese people is an appreciation for and the pursuit of fine food. It is a way of life, perhaps a philosophical approach to cushion the harsh realities of everyday living. Perhaps too, this is why we Chinese like to serve our banquets on a *round* table, so that everyone really is gathered around, all sharing the spread of dishes.

Another example of the Chinese philosophical interpretation of food is the custom of serving noodles *(Mein)* every birthday or feast day. Noodles, because of their length, are a symbol of longevity. *Every* guest at a party partakes of *Mein* to express his desire to wish happiness and long life to the person being honored at the festive occasion.

*Tsao Shen,* according to Chinese mythology, is the Kitchen God sent to earth to supervise people's cooking and watch their behavior. A paper image of him is found in all kitchens. At the end of each year, before he goes up in flames to report to the Jade Emperor in Heaven, a prudent housewife will rub his lips with honey so that he will have a few sweet words to say about the family's food and wine.

We hope that EIGHT IMMORTAL FLAVORS has encouraged you to understand and appreciate Cantonese cookery, and that henceforth you will share with us the smiling approval of the Kitchen God.

# *Index*

*For further inquiries regarding menus or ingredients write to
Kan's Restaurant,
708 Grant Avenue, Chinatown, San Francisco, CA 94108.*